The Latina Survival Guide

A Memoir of Drama, Trauma and Telenovela Logic

by Charo Toledo

Title: The Latina Survival Guide
Subtitle: A Memoir of Drama, Trauma and Telenovela Logic

ISBN: 978-1-969745-08-9 (English Paperback)
ISBN: 978-1-969745-09-6 (English eBook)
Library of Congress Control Number: 2026913992
Categories: Memoir, Hispanic Latina Women, Autobiography
Cover design by: RMPStudio™
Interior design: RMPStudio™ Team
Photography Cover Image: Charo Toledo
Editor: RMPStudio™ Editorial Division

ORDERING INFORMATION: **https://thelatinasurvivalguide.org**
This work is a memoir based on the author's personal experiences and recollections. Certain names, places, and events may have changed for privacy or narrative purposes. While every effort has been made to ensure accuracy, the author and publisher make no representations or warranties regarding the completeness or accuracy of the content and disclaim all liability for any loss or damage arising from its use.

Printed in Las Vegas, Nevada, United States of America
Manufactured in the United States of America, Rosales Mavericks Publishing Studio™| 1180 N. Town Center Dr., Suite #100, Las Vegas, Nevada 89144

PRAISE FOR THE LATINA SURVIVAL GUIDE

"With *The Latina Survival Guide*, Charo Toledo has reinvented the memoir, creating something unique, rich, and distinctly her own... a multitude of incredible tales that are mini movies within themselves, all tied together by a fun and exuberantly innovative conceptual structure."

—Mark Valadez, Writer-Producer, Queen of the South

"Vivid, funny, and unforgettable — 1970s Puerto Rico in sequins, cologne, and madness."

— Jennifer Joyce, TV Writer

"Warm, sharp, wickedly funny, a lush portrait of Puerto Rican life."

— Victor Duenas, TV Writer

"Electric and hilarious stories about growing up in Puerto Rico in an amazingly cinematic way."

— Annabelle Mullen Pacheco, CEO Belle Films

"From the very first chapter, I was transported back to Puerto Rico. Toledo's telenovela lens is brilliant."

— Norma Maldonado, Actress

"A piercing and insightful portrait that challenges stereotypes and invites empathy."

— Jasmin Espada, Producer, 333 Pictures · Rebel 6 Films

"I was literally laughing out loud just reading the Program Schedule... Amazingly written and so entertaining!"

— Wendy Payne, Retired IRS/Enrolled Agent

"Bold, heartwarming, and unforgettable — a memoir that reads like its own novella."

—Noelia German, Gen Z Reader & TikTok Creator

"What stayed with me most was the author's courage. The way she unpacks identity, family, and the inherited scripts we grow up with takes real vulnerability, and she does it with humor, honesty, and heart. She didn't just write a memoir. She gave people permission to reflect on their own story. Highly recommend."

— Joseph Garcia, Actor

"Beautifully told with wit, vibrancy and with the right balance of succinctness that makes you want to know more!"

—Karolina Montenegro, Contract Administrator

A SPECIAL PRESENTATION
THE LATINA SURVIVAL GUIDE

Presented by Rosales Mavericks Publishing Studio™

A Charo Toledo Production

Filmed in spirit on location in Puerto Rico, the original network of my life.

For Papi (the signal)

For Mami (the static)

Friends and Family (the reruns that saved me)

And for every street, storm, and song still playing back home.

AUTHOR'S NOTE

Trauma doesn't tell stories in order. It reruns them.

Some episodes air out of sequence. Others get cancelled halfway through and return as spin-offs.

This book isn't meant to be read front to back but tuned into, like late-night television when you can't sleep.

Each chapter is a broadcast from the same signal; a girl learning to survive her own telenovela.

The Decoder and Survival Laws are the commercials between acts: reminders, translations, coping mechanisms.

Think of this as syndication therapy.

If you start laughing halfway through an old wound — congratulations. You're already fluent in recovery.

Now, cue the static.

FOREWORD

Some stories entertain us, and some accompany us. *The Latina Survival Guide* is a rare memoir that does both, while honoring something sacred: the lived experience of Puerto Rican women navigating the world with humor, resilience, and an unshakeable sense of identity.

As I read Charo Toledo's pages, I found myself transported, not only to her family's living room in Guaynabo, but to the memories of my own childhood, my mother's voice and my own journey from the island into spaces where I would often be "the first," "the only," or the one expected to explain who we are. This book understands that displacement and belonging can coexist, that we carry our homes with us even when the world insists that we leave them behind.

Toledo's brilliance lies in how she frames survival not as a tragedy but as an art, inherited from generations of women who learned to endure with elegance and fire. Her episodic structure, program schedules, survival laws, reruns, and flashbacks are not merely creative devices. They reflect a cultural truth. Puerto Rican women do not experience life in a straight line. We experience it as memory layered upon memory, lessons passed down in kitchens and whispered over coffee, humor braided tightly with grief.

What makes *The Latina Survival Guide* extraordinary is its refusal to flatten that complexity. Toledo writes with clarity and compassion about family, faith, ambition, and contradiction. She understands that humor is not avoidance; it is a strategy. That nostalgia is not indulgence; it is preservation. And that remembering is not weakness; it is power.

This memoir is also an act of reclamation. Toledo reclaims the stories that shaped her, the women who raised her, and the cultural logic that taught her how to survive long before she had language for it. Her voice is sharp, generous, irreverent, and deeply loving. She invites us into moments that are tender, uncomfortable, hilarious, and holy, always with honesty, never with apology.

For many Latinas, survival has meant learning to adapt to systems that were not designed for us while holding fast to who we are. Toledo's journey, from a Puerto Rican childhood rich with myth and ritual to leadership in creative and public spaces, reflects the paths of so many women who learned to navigate multiple worlds at once, translating themselves while refusing to disappear.

The Latina Survival Guide is not a manual for becoming someone else. It is a permission slip to become more fully yourself. It reminds us that survival is not only about endurance but also about creativity, faith, and joy. About choosing to live visibly, honestly, and on our own terms.

I am grateful for this book. I recognize myself in it. And I know many others will too.

Carmen G. Cantor

U.S. Ambassador (Ret.)

Author of *The Ambassador: Two Hats. Two Presidents*

PROGRAM SCHEDULE
THE LATINA SURVIVAL GUIDE ~ SEASON ONE

DAY 1 ~ DECEMBER 25
ACT I ~ HURRICANES, HANDGUNS & HOLY GHOSTS

7:00 AM - 5:00 PM | EPISODES 1-11

DAY 2 ~ DECEMBER 25-26
ACT II ~ MADRID STREET: DYNASTY WITH BEANS
6:00 PM - 4:00 AM | EPISODES 12-22

DAY 3 ~ DECEMBER 26
ACT III ~ FROM DISCO BALLS TO CHICKEN INN

5:00 AM-1:00 PM | EPISODES 23-31

DAY 4 ~ DECEMBER 26
ACT IV ~ CATHOLIC PREP SCHOOL, PUBERTY & OTHER NATURAL DISASTERS

2:00 PM-10:00 PM | EPISODES 32-39

DAY 5 ~ DECEMBER 26-27
ACT V ~ CATS, CURSES & OTHER INHERITANCES

10:00 PM-7:00 AM | EPISODES 40-49

DAY 6 ~ DECEMBER 27

ACT VI ~ SEQUINS, SURVIVAL & CLOSURE

8:00 AM – 1:00 PM | EPISODES 50–55

— COMING ATTRACTIONS —

Even books deserve post credits

ACT I

HURRICANES, HANDGUNS & HOLY GHOSTS

(Episodes 1-11)

EPISODE 1 – DISCLAIMER

12/25 — 7:00 a.m.

Rating: PG

Episode Description: *My lawyer made me write this.*

This is not a self-help book. It is a survival *novela* — filed under comedy, trauma, and sequins.

The stories you are about to read are inspired by real events, but names, timelines, and incriminating details have been blurred, altered, or shamelessly dramatized. Any resemblance to actual tyrants, gossipy titis, or polyester uniforms may or may not be coincidental. Consider this my legal way of saying: sue the telenovela industry, not me.

The names may be changed but the chancletas[1] are real.

My legal counsel suggested I use a pseudonym. I suggested she try surviving a Puerto Rican mother with good aim.

I was born in Puerto Rico — not the postcard-perfect San Juan of cruise ship brochures, but in an enclave of privilege most people pretend doesn't exist.

It's a world of old money, European vacations, and private Catholic schools designed to ensure you never interacted with the "wrong kind of people." It smelled like leather briefcases, gardenias, and my titis' Aqua Net — the true perfume of San Juan privilege.

[1] **Chancleta(s):** A slipper; the aerodynamic disciplinary device wielded by Latina mothers with terrifying accuracy. See LSG Decoder.

My life was excess personified:

- Private Catholic school: Academia San José[2]
- Designer clothes: Valentino, Oscar de la Renta, Balenciaga — on a child who still had braces
- Summer trips abroad: Paris, Madrid, and Rome, all curated to prove we were not like the others

In other words, I was born into a portfolio that traded heavily in $ABUELA (matriarch dividends), $INFIDELIDAD (affairs-as-assets) and $CHISME futures, (always bullish).[3]

It was Beverly Hills — but make it Spanish aristocracy.

Puerto Rican elite institutions[4] marked your rank in life. Lineage wasn't dinner table talk; it was blood sport.

Suitors weren't judged on love, but on last names.

"Rodriguez? From where? Ponce? Bayamón? New York?"

Cue the ancestral side-eye.

And then, I broke the script. I left.

Leaving meant exile.

No velvet gates.

No pedigree suitors.

No whispered roll calls of surnames.

Leaving meant losing rank.

But it also meant survival.

Freedom.

---

[2] **Academia San José:** Elite Catholic school. Polyester uniforms, Ivy ambition, and abuelas as admissions officers. Gossip Girl with rosaries.

[3] **Novela Stock Exchange:** Market trends include rosaries, betrayal and slaps across the face. Regulation: nonexistent.

[4] **Puerto Rican elite institutions**: Holy Trinity: Academia San José, Caribe Hilton, El Zipperle.

Oxygen.

Because every telenovela heroine knows — you don't find yourself until you walk out of the mansion, slam the wrought-iron door, and disappear into the night.

Next episode? Survival with a price.

From Gilded Privilege to Hollywood Hustle

I went to Swarthmore (exclusive, yes, but not Harvard or Yale, which scandalized the relatives). I trained at A.C.T., the American Conservatory Theater.

I chased the dream:

- Worked in soaps in Hollywood.
- Worked in soaps in Mexico.
- Came back to Hollywood to write for *East Los High*, a show about working-class Latinos; ironic, since I hadn't stepped foot in a barrio until I got to the U.S.
- Then, plot twist: I worked for the DEA. (Cartels, files, classified. More on that in another book.)
- Then I wrote another show and another.

And then? I hit a wall.

The Shocking Truth: The American Dream Is a Scam

After years of hustling in Hollywood, Mexico, and government agencies, I realized something horrifying:

In the United States of America, I was a second-class citizen.

- Not for lack of education.
- Not for lack of talent.
- Not because of my overinvestment in soap-opera love triangles.

No.

Because I was Puerto Rican.

Let's pause for the cosmic irony.

I am an American citizen.

By birth.

By law.

By every constitutional definition possible.

And yet…

- I was treated like an immigrant.
- Seen as a foreigner.
- Forced to "prove" my Americanness to people whose ancestors had arrived at Ellis Island centuries after mine had settled in Puerto Rico.

It didn't matter that my father held two Ivy League degrees in the 1950s — an unheard-of feat before the Americans with Disabilities Act and before the Civil Rights Act.

It didn't matter that our Rolodex was stacked with Ivy grads and inherited wealth.

None of it mattered.

Because in America, people saw a Latina and made their assumptions accordingly.

The twist?

Survival here would require a new law.

A Memoir of Madness, Privilege & the Loophole of the American Dream

Let's address the elephant in the room.

When people think about a Puerto Rican success story, most people think J.Lo.

I am not J.Lo.

This is not: "Started from the Bottom, Now We're Here."

This is:

"Started at the Top, Fell Down a Flight of Stairs, Hit My Head, and Woke Up Wondering What the Hell Happened."

Because that, dear reader, is the American Dream's fine print.

THE DECODER

Survival Law #1: *The American Dream has no warranty — especially if you're Puerto Rican.*

EPISODE 2 — THE HURRICANE BIRTH

12/25 — 8:00 a.m.

Rating: PG

Episode Description: *Because, of course, my entrance to this world was dramatic.*

Some people are born in quiet hospital rooms, swaddled in love and soft lullabies.

I was born in a hurricane.

The day Hurricane Cleopatra ravaged Puerto Rico — a tempest so monstrous that it tore through the Caribbean like an uninvited chilla,[5] flipping tables, ruining hairstyles, and leaving destruction in its wake.

Forget the storm stats. All you need to know is this.

It was chaos.

And it was literally my first lullaby.

The air was so thick with humidity you could drink it. Candle wax dripped onto tile. Smoke curled like prayers. Picture my poor mother: petite, porcelain, Catholic-school tough, nine months pregnant as shutters rattled and windows shook.

The hospital was in blackout. Doctors darted like stockbrokers on Black Monday. Instead of losing portfolios, they were losing patients.

[5] **Chilla:** The sidepiece. The mistress. The one not invited to Christmas dinner, but for sure blowing up someone's phone on Nochebuena.

And my father? He would've preferred sipping J&B at El Zipperle,[6] but bars were shuttered, so he reluctantly showed up.

As the hurricane howled and the hospital lost power yet again, I arrived — a nine-pound, twenty-two-inch Amazonian baby, screaming louder than the storm itself.

The obstetrician crossed himself.

The chandelier fell.

The generator crossed wires.

I debuted with thunder and poor timing.

My mother fainted like a soap-opera heroine. In the dark, I heard Mami whisper to no one — maybe to God:

"*¡Que no se la lleve el viento!*"[7]

No crib could contain me. So, the staff, exhausted, resourceful, placed me in a cardboard box.

Yes. A hospital-sanctioned manger.

Maybe that's why I never trusted comfort. It always felt temporary — one gust away from collapse.

And Papi? He lit a Cohiba inside the maternity ward as casually as most people lit candles, then muttered:

"*¡Ay, Virgen, ¡esta va a ser un problema!*"[8]

He wasn't wrong.

Drama had already claimed me as its favorite child.

Some babies get a silver spoon.

I got a Category 4 entrance cue.

---

[6] **El Zipperle:** Restaurant where Hato Rey's power players came to eat, drink and casually broker $30 million contracts between bites of schnitzel and arroz con pollo.

[7] **¡Que no se la lleve el viento!** Let her not be *Gone with the Wind*...

[8] **¡Ay Virgen esta va a ser un problema!** Oh, Blessed Virgin of Botox and Bad Decisions, we're entering full telenovela territory!

Now tell me — do you remember the day you were born?

No?

That's because it wasn't nearly as dramatic.

THE DECODER

Survival Law #2*: Born in a storm? Congratulations! Chaos is your sibling. Learn to braid the wind.*

EPISODE 3 – TELENOVELAS AS A SURVIVAL GUIDE

12/25 — 9:00 a.m.

Rating: PG

Episode Description: *Everything I needed to know about life, I learned from telenovelas.*

Why I Left My Island

Why did I leave my Puerto Rico? My sun-drenched island of flamboyant *flamboyanes*,[9] long afternoons sipping café con leche, and family gossip that travels faster than hurricane alerts?

The official answer: *el sueño americano.*

Bigger.

Better.

Freedom.

The real answer?

I was suffocating.

I wanted out of a telenovela that wasn't mine — a multi-generational saga, with impossible love, misplaced loyalties, and villains who could give *Catalina Creel*[10] a run for her pearls.

[9] **Flamboyanes:** Puerto Rico's drama-queen tree. She doesn't bloom; she arrives. Every summer she throws on a red gown, blocks traffic and reminds the island who the real diva is.

[10] **Catalina Creel:** The O.G. telenovelas villainess from *Cuna de Lobos*, (1986). High-glam evil in silk eye patch. She made vengeance look couture and proved with enough pearls and poison even homicide can be high fashion.

I wanted to flip the script.

Raised by Telenovelas

Sure, I consumed American pop culture, but my moral compass came courtesy of Televisa. Verónica Castro's trembling lip. Thalía's tragic glow.

My first theology was *Cuna de Lobos*,[11] where the gospel read: **Never, ever trust anyone with an eye patch that matches their outfit**.

Catalina Creel didn't just wear an eye patch — she weaponized it. In a family of Catholics, she was my first saint. She turned disability into Dior, poisoned husbands between facials and proved evil could arrive in a Mercedes with perfect lipstick.

At nine, I taped a silk scarf over one eye and practiced glaring into the mirror. Catalina was my first acting teacher. Catalina taught us that villains flaunt their flaws—and we applauded.

In my family, we didn't discuss emotions.

We broadcasted them.

The living room was a soundstage with unpaid extras and no commercial breaks.

Cristina Bazán[12] taught us heartbreak, redeemed only when she landed El Puma.[13] I believed it. Mami watched Cristina cry with the reverence of a Mass. Bills arrived, the power company (LUMA's spiritual ancestor) charged what could've bought three Birkins, and Mami still wept like Verónica Castro — luminous, tragic, air-conditioned.

---

[11] **Cuna de Lobos:** The 1986 Mexican soap that made evil fashionable. One woman, one eye patch, and more gaslighting than a presidential debate. Everyone's aunt secretly thought she was Catalina Creel minus the budget.
[12] **Cristina Bazán**: Puerto Rico's patron saint of emotional repression. Johanny Rosaly cried so elegantly she made trauma look like a skin care routine.
[13] **El Puma:** Venezuelan singer José Luis Rodriguez proof that conditioner and confidence can build an empire. My first crush and first lesson that volume=power.

I took notes.

I learned early that tears became currency. My exchange rate beat Wall Street.

When I was eight and refused to leave Titi Alba's weekend getaway. I cried and told my father, "¡*Tu te quedas ahí feo*!" They laughed.

That's when I realized drama could halt authority.

It was my first close-up.

The Gospel According to Soraya

Telenovelas were my emotional bootcamp.

Soraya Montenegro from *María la del Barrio*[14] taught us betrayal like an AP course. Treachery wasn't always an eyepatch; sometimes it wore couture, complemented your shoes and then shoved you — literally — in the trash.

For the record, this happened to me.

Field Day. Third grade. I stomped on the rival team's yellow hat like it owed me money. The sixth-grade queen yanked my hair and tossed me into the trash can.

Not couture — just Gloria Vanderbilt jeans — but pure telenovela energy.

Survival Law X: Never stomp on a queen's hat unless you're ready for the dumpster.

Lessons in Glamorous Suffering

---

[14] **María la del Barrio:** Thalía's crowning telenovela achievement, part saint, part street fighter. She cried in contour and weaponized poverty chic. Her defining moment? Tossing her rival straight into the trash, proving sometimes the recycling bin is the only safe place for a man.

Los Ricos Tambien Lloran[15] insisted life was suffering — mascara-streaming, staircase-tumbling suffering. Even mansions couldn't cry-proof their marble floors.

By comparison, my teenage heartbreaks, ugly crying into an off-brand pillow, felt like reruns on a student budget.

American girls had Barbie's Dreamhouse.

I had Catalina's villain arc.

Catechism taught me sin.

Thalía taught me sequins.

Later, came *The Rules*,[16] a pastel dating "Bible" commanding women to disappear in pearls. Don't call. Don't eat. Don't exist.

Allegedly it worked — until you farted or told the truth.

Honestly, if a book tells you to vanish to be loved, donate it and buy a sandwich. Sandwiches never gaslight you.

Moral of the Episode

Forget school. Telenovelas were my survival flashcards —less education, more emotional disaster preparedness.

They taught me that chaos could be scripted, that every tragedy had a theme song, and that survival could be fabulous.

Maybe that's why I clung to them. They offered continuity when my life was just commercial breaks between traumas.

If life insists on drama, you might as well make it binge-worthy.

---

[15] **Los Ricos También Lloran:** The 1979 telenovela that taught Latin America that even the rich cry, though preferably near marble staircase and within reach of a yacht. A masterclass in humid suffering: mascara bleeding, pearls clutched and someone always tumbling down a banister of emotions.

[16] **The Rules:** The 90's dating bible that taught women to behave like elusive cats in pearls. Basically, a masterclass in emotional starvation rebranded as elegance. Many of us treated it like scripture, only to discover it was less *Genesis* and more *Gaslight*.

THE DECODER

Survival Law #3*: When life feels impossible, pretend you're in a telenovela. If you can't survive it, at least give it ratings.*

EPISODE 4 — THE MATRIARCH AND THE GENERAL

12/25 — 10:00 a.m.

Rating: PG

Episode Description: *Power, survival and the fine art of outliving your enemies.*

I inherited this love for drama, but I also inherited something else: the quiet strength of women who survived by making themselves indispensable.

Take my grandmother: **Doña Eulalia Mercedes Rivera de Nazario**, known to all as Maman. Maman who married a tyrant and outlived him out of sheer spite.

My grandfather, **Don Apolonio Nazario**, El General[17] was the kind of man whispered about in hushed family gossip. A *viejo tirano* who built an empire with one hand and ruled his home with the other — usually swinging a belt. A man who believed in discipline the way other men believed in God.

A dictator in guayabera, the kind of man who thought kneeling on gravel-built character — and maybe orthopedic bills. His belt had more cameos than Cantinflas. We should've given it its own SAG card.

And my grandmother?

[17] **El General:** Not an actual general, just a domestic dictator with a belt and a God complex.

She carried nine children while chain-smoking Chesterfields like it was prenatal yoga. She waited all day long for the 8:00 p.m. telenovela, because at least there, justice existed.

By the time I came along, Maman was a relic of another era — still in widow's black like it was Chanel couture, still refusing to drive because, as she put it, "*Eso es lo que hacen las putas.*" According to Maman, women who drove weren't fast; they were fast.

I froze.

I drove.

A lot.

Did that make me… a floozy with a license?

My mother—cool as an ice cube in a Cuba Libre —explained that back in the day, El General bought Maman a Cadillac. Maman detonated because she knew his mistress, La Gata, was already test-driving the same model.

Nothing says romance like synchronized infidelity.

From that day on, Maman's logic calcified: driving equaled debauchery. A respectable lady got *driven.* Preferably by the Holy Spirit in a Cadillac.

Meanwhile, there I was cruising in my Porsche 911, dragging our family honor behind me like an oil leak in heels.

But here's the thing.

Every time I pulled into her driveway — that crumbling Baldrich mansion with iron gates and judgmental orchids — I felt like I was looking into a crystal ball.

If I stayed.

If I obeyed.

If I married the kind of man, El General would have approved of.

I could end up just like her.

Imprisoned in widow's black.

Silenced by tradition.

Surviving, but never living.

Maman endured. She survived — but she never *gozó la vida.*

She survived a husband who mistook control for devotion. She survived a society that prized silence over selfhood — a world that never once asked what she wanted, only what she could endure.

I wondered…

Is survival enough, if it comes at the cost of joy?

Years later, when she passed, I wasn't at her funeral. I was too busy acting in San Francisco, chasing a stage dream while missing the woman who had defined so much of my script — a fact I regret, and one I carry like a footnote nobody asked for but that never stops echoing.

As a teenager, though, I didn't see her as tragic.

I saw her as mortifying.

She lived with us, and whenever a *pretendiente*[18] came calling, Maman would shuffle out in her widow's-black *bata,*[19] like death's chaperone. She'd fix her eyes on my date and demand, with courtroom gravitas:

---

[18] **Pretendiente:** Literally, "suitor," but in Puerto Rican households, it meant any male with a pulse within five miles of your daughter. Ranking system: harmless crush, mild threat, potential scandal in sneakers.

[19] **Bata**: A shapeless housecoat: half comfort, half weapon. In a grandmother's hands, it was tactical gear; ideal for surprise attacks on teenage boys and instant moral correction.

"*¿Quién es ese hombre? ¿Qué quiere?*"

Who is that man? What does he want?

At the time, I rolled my eyes and prayed for the earth to open.

Now, looking back, I see it.

She wasn't trying to humiliate me.

She was trying to protect me.

It was her way of making sure I didn't end up with a tyrant like hers.

Leaving the island wasn't rebellion.

It was self-preservation.

I wasn't just escaping a place.

I was dodging destiny.

That's the paradox.

I left because I didn't want to become her.

However, I carry her anyway — the fire, the fury, the questions no man could wiggle out of.

I was literally born in a hurricane; Category 4, tear-your-roof-off-your-life kind of storm.

Tell me that's not divine foreshadowing.

But I didn't stay stuck.

I flew away.

And this book?

This is for the women like me — the ones who refuse to play nice or play small. The ones who carry chaos in their blood but still manage to build, to love, to laugh.
Because no matter where you land...

La supervivencia es un arte.[20]

Mi amor, we were born to master it.

THE DECODER

Survival Law #4: *Survival isn't muscle; it's stamina. Outlast everyone at the table.*

---

[20] **La supervivencia es un arte**: Survival is an art. Said when life explodes but the eyeliner doesn't. Proof that our ancestors passed down high-functioning trauma, and impeccable accessorizing.

EPISODE 5 — THE GUN INCIDENT IN MAMAN'S HOUSE

12/25 — 11:00 a.m.

Rating: PG

Episode Description: *Wealth, chaos, and a high-stakes game of armed misunderstanding bingo.*

Now, dear reader, if you take nothing else from *The Latina Survival Guide*, let it be this: sometimes the universe hands you a pass, sometimes it does not.

In our case, on a Christmas that should've been filled with sugar-dusted *mantecaditos*[21] and ill-advised gifts, the Universe — by sheer cosmic oversight or divine intervention — decided we would live to tell the tale.

It all started with the guns.

It was the 1970s, a time when questionable parenting choices were not just common, but practically mandatory. That year, my sister, Veronica (Vero) and I received a pair of plastic toy guns — a festive endorsement of Cowboys and Indians[22], that deeply problematic, colonialist pastime in which my sister, naturally, assigned herself to the role of the heroic cowboy, while, I, the younger, more pliable one, was relegated to the Indian.

---

[21] **Mantecaditos**: The Puerto Rican cookie world's ultimate little seductress. Also called polvorones but only amateurs call it that.

[22] **Cowboys and Indians**: The ultimate childhood role-play game where one kid gets a shiny badge and the other gets a paper feather and generational trauma.

Despite the fact that, with her very Taína cheekbones, she was the obvious candidate for historical accuracy.

The script was simple: she would hunt me down, scalp me metaphorically, and bask in the glory of victory, while I — doomed to historical erasure, would perish in silence.

At least that was the plan.

Enter: The Adults

My parents, in an impressive act of Latino parental obfuscation, whisked themselves away to Washington D.C., allegedly because *my father had to testify before Congress* — a vague yet dramatic claim that, to this day, remains shrouded in mystery.

What, exactly, my father had to say to Congress? I still don't know.

But of course, my mother — a woman who believed children should be seen, not informed — kept us blissfully unaware, ensuring we continued to exist in our perfectly curated alternative reality, where parental disappearances were normal, and facts were mere suggestions.

With them gone, Vero and I were deposited at Maman's mansion, a sprawling Baldrich estate where survival skills were tested, but decorum was law.

Maman was a formidable grandmother who ran the house with the efficiency of an *ancien-régime* French countess and the paranoia of an early 2000s tech billionaire.

Case in point?

The *life-size* cardboard cutout of my *cabrón*[23] grandfather positioned by the telephone table to scare off potential

[23] **Cabrón:** Puerto Rican for man, idiot, or legend depending on tone and eyebrow height. Once meant "male goat" (horns, obviously). Now: your bro, your ex, or both.

intruders. A man so spectacularly unbothered in life had, in death, been repurposed into an improvised security system.

Macabre? Yes.

Effective? Also, yes.

Alexa could never.

Bingo, But Make it Armed

The real action, however, was happening in the dining room, where my tías — a coalition of Catholic high-stakes gamblers — were deep in the throes of Bingo Night.

Forget parish basements. These women played for real money.

The *bolos*[24] — sacred bingo numbers — were kept in an antique French-linen pillowcase because why store them in plastic like a peasant? Maman would stir the bag and call out the numbers with all the solemnity of a high priestess conducting an exorcism.

"*¡Seis! ¡Treinta y seis! ¡Setenta — el bolo del pretendiente de la Tía Ramona!*"

The rule was ironclad: do not interrupt the game; unless you had a death wish or a winning card.

The Incident

Meanwhile, Vero and I escalated our Cowboy-versus-Indian showdown in the guest bedroom reserved for Tío Rubén —our beloved uncle who never arrived on time but always brought the best gifts and disappeared for long stretches with suspicious ease.

---

[24] **Bolo(s):** Not an acronym, not a fugitive alert; just the number you scream when B-11 is called, because "B11" lacked the necessary chaos.

Left to our own devices, Vero and I decided to escalate our Cowboy-versus-Indian reenactment.

The game had started harmlessly enough chasing each other around the room, ducking behind armchairs, fake shooting, fake dying…

At some point, I vanished.

I wedged myself into a closet behind an impenetrable wall of guayaberas and Panama hats, my heart pounding as Vero searched.

And then, she found something else.

A .38 revolver.

Not a toy.

Not a prop.

A real, fully loaded revolver.

Vero picked it up, gleeful. She pointed it at me. Then at herself.

Then, she pulled the trigger.

BOOM.

The sound was like the television had exploded.

For a split second, I saw the headline: *Eight-Year-Old Shot at Bingo Night.*

We stared at each other, stunned.

Then the blood.

A crimson geyser bursting from Vero's left hand.

Some screamed.

Some ducked.

Maman lit another Chesterfield.

Just another Tuesday.

I wasn't afraid of dying.

I was afraid of Mom.

Catholic guilt doesn't need bullets; it comes preloaded.

Because *Dios nos libre*,[25] surviving a gunshot only to be murdered by our own mother for misbehaving was a very real possibility.

Aftermath

We ran to the bathroom, hysterical, wrapping her hand in toilet paper, like a two-ply Charmin[26] could stop an arterial bleed.

Enter Titi Lía, *La Boticaria* — the family's pharmacist and designated voice of reason. She took one look at the blood-drenched crime scene, wrapped Vero's hand in a proper towel, and started yelling for 911.

God bless a pharmacist in a family full of lunatics.

The rest was a blur: ambulance, cast, Maman's disapproving tsk-tsks, my mother's absolute meltdown upon return.

And the gun?

It belonged to Tío Rubén. He had left it there "just in case" someone tried to rob Maman. Because, back in the day, people didn't believe in safety boxes or trigger locks.

If you needed a gun, you needed a gun.

Vero survived, emerging with a cast, a permanent V-shaped scar—V, for Vero, Violence, and Vatican-level guilt—and a level of celebrity at school usually reserved for war heroes and child actors.

I, her unpaid assistant, was conscripted to wrap it before showers and fetch juice boxes on demand.

---

[25] ***Dios nos libre***: "God deliver us" usually from your own choices. Always said out loud, never works. See LSG decoder.

[26] **Charmin**: Mr. Whipple begged America not to squeeze it. He never mentioned not using it for arterial bleeds.

It was funny.

Until it wasn't. Until you realized chaos was the baseline, and calm was the anomaly.

The Latina Survival Lesson

- Lock up your damn guns. This should not even need to be said.
- Sometimes survival is just chaos hitting pause—not mercy.
- Survival in a Latino family isn't quiet. It's dramatic, bloody, and somehow stylish.

In the end, we should have died.

We didn't.

THE DECODER

Survival Law #5*: Family feud? Duck first, ask questions later.*

EPISODE 6 – PAPI: THE FINAL BOSS

12/25 — 12:00 p.m.

Rating: PG

Episode Description: *Or, how a disabled man outplayed an entire Puerto Rican telenovela.*

Let's be honest. If my father had been born in almost any other country, in almost any other family, he might have spent his life locked away in a dark room, hidden behind curtains and shame.

But this was Puerto Rico.

My father, **Don Leopoldo Santos Oliviano de Vizcaya**, was born into a world where people made things work. Obstacles were merely suggestions. Pity was for other people. A man with cerebral palsy could become the suavest, smartest, most legendary womanizer in our family's history.

Yes, I said womanizer.

Because God gives with one hand and takes with the other. While my father came to this world with twisted legs and one arm that wouldn't cooperate, he was also gifted with something far more powerful: an unshakable confidence, a razor-sharp wit, and a photographic memory.

Papi could quote Shakespeare and Cervantes —sometimes in the same sentence, in two languages, and still remember what he had for lunch in 1962.

He was the kind of man who could disarm you with a joke, seduce you with a poem, and leave you wondering why you'd never dated a guy who walked with crutches before.

For me, watching Papi meant realizing disability didn't cancel desire. It rewired it into strategy.

I watched strangers lean in when he spoke and I thought: *So, this is power.*

Act One: Born to Crawl, Destined to Rise

He was born in Villalba, a small town in the mountains, a day a midwife was late, and the baby refused to come out. My grandfather, chain-smoking outside the house, was probably muttering: *¿Pa' qué me metí en esto?*

From birth, his legs were fused. He crawled until twelve.

Even as a crawling child, there were signs he was different — not broken, just brilliant.

His best friend, **Toro Vélez**, carried him to school every day. Toro was built like a Puerto Rican rhinoceros and later became a millionaire, because in this family, even side characters come with plot twists.

At school, my father inhaled books like other kids inhaled candy. He didn't read. He devoured. By his teens, he was quoting Tolstoy, Weber, and Molière. He graduated *summa cum laude*. Of course he did.

The Surgery

(And the Slight Risk of Being an American Experiment)

When he was twelve, a team of American doctors arrived in Fajardo with gleaming white coats and suspiciously high hopes. They said things like:

- We can separate his legs.
- Trust us — this isn't experimental.

Desperate to stand in a world built for walkers, he agreed.

They operated.

He spent two years recovering, unable to attend school. So, he read. Classics. Philosophy. Psychology. Literature. Memorizing passages like prayers. Gripping words the way others gripped rosaries.

But recovery wasn't just scripture and solitude.

He was thirteen.

She was American. Red hair. Green eyes. Starched white uniform.

A nurse.

She leaned down — maybe to check a chart, maybe to fluff a pillow — and then, without warning, kissed him. Just a brush of lips but for a thirteen-year-old in traction, that was basically third base.

Papi would later claim that was the moment two things happened:

- He realized he could be desired.
- He developed a lifelong thing for women in nurse uniforms, which eventually became my mother's problem.

By the time he finished recovering, he could walk with crutches. To him, that meant freedom.

Thanks to that redhead, it also meant something else.

He was back in the game.

Confidence as Survival

That's when Papi found Raymond Chandler.[27]

---

[27] **Raymond Chandler**: The man who convinced a limping Puerto Rican kid that sarcasm was mobility and a trench coat counted as therapy.

Marlowe's trench coats and one-liners became his armor. He wasn't just a boy on crutches anymore. He was the Puerto Rican Philip Marlowe, swaggering into rooms with sarcasm and smoke, as if life itself were a case he could crack.

Charm was Papi's shield, but it didn't erase the pain of being trapped in a body that betrayed him.

He taught me survival wasn't about strength.

It was about confidence so unshakeable that the world bent around it.

Whenever I start auditioning for the role of *Poor Me*, I remember Papi — half muscle, half miracle — outsmarting gravity with a grin.

He didn't have time for self-pity. He was too busy rewriting physics. So, I shut up, pour some café and keep moving.

The man crawled till twelve.

I can survive 2026 in the United States.

From Crutches to Cap & Gown

He left Villalba for Hato Rey, studied law, became president of his class, and received a standing ovation at graduation.

He didn't stop there.

He applied to Wharton Business School in Philadelphia in the 1950s — when there were no disability accommodations. He was accepted.

Picture it: a Puerto Rican man with crutches, alone on icy sidewalks, carrying books in one hand, slipping in the snow, hauling himself up — day after day.

At Wharton, the ice cracked under his crutches. Every step was a gamble against gravity. There were no elevators, only stairs. He stayed in the library until closing. Stubbornness or resilience, I could never tell the difference. He made both look like love.

He studied until he bled brilliance.

He graduated with honors.

Again.

Because in our family, success was a hereditary disease.

Enter Mami: The Final Mission

He saw her across campus:

Doña Solángel Nazario de Díaz.

Not a nurse—but a dietician. In the 1950s, however, uniforms were very postwar cosplay chic.

Love at first sight.

There was just one problem.

He couldn't exactly run after her.

So, Papi recruited a wingman.

Enter **Cundo Flechazo**.

Yes, that was his name.

A *carro público*[28] driver with ruddy cheeks, green eyes, a tragic comb-over and a solid F in my father's Business Administration class.

My father made him an offer he couldn't refuse:

"Deliver an orchid and a poem to Solángel every day of a month. Do that, and I'll turn your F into a miracle."

Deal.

---

[28] **Carro público:** Not a taxi, not a bus. The original Uber, but with more rosaries, gossip and the faint smell of gasoline mixed with Aramis cologne.

For thirty days, my mother received:

- One orchid
- One original poem (often quoting Neruda and Borges)
- One sweaty, grinning Cundo shoving it into her hands.

Eventually, Mami gave in.

Because if a man sends orchids and poetry for thirty straight days, you either call the police or go on one date.

She chose love.

Or exhaustion.

Then entered El General, my grandfather, a man who took one look at my disabled, poetry-writing, orchid-sending suitor arriving in carro público driven by Cundo — whose hobbies included failing classes and dating Dominican woman from el *caserío*[29] — and declared, with all the grace of a falling anvil:

"*Sobre mi cadáver.*"[30]

(To be continued…)

THE DECODER

Survival Law #6: *Never underestimate the counted out. Disability doesn't cancel strategy.*

---

[29] **Caserío**: Puerto Rican housing projects. Mami called them "the jungle," warning us about *los titeritos del caserío,* baby mafiosos in Nike slides. To her, *Lloréns Torres* was less a neighborhood, more a moral threat than a zip code.
[30] **Sobre mi cadáver**: Over my dead body. Translation for non-Spanish speakers: Permission granted posthumously.

EPISODE 7 – MAMI: RADIANT RAGE IN PASO FINO ANKLES

12/25 — 1:00 p.m.

Rating: PG

Episode Description: *Or, how a woman weaponized paso fino ankles, silence and survival itself.*

My mother didn't shout in public.

She didn't throw plates.

She didn't raise her hand where anyone could see.

In private?

She did.

She let the walls absorb what society never could.

Her fury was silent in salons, seismic in kitchens. Some people bake cookies; she baked consequences.

When **Doña Solángel Nazario de Díaz** walked into a room, rage traveled with her like perfume — invisible, intoxicating, impossible to ignore. Her heels struck marble, each step leaving a trail of Ralph Lauren, intimidation, and intention.

Her beauty was legendary: luminous skin, pearls at her throat, a waist so tiny it measured just seventeen inches, and ankles as delicate and precise as a paso fino horse.

However, those same ankles could summon thunder.

Her elegance was armor.

Her rage was the weapon strapped beneath it.

Yet she was more than rage.

Solángel was *La Generala de la Cocina.*

In the kitchen, her culinary witchery was a legend: *manjares*[31] that could seduce a bishop, calm a child, or silence a rival. Her food was medicine, indulgence, absolution.

She could've held her own on *Chef's Table*— if *Chef's Table* featured women who cooked in high heels while quoting Sor Juana Inés de la Cruz,[32] and planning the next charity luncheon.

When sickness came, she became balm: cool hands-on hot foreheads, broths sick with love and control. Pampering that bordered on royal protocol.

The Generala

To her children, she was protector and drill sergeant.

She held the house together without yoga, meditation apps, or podcasts telling her to breathe. Her downward dog was a slap. Her therapists were her sisters, their *cua-cua-cua* laughter was the only group session available.

Discipline was her gospel.

Sometimes it went too far.

But in her mind, softness was a luxury, and survival was duty.

Survival required order.

---

[31] **Manjares:** Puerto Rican desserts so decadent they blur the line between pastry and spell work. Think flan, tembleque, brazo gitano but also a mother's coded way of saying " *I love you and I control you*" in one custard. In our house, manjares weren't recipes, they were negotiations: sugar + eggs + condensed milk = obedience, forgiveness, and a side of diabetes.

[32] **Sor Juana Inés de la Cruz:** The original Latinx feminist. A 1600s nun who clapped back the patriarchy with a quill. "*Hombres necios que acusáis a la mujer sin razón...*" The 17th Century version of: "Boy, bye!"

Ivy League degrees and master's programs are not forged from cuddles. They're forged by mothers who stomped, who scolded, who demanded.

If I braved Swarthmore alone, California alone, and this book alone, it's because she drilled into me that you do not quit.

You finish with grace.

Sometimes stubborn. Sometimes fateful. Always graceful.

The Darkness & the Laughter

As the youngest, she had witnessed El General's punishments — swift, humiliating, unforgettable.
Yet, what she remembered more clearly was the aftermath.
Maman and her sisters slamming the door.
Then exploding into *cua-cua-cua* laughter — ducks mocking pain.

That became her inheritance.

Rage pressed down like fine china. Laughter as rebellion.

She carried both legacies forward — radiant one day, cruel the next.

Silent. Explosive. Human.

Recognition

For me, the survival lesson was recognition.

Beauty and violence can live in the same body.

Silence hums with history.

Sometimes the only release is to stomp.

Sometimes it's to laugh.

Sometimes it's both.

I pretended not to stare at her ankles, but in that moment, I understood quiet power.

To this day, when I hear heels echo on marble, my spine straightens.

Not out of fear.

Out of recognition.

Because I know the sound of rage disguised as grace.

And I know it works.

THE DECODER

Survival Law #7: *Beware of the mother who stomps. Her ankles hold ancestral fury, culinary sorcery, and the discipline of a general.*

EPISODE 8 — FORBIDDEN ROMANCE

12/25 — 2:00 p.m.

Rating: PG

Episode Description: *Or, how a serenade became a siege.*

Love stories are often messy, passionate and full of questionable life choices. But rarely do they involve a midnight musical ambush — and a grandfather who, in a fit of rage, weaponized his own dignity.

My parents were not normal people.

They were characters in a high-budget, over-the-top forbidden-love telenovela, complete with a dramatic villain, a soundtrack by Los Panchos, and a midnight act of war disguised as romance.

Phase One: Operation Seduction

Once my father successfully infiltrated my mother's heart, the grand, no-holds-barred, money-is-no-object courtship began.

He wined and dined her at San Juan's most exclusive temples of old money — places where men smoked cigars the size of their self-worth and women sipped cocktails while plotting social assassinations.

- **Caribe Hilton**[33] — Nothing says romance like the faint scent of colonialism.

---

[33] **Caribe Hilton**: Where piña coladas were born; I lost my first kiss, and Puerto Rico's unofficial embassy of 80s disco glamour. Picture it: a private beach, Julianna's velvet-roped club, and enough sequins bright enough to guide ships home.

- **El Zipperle** — For when you want a steak and a side of European disdain.
- **La Cueva del Chicken Inn**[34] — Where the pizza was holy, but nothing else was.

Each date was lavish, clandestine, and absolutely forbidden.

Because Don Apolonio — my mother's father — was *not* having it.
One look at my father — his crutches, his twisted legs, his dangerously high levels of confidence — and he decided this man was a threat to the bloodline.

A cripple? In *his* family?

¡Jamás!

Never mind that my dad was Wharton-educated, a legal and financial mastermind, a world-class manipulator with the seductive powers of a golden-era movie star.

To Don Apolonio, none of it mattered.

Disabled men did not inherit daughters.

Phase Two: The Midnight Coup

So, like every romantic hero faced with adversity, my father did what any self-respecting, semi-disabled genius would do.

He turned it up.

At precisely midnight, he staged the most reckless grand gesture of the century.

He hired a trio of musicians.

---

[34] **La Cueva del Chicken Inn**: Raúl Juliá's father opened it in 1947. (yes, Gomez Addams had a dad).The pizza was divine, the lighting suspiciously spiritual. You didn't dine at La Cueva, you crossed over.

Then a pianist.

After all, why stop at guitars when you can roll in a baby grand for maximum drama?

Nothing says love like violating a noise ordinance.

He loaded them onto a massive truck and stormed my mother's house like a musical coup d'état.

That night's serenade reeked of rum and night jasmine —danger in 4/4 time.

There, beneath the Caribbean stars, he sang her the most gut-wrenching bolero of all time:

Sin ti,[35] *no podré vivir jamás...*
Y pensar que nunca más,
estarás junto a mí...

Without you, I could never live...
And to think that never again,
you will be by my side...

It was spectacle. Delirium. Broadway in Baldrich.

Puerto Rico's version of holding up a boombox blasting *In Your Eyes* — except with a live orchestra and hazardous levels of moonshine.

My mother?

Swooning.

Her lipstick smudged on a borrowed glass.

Her rage glowing as brightly as her loneliness.

My father's confidence?

---

[35] **Sin Ti:** Bolero immortalized by Los Panchos, weaponized by my father when orchids and Neruda weren't enough.

Peaking.

And then —

Don Apolonio woke up.

THE DECODER

Survival Law #8: *If love knocks, don't just open the door. Expect the full orchestra.*

EPISODE 9 – THE GOLDEN SHOWER OF RAGE

12/25 — 3:00 p.m.

Rating: PG

Episode Description: *Or how my father survived piss, patriarchy, and exile.*

Phase Three: The Great Piss War of 1957

My grandfather, already running on zero patience and a lifetime allotment of machismo, staggered to his window, surveyed the circus unfolding below, and barked:

"¿Quién es ese gato esgalillao?"

Who is that screeching cat?

In Puerto Rico, even insults come with animal metaphors.

Because this man was a man of swift action and questionable judgment, he grabbed the nearest object at hand:

A *palangana.*[36]

Without hesitation, El General dumped the entire thing out the window onto my father.

Cue:

- Screaming
- Chaos
- Musicians fleeing

---

[36] **Palangana**: A washbasin, Victorian "toilet" for midnight emergencies; a.k.a. *pato*, which insulted ducks, gays, and anyone with a nose.

- A pianist gamely trying to finish the song

And my father?

Drenched.

Soaked in ancestral vengeance, hierarchy, and bodily fluids, laughing his absolute ass off.

Because nothing says *I'm winning* like getting baptized in rage water and still walking away with the girl.

Here's the thing.

This wasn't just slapstick.

For my father, humiliation was a weapon he flipped inside out. If he could laugh — drenched, steaming, publicly shamed — he could survive anything.
Classism.
Ableism.
Exile.

Rage only works if you let it shame you.

He never did.

Phase Four: The Nuclear Option

By sunrise, Don Apolonio had decided escalation was required.

So, like a 19th century aristocrat cosplaying banishment, he shipped my mother off to Virginia.

Alone.

No warning.

No discussion.

The mission was clear: marry her to a tall, able-bodied American doctor and erase the problem.

And guess what?

She did.

Mami vs. The Deep South

Now imagine this:

A Puerto Rican bombshell with a seventeen-inch waist, doll eyes and ankles delicate enough to be insured by Lloyd's of London — parachuted into pre-Civil-Rights-era Virginia.

Spoiler: the Southern debutantes did **not** take it well.

This was:

- Jim Crow America
- Before Civil Rights
- Before anyone knew what to do with a caramel-skinned goddess crossed her legs like an eviction notice.

Doors closed.

Seats emptied.

Smiles turned to frost.

Yet she endured.

Exiled, Mami sat alone; her rage as bright as her loneliness. She sat. She ate. She waited. She endured. And she still looked better than all of them combined.

She was this close to settling.

To marrying her tall, white, doctor fiancé.

To trading passion for safety.

Until —

The Accident.

What was it?

Oh, *dear reader.*

Just you wait.

THE DECODER

Survival Law #9: *In Puerto Rican families, every victory comes with collateral damage.*

EPISODE 10 – THE FUNERAL PROPOSAL

12/25 — 4:00 p.m.

Rating: PG

Episode Description: *Because nothing says romance like a corpse within arm's reach.*

Let's set the scene.

My grandfather, El General, **Don Apolonio Nazario** — a man built entirely out of pride, cigar smoke and unnecessary risk-taking — decided one day that he, and he alone, was going to fix a faulty electrical pole.

Now, you might be thinking, *shouldn't an actual electrician be handling that?*

You would be correct.

But Don Apolonio was a man who didn't believe in weakness. He thought hiring a professional was for cowards. And, unfortunately, he was a man who did not understand electricity.

And that, dear reader, is how he electrocuted himself to death.

The Most Aggressively Puerto Rican Death Imaginable

This was not a quiet, dignified passing.

There was a blinding blue spark that lit up the night sky, and a sizzling crack that haunts local pigeons to this day. And just like that, Don Apolonio was no more.

A tragic loss? Yes.

An absolutely on-brand way for a Puerto Rican patriarch to die? Also, yes.

Enter My Father: The Opportunist

In the wake of this shocking tragedy, my mother — eyeliner smudged, pearls loose at her throat — called one person.

My father.

And my father? Oh, he saw his moment.

Like the Machiavellian mastermind he was, he:

- Dumped his redhead American girlfriend (goodbye, Becky — who went on to invent Pilates. Probably.)
- Grabbed Cundo, human bad idea factory.
- Boarded the first plane back to Puerto Rico.
- Showed up at the funeral with a bottle of *pitorro* tucked under his arm, because why grieve sober?

Picture the scene.

A solemn wake at Maman's house. The air thick with incense, candle wax and the acrid bite of moonshine. Relatives in black fanning themselves. One aunt, collapsing onto a couch in operatic faint. The hum of women praying the rosary and weeping blurred into static.

Then, through the heavy wooden doors, walks my father.

Dressed to kill.

Crutches clicking against the tile like punctuation marks. Flanked by Cundo, nodding solemnly while sipping straight from the bottle.

It was pure telenovela staging: the villain thought defeated returning at the worst possible moment.

And my mother?

Teary-eyed. Fragile. Caught between the casket and the man who refused to be erased.

She looked less like a society beauty than a girl desperate to be carried away.

The Proposal

My father locked eyes with her.

Then glanced at the casket of the man who had fought so hard to keep them apart, and said, with the shamelessness of a survivor who never knew when to stop:

"Well, now that *El Viejo's* gone, why don't you marry me?"

Reader.

She. Said. Yes.

Puerto Ricans are nothing if not efficient with grief.

Not because it was the perfect moment.

Not because grief makes good soil for romance.

But because she was exhausted.

Because love and survival often come disguised as surrender.

Because sometimes, in the middle of death and chaos, you choose the man who refuses to let you go.

Latina Survival Wisdom

My father never took *no* for an answer.

My mother never stood a chance.

And Cundo? That man probably graduated valedictorian from the School of Stubbornness.

Because in our family, courage and ingenuity weren't just traits.

They were competitive sports.

Even in death.

THE DECODER

Survival Law #10: *Laugh at death once, and marriage feels less like destiny than endurance.*

EPISODE 11 – GHOSTLY CONSULTANTS

12/25 — 5:00 p.m.

Rating: PG

Episode Description: *When your family treats the afterlife like a business conference & a high stakes telenovela.*

Death in my family was not a sacred mystery.

It was an industry.

A well-oiled, cross-generational, full-service operation run with the cutthroat precision of a luxury real-estate firm and the supernatural flair of a low-budget horror movie.

While other families gathered for Sunday dinners, we gathered for séances. While other children were taught about the birds and the bees, I was taught about the dead and the restless.

Other kids played Monopoly.

We played, "*Guess Which Ancestor is Haunting the Kitchen*?"

Spoiler: It was always someone named Carmen.

The ghosts weren't gone.

They were just nosy.

And very Puerto Rican.

Ancestors lingered in doorways, occupied kitchen chairs, and whispered unsolicited advice like uncles who couldn't resist weighing in.

The most haunting story belonged to **Lito** — my cousin, the child with a beard and a very bad premonition.

Lito: The Child with a Beard and a Countdown Clock

Lito was nine years old when he started growing a mustache and a beard.

This was not normal.

Even in our gene of prematurely graying, over-dramatic ancestors, a child who looked like a forty-five-year-old accountant was unsettling.

Add the doomed aura of a cursed Disney prince, and you have the makings of a family legend no one wanted but everyone repeated.

Naturally, my **Tía Alba Morales** and **Tío Rubén Nazario** — who happened to own *Casa Eterna* Funeral Home, of course they did — took him to a doctor.

The diagnosis: a brain tumor causing his body to age too quickly.

He died soon after.

I never met him.

But I felt him every time I visited Tía Alba's house in Vega Alta.

Why?

Because her house was on top of a funeral home.

A Childhood Among Caskets: My First Work Experience

Most kids visited aunties with cookie jars and VHS tapes.

I visited an aunt with a walk-in embalming room and a stockroom full of premium caskets.

By six, I was running wakes like a pint-sized Kris Jenner with a prayer card.

- Age six: Handed out *estampitas* with concierge poise.
- Age seven: Poured hot chocolate for the grief-stricken like a barista in purgatory.
- Age eight: I could stage an altar with flowers, candles and a strategically placed rosary as if opening night in Bellas Artes.

One day, I scraped my knee in the cemetery and collapsed in an Oscar-worthy meltdown.

Titi Alba — equal parts pharmacist and retired beauty queen — patted my head and asked:

"Cha-cha, ¿qué tu quieres?"

Through snot and tears, I screamed:

"¡Un Whopper de Burger King!"[37]

That dear reader, is when I discovered my ultimate survival mechanism.

Fast food over feelings.

The Refrigerator, the Repairman & the Ghost Who Gave Permission

When the refrigerator died, most families called Sears.

We called a spirit medium.

---

[37] **Whopper de Burger King**: The post-mass treat of choice, plus a giant metal slide that doubled as skin-removal device. See LSG Decoder.

Evaristo, bald and stoic, came to fix it.

Hours later, we returned from a burial to find him calmly eating a sandwich at our kitchen table.

Titi Alba froze.

"¿Quién te preparó ese sándwich?"

Who made you that sandwich?

Evaristo, mid-chew, pointed towards a framed photograph.

"El nene."

The boy.

He was pointing at Lito.

The child who had been dead since Kennedy was in office.

The Weekends That Saved Me

Not every memory at *Casa Eterna* was embalming fluid and *estampitas.*

Weekends with Tía Alba and Tío Rubén were some of my happiest. They spoiled me as if I were an only child — gifts plucked from shelves without hesitation. Tenderness disguised as indulgence.

Her *sopa de plátano*,[38] steam curling like incense, broth salty-sweet and thick enough to haunt me in dreams.

Her altar to **San Judas Tadeo** (St. Jude) flickered constantly; candles lit for impossible causes, and eventually, for me.

---

[38] **Sopa de plátano:** Basically, Prozac with cilantro. Titi Alba's cure-all; green plantains boiled into submission until the broth tasted like comfort. Forget therapy, forget Xanax; one bowl and suddenly your soul was moisturized, your grades improved, and your enemies tripped on the sidewalk.

Even years later, when I was up for an audition in New York or a job in L.A., I knew that somewhere in *Casa Eterna*, a *velón* was burning with my name on it.

Between caskets and candles, I learned that survival wasn't only about ghosts. It was also about being loved enough to believe the impossible might just bend in your favor.

Con fé todo se puede.

With faith, everything is possible.

Doña Lucrecia: The Witch Who Loved Me Too Much

Every telenovela needs a witch. Ours was **Doña Lucrecia**.

Her hair was fire-engine red, like she dyed it with the blood of men who'd looked at her twice. Her skin was powder-white, as if sunlight had a restraining order. Her lipstick—crimson armor—drawn on with the confidence of a woman who hexed for sport.

She scared me. She scared everyone.

Adults whispered that she'd put spells on married men—love potions, candle work, the whole Loíza starter kit. Even priests crossed the street when they saw her coming, clutching their rosaries like pepper spray.

Yet she adored me.

"Tienes una gitana siguiéndote."

A gypsy is following you.

She wanted to read my tarot cards. Titi Alba said no. Even in that world, there were limits.

Doña Lucrecia also ran a *picas*[39] betting ring from her house. She always won. I still wonder if the spirits gave her the winning horse — or if the horses were too afraid to lose.

I never understood gambling or her flirtation with darkness. How can she be the mother of Titi Alba, who hosted priests for dinner upstairs, while downstairs — by the funeral home — Doña Lucrecia made deals with the other side?

There was a time in my life that I wished I had let Doña Lucrecia read my cards. Maybe she would've made sense of the zigzag path my life became — the risks, the obsessions, the men I barely survived, the strange jobs, the impossible dreams that somehow kept me alive.

Maybe Titi Alba already knew what the cards would say and didn't want me spooked by all the twists and heartbreaks ahead.

Maybe, the red-haired witch was trying to warn me about the gypsy she said followed me. Has that spirit been steering me ever since? Is that why I've moved so often, chasing art as if it were both a blessing and a curse?

What if Lucrecia's message was never a warning at all, but an invitation — to live every spell, every mistake, every miracle, until I could write my own prophecy?

My Own Gift

The spirits weren't just theirs. They were mine, too.

While other kids rode bikes, I saw aura colors like traffic lights. I knew who'd break up, who'd get sick, who'd never pay back a loan. I didn't ask for it; but the whispers came anyway, nosy, relentless, oddly comforting.

---

[39] **Picas:** Puerto Rican mechanical horse-racing game in which miniature horses race in circles while adults shout, smoke, and temporarily forget God.

Basically, I was the family's personal Netflix; dropping spoilers before anyone else had even logged in.

These days I'm more like a radio; Whoopi Goldberg in *Ghost* with better hair and worse boundaries.

The departed find me, hijack my frequency, and insist I deliver their messages.

It always happens one-on-one, when the living least expects it.

I just repeat what I hear — sometimes in strange syntax, sometimes with uncanny detail — and people freeze like I've said the password to their grief.

Once, a spirit told me to tell a friend about an ex-lover she'd missed in the 1980s because she was making a phone call in a San Francisco booth (coordinating a weed deal) at the exact wrong moment. She didn't smile; she went pale like I'd just live-streamed her 1987 weed deal.

Another time, I repeated a phrase a father used to whisper to his daughter before school… and she burst into tears.

It doesn't happen on demand. The dead are like influencers; they don't post on schedule. They show up when they want attention.

My ancestors, of course, are the pushiest. They slide into my dreams, my playlists, even my photo roll — numbers flashing like 444, 333, 222, 555, like celestial spam. They show up in songs, in power outages, in perfectly timed coincidences.

The truth? They're never gone. None of them are. You just have to tune in to the right frequency — somewhere between AM nostalgia and divine interference — and be willing to listen.

Lessons from a Family That Branded Death

While other kids learned to make grilled cheese, I learned to:

- Run a wake like a Four Seasons event planner with a liquor license.
- Treat ghosts like unpaid consultants with opinions.
- Understand that a premium casket is a beachfront property — invest early, get the best view.

Most people fear death.

We monetized it.

Most people avoid ghosts.

We asked if they wanted sugar with their coffee.

Some families inherit jewelry.

I inherited the dead and learned how to accessorize accordingly.

Because if the ghost of Lito proved anything, even in the afterlife…

You're never off the clock.

THE DECODER

Survival Law #11: *Ghosts don't scare me. Relatives with business plans do. But a sopa de plátano and a San Judas candle can make even death feel negotiable.*

ACT II

MADRID STREET: DYNASTY WITH BEANS

(Episodes 12-22)

EPISODE 12 – EL CAMINANTE

12/25 — 6:00 p.m.
Rating: PG

Episode Description: *Every neighborhood needs a ghost. Ours wore corduroy.*

Our house was on Madrid Street in Torrimar, Puerto Rico — one of those gated communities where every cul-de-sac borrowed gravitas from Spain. Toledo. Segovia. Córdoba. As if naming a dead-end "Salamanca" could erase the fact you were still in Guaynabo, surrounded by cement.

Naturally, we lived on Madrid — the capital.

Coincidence? Please.

My family was tailor-made for the crown jewel of Torrimar snobbery.

The houses were ranch-style cement bunkers, *modern* in brochures, and hurricane-proof in practice. My father who navigated life on crutches with tragic conquistador gravitas, sneered at American houses.

Casitas de cartón, he scoffed.

Cardboard boxes fit to blow away.

He tolerated American toothpaste but not the reindeer usurping the Three Kings.

Maman, who lived with us when she was older, was born in 1900. She oscillated between bingo ecstasy and death mask solemnity, lighting Chesterfields while looping the same hurricane stories — villagers flying like papier-mâché Dorothys during San Felipe and San Cipriano.

I found it mesmerizing.

My mother, meanwhile, could not have cared less about hurricanes.

She worried about my knees.

Every scrape from rollerblading was a blow to my marriage prospects. Worse, she feared they'd turn me into a *machota*,[40] her whispered panic code for lesbian.

To her, a pleated skirt was wasted on a girl with skinned knees.

Looking back, I understand now: it wasn't about knees or bandages.

It was about control.

A girl who skates, who falls, who dares, is harder to contain.

My mother wasn't policing my skin. She was policing my future.

That control followed me long after the scrapes healed.

Even when I left for Swarthmore, Mami kept my room frozen in time, exactly as if I were still eight — pink covers, antique bedframe, stuffed animals, trophies lined up like evidence of obedience.

When I came home, it felt like walking into a museum dedicated to the child she wished I had remained.

She often urged me to abandon Hollywood, abandon the States, abandon my life and return to her.

I couldn't.

I rebelled.

Maybe foolishly. Maybe bravely.

---

[40] **Machota**: Proof that queerness survives tías, polyester, and Catholic guilt.

The truth is I'm still fighting the ghost of my mother—her unreachable standard, her perfect discipline.

Aren't we all fighting some version of that?

The Madrid Street Spy Agency

My sister Veronica, our neighbor Catalina "Cata" Vélez Arrieta, and I founded the **Madrid Street Spy Agency**.

Still in our crisp white blouses and cerulean pleated skirts, we crouched behind hibiscus hedges with Cold War seriousness.

Picture Nancy Drew — but bilingual, sweaty, and wearing knee socks.

Catalina was our aristocrat-by-association. Her Spanish mother's Castilian lisp made "zapato" sound like a property deed.

Destiny clung to her.

Years later, she would rule her own empire from the Obama White House. Then, she ruled a Chihuahua named Tuki, who identified as a Doberman and barked accordingly.

Excellent preparation for bipartisan delusion on the Hill.

Enter El Caminante

Every neighborhood needs its mystery.

Ours was *El Caminante*.[41]

A teenage boy. Sixteen? Seventeen?

An afro that bounced like it kept its own metronome. Rust-colored corduroys in Puerto Rico's heat. Unforgivable.

Black T-shirt. One-strap backpack.

---

[41] **El Caminante**: Lit. The Walker, but less Nordic track, more ghost with commitment issues.

Every day, he walked past our house.

Silent.

Eyes forward.

Never looking at us.

Even the coquí seemed to pause mid-song as he passed.

He was always headed towards *Marista*,[42] the all-boys Catholic school.

We obsessed.

Catalina sighed, "He must be in love with one of us."

Veronica countered, "He's secretly rich, pretending to be poor."

Me?

I whispered, "He's a ghost."

Because in Puerto Rico, the boundary between the living and the dead is famously porous.

Every family has one — someone who keeps walking because no one ever asked them to stop.

And then, one day, he was gone.

No farewell.

No corduroy procession.

Just absence.

Only later did I understand what we were really doing.

Projecting.

Catalina projected destiny.

---

[42] **Marista**: The all-boys Catholic School in Torrimar, perennial rivals to Jesuit powerhouse San Ignacio. Think Sharks vs Jets in uniform ties, except the turf war was played out on basketball courts, soccer fields and quinceañera dance floors.

Veronica projected wealth.

I projected death.

Children don't interpret strangers.

They cast them.

El Caminante became our rehearsal — a blank screen on which we practiced the stories we would later live.

Maybe that's why I became a writer — to bridge the reality that never made sense, to stitch contradictions into something coherent.

When the answers didn't come, I invented them.

At every dinner table, I was the one saying, "*¿Te acuerdas?*" Do you remember?

As if memory itself could turn chaos into narrative.

Puerto Rico raised me to believe melodrama was survival.

Only in the exaggerated logic of telenovelas could I decode my family, my country, myself.

When the boy disappeared, Madrid Street revealed itself fully.

Widows dressed in mourning like couture.

Vendettas aging across generations.

Gossip traded like stock tips.

Who needed a silent boy in corduroy when every driveway staged a telenovela by breakfast?

The truth is, I still think about him.

About vanishing without explanation.

About how so many women in my family turned absence into fuel.

When answers don't come, you build a myth — and then you live inside it.

That's survival.

It's also storytelling.

And storytelling became my rebellion, my inheritance, my way of surviving the unsolvable.

When *El Caminante* vanished, Madrid Street stopped pretending it had mysteries.

It became what it always wanted to be.

A full-blown telenovela.

No commercial breaks.

That's when the chaos really began.

THE DECODER

Survival Law #12: *Respect the neighborhood ghost. He always knows more secrets than the living.*

EPISODE 13 – MADRID STREET: A CINEMATIC UNIVERSE OF ITS OWN

12/25 — 7:00 p.m.

Rating: PG

Episode Description: *A dysfunctional ensemble that could fuel five telenovelas.*

Some streets are just streets.

Madrid was not.

It was Beverly Hills with rosaries; *Crazy Rich Asians* with bingo cartels, *Dynasty* with Thom McAnn lift shoes.

After the mysterious disappearance of El Caminante, neighborhood surveillance became a civic duty. Our agency took it personally. By December, the Madrid Street Spy Agency had gone pro.

Our mission: surveillance, gossip, and defense against emotional terrorism.

Headquarters: My porch.

Assets: Folding chairs, Woolworth's binoculars and a half-empty can of Goya Vienna sausages. Code names were classified — until Mami leaked them on the phone.

Case File 001: The Caracas Contingent

Operation Arepas & Assets

Every spy agency needs an international scandal and ours came from Caracas.

We logged it in the binder as Case File 101: *The Caracas Contingent.*

Mission Objective: determine why the Fernández-Lamberti palace received more deliveries than Santa Claus and then vanished faster than a Caribbean tax break.

Every week brought a new delivery: imported tiles, chandeliers the size of Volkswagens and once — allegedly — a marble Virgin Mary with her own air conditioner.

Their parties were legendary; *quinceañeras* choreographed like Televisa specials. Mercedes, Lamborghinis, Venezuelan pop stars sliding through. It was the kind of glamour that made even San Juan's humidity feel imported.

And then, one day, they were gone.

Just...gone.

No goodbye. No moving truck. Only FBI agents, yellow tape, and unmarked sedans cordoning off Madrid Street.

The Spy Agency convened an emergency meeting under Cata's *uva de playa* (Sea grape) tree.

Possible theories were debated with full 1980s Cold War seriousness:

- Drug lords
- CIA
- Secret Venezuelan royal family.

We never solved the case. We did conclude one thing: adults were terrible at keeping secrets and even worse at hiding evidence.

(Outcome: Unresolved. Glamour vanished. FBI remains unimpressed.)

Case File 002: The Dynasty Kids and The Impossible Mission

Operation Onion Tears

Cata and I were agents of chaos.

Our Impossible Mission? For Cata to walk home past Adrián Gutierrez de los Engranados — heir to bulldozers, ice cream shops, and questionable ledgers.

Adrián had decided she was his prom date. Cata disagreed.

Our plan: Disguises.

Two *Amigo*[43] grocery bags. Two holes cut for eyes.

Surely, Adrián would be fooled.

He was not.

He recognized Cata instantly. He already knew her legs.

Meanwhile, mine, were a national park of adolescent neglect — a detail that made me both invisible and invincible.

He ripped off my bag. I bolted home.

Cata trapped inside hers (which recently held onions), coughed and teared up. Adrián mistook it all for passion and paraded her home like a victorious general, onion tears glistening in the sun.

Survival Commentary: If a man confuses allergies with devotion, he's not your Romeo. He's your red flag with legs.

(Status: compromised. Agent Cata emotionally contaminated.)

---

[43] **Amigo Supermarkets:** Puerto Rico's cheeriest grocery chain (literally "Friend"), locked in a bitter rivalry with Pueblo ("People"). It was the island's longest-running telenovela. Friend vs People, featuring dramatic price wars, seductive jingles, and more betrayal than a Univision finale.

Case File 003: Papito, the Cadillac Casanova

Operation Cushion Control

Objective: Identify how one man can weaponize feathered hair, platform shoes and three sofa cushions into delusional sex appeal.

Papito was Madrid Street's Shaun Cassidy — according to himself.

Feathered hair. Mirrored sunglasses. Thom McCann lift shoes. A 1978 Cadillac DeVille, a mobile ego requiring three sofa cushions to operate.

From the curb, we observed.

"Subject approaching," I whispered into my hairbrush walkie-talkie.

Papito revved his engine.

We laughed.

I dove into the hibiscus hedge, mimicking him: sunglasses, swagger, and limited visibility.

Papito caught me.

Slowly removed his shades.

That was the day he declared war on the Spy Agency.

Case File 004: La Piscinita: Papito Strikes Back

Operation Chlorine and Shame

Objective: Assess psychological damage caused by public nicknaming and splash-zone humiliation.

Caribbean heat: 100 degrees in the shade.

Too old for dolls. Too young for dignity.

Vero and I dragged out a plastic kiddie pool. Two inches of hose water became our private spa. We posed like dethroned Miss Universe contestants because humiliation, if well-lit, is practically pageantry.

Then Papito arrived, followed by a Greek chorus of cousins.

He stopped. Smirked.

"*¡Las niñas de la piscinita!*"[44]

The nickname stuck harder than mosquito bites in August. Whisper it at a party, and we'd implode.

Papito had won.

Survival Commentary: On Madrid Street, you can survive hunger, heartbreak, even heat — but never a nickname.

Case File 005: The Vanishing House

Operation Nostalgia Recon

Objective: Return to the scene of emotional origin without imploding; results inconclusive.

Madrid didn't raise us.

It trained us.

The Spy Agency was never really about espionage. It was rehearsal for adulthood, where the lies got bigger and the costumes subtler.

It was a writer's room disguised as a cul-de-sac. A trauma factory. A telenovela franchise. A neighborhood that believed in divine retribution and weekly lawn care.

When Mami, died, the headquarters closed.

---

[44] **Las niñas de la piscinita:** Literally "the little pool girls," figuratively, "the ones with floaties made of generational wealth."

I haven't walked that street in over ten years—not because I couldn't, but because I know my heart would break if I went back and found it gone.

Or worse.

The same without me.

"*Pero el tiempo pasó y no pude volver al San Juan que yo amé...*"[45]

But time went by and I couldn't return to my beloved San Juan...

So, this book becomes my way back.

A declassified file.
A paper piscinita.

An onion-bag disguise.

Madrid Street survives here — under better lighting, with fewer mosquitoes, and no commercial breaks.

THE DECODER

Survival Law #13: *If your street runs like a telenovela, lean in, even your nostalgia deserves a theme song.*

---

[45] **En Mi Viejo San Juan:** (1942) by Noel Estrada, became the unofficial national anthem of the Puerto Rican diaspora. It's the song you belt out at 2 a.m., drunk, arm-in-arm with cousins and strangers alike. No wedding, no quinceañera, no family party ends without it; and nobody sings it dry-eyed.

EPISODE 14 – THE BINGO CARTEL & DOÑA AZUCENA'S PLOT

12/25 — 8:00 p.m.

Rating: PG

Episode Description: *Where beans, vendettas, and cake decide fate.*

Thursday nights on Madrid Street weren't quiet.

They were blood sport.

Doña Jacinta Bolaños reigned as hostess, her terrace dressed in lace and gossip, widows in mourning black coughing strategically over their bingo cards as if to hex one another. The air was thick with Chanel No. 5, mothballs, and vendetta.

Maman never missed a round.

She arrived with her *sandwichitos de mezcla*[46] cut into "classy" triangles and her sacred *habichuelas*[47] used as markers. To her, beans equaled luck. To everyone else, they equaled scandal.

"¡Habichuelas en la mesa de bingo!"

They gasped, as though she had unleashed livestock at the Vatican.

---

[46] **Sandwichitos de mezcla:** Neon cheese + Spam + white bread = Puerto Rican party cocaine.

[47] **Habichuelas:** Puerto Rican beans. Maman's bingo markers, also delicious with rice.

Jacinta wasn't Maman's fiercest rival.

That crown belonged to **Doña Azucena,** the society's baker.

Her wedding cakes were architectural masterpieces: tiered towers, spun-sugar roses, white icing so smooth it could double as a Botox commercial.

Maman's review?

A shrug.

Then the dagger.

"Está bonito, pero seco."

Pretty but dry.

Azucena's cakes were like rich husbands: all presentation, zero substance.

Worse, Maman was convinced Azucena would poison her one day — just to clinch a bingo win.

Paranoia? Maybe.

But paranoia grew legs the night Doña Azucena — working woman, doctor husband, double scandal —brought one of her confections to bingo.

That night, Maman lost a great deal of money.

By the next morning, she also lost her dignity.

And everything in her stomach.

The doctor diagnosed *E. coli.*

Coincidence?

Bad refrigeration?

Expired eggs?

Or Azucena's long-awaited act of cake-assassination?

Madrid Street still debates it.

Maman never touched another slice of bingo cake again.

Survival Commentary: Forget *Game of Thrones*, Doña Azucena's chocolate cake had higher stakes and more casualties.

THE DECODER

Survival Law #14: *Paranoia counts as survival. Uno nunca sabe.*[48]

---

[48] **Uno nunca sabe:** A Puerto Rican proverb that covers everything from taking an umbrella on a sunny day to hiding jewelry before your cousin visits. Translation: "One never knows." Function: instant paranoia, often justified. It's the island's version of Murphy's Law, only with more rosaries and gossip.

EPISODE 15 – FIRST COMMUNION EST GURUS & QUEEN OF SHEBA CAKE

12/25 — 9:00 p.m.

Rating: PG

Episode Description: *Because salvation comes in wafers, focus mantras, and chocolate.*

Every telenovela needs a dramatic device to keep the audience hooked. In Catholic Puerto Rico, that device was **First Communion.**

The logic was simple: once you received the tasteless wafer, you were spiritually insured. If you died young —struck by lightning, drowned in a freak *piscinita* accident, or impaled by a rogue piña colada umbrella — you had your ticket stamped.

No eternal hell, just express check-in to heaven's VIP lounge.

Think of it as a theological seatbelt, a sacrament you acquired early in case you didn't make it to the season finale.

So, when I lined up in my white lace dress and satin gloves, I wasn't just an eight-year-old in ruffles.

I was a child actress performing for eternal stakes.

Then, my father entered stage left.

My father — disabled Ivy-Leaguer, business mogul, philosopher tyrant — decided he too would take his First Communion.

At forty-something.

On crutches.

Alongside me and a gaggle of itchy-socked children.

The priest sweated.

The kids gasped.

Mothers clutched rosaries as though repelling an exorcism. Why would a grown man crash the holiest milestone of childhood?

Maybe it was his spiritual IPO — a late-stage investment in eternal dividends.

Maybe it was his ultimate power move: *See? Even God* answers to me now.

Or maybe he was just bored and needed a new institution to dominate.

Either way, it was a scene.

The Eucharist as telenovela plot twist.

And me?

Standing there in my tiny gloves, realizing that even in the house of God, I was supporting cast.

In hindsight, I think that strange Communion duet with my father was less about ego than about us.

He was a man who lived by "when there is a will there is a way." A man who had only been present at my hurricane birth and who, in his crooked way, wanted to do something sacred with me.

Maybe it was his way of saying: you're my favorite. We share the same wicked sense of humor. And if you're going to be dressed as a child bride to eat the body of Christ, I'll stand beside you.

At eight, I was scared and annoyed.

At forty-eight, I see it as love disguised as spectacle.

The EST (Erhard Seminars Training) Guru & The Gospel of Focus™ [49]

Enter the 1970s: avocado kitchens, polyester pants, and fraudulent enlightenment.

My father discovered Dr. Milián,[50] self-help messiah, part-time hypnotist, and a man whose main credential was Focus™.

Bad grades? Focus.

Marital screaming match? Focus.

Democracy collapsing? Not enough focus.

Our house turned into a low-budget monastery of productivity. No laughter, just Focus™ and someone hyperventilating self-discipline.

In hindsight, it was probably his home-grown treatment of my undiagnosed ADHD, known in the 1970s as *being a child.*

Anyway, I still have ADHD.

I just prefer to call it **multi-dimensional focus.™**

The Kitchen Illuminati & The Queen of Sheba Cake

Meanwhile, my mother found her own guru: Doña Pons, Puerto Rico's Julia Child, high priestess of butter and béchamel.

From her kitchen emerged dishes that bordered on sorcery:

- *Pan halado* — sticky monkey bread that could raise the dead
- *Pesto à la Genovese* — Puerto Rican basil that shamed Liguria

---

[49] **Focus:** Not a household word, but a cult in ours. Capitalized, trademarked, and weaponized.

[50] **Dr. Milián:** Motivational guru, tax write-off, and man who once claimed to levitate a stapler.

- **El Bizcocho Reina de Saba** (The Queen of Sheba Cake, Reine de Saba)[51]— a chocolate monument to excess, so rich it deserved Vatican approval as a new sacrament.

Forget wafers.

This cake was the true body of Christ.

In the Nazario clan, power wasn't measured in Cadillacs or land.

It was measured in food.

Each sister had a signature dish — a culinary weapon that secured her place in the family hierarchy:

- Titi Lía: *Habichuelas Coloradas* — rumored to resurrect marriages on life support
- Titi Marina: Spaghetti and coconut flan — an unholy combo, but money silenced the critics
- Titi Ofelia: *Arroz con jueyes* — narco level luxury
- Titi Estela: *Surullitos de maíz* — golden, crispy, legal crack
- Maman: *Arroz con dulce* — so sweet it came with an insulin pen
- Titi Ramona: *Sofrito* to dominate, *dulce de papaya* to seduce

Then there was **Titi Aurelia.**

The scandal.

The childless one.

The woman who didn't cook.

An act so radical it qualified as witchcraft in San Juan.

---

[51] **El Bizcocho Reina de Saba:** Julia Child's chocolate cake so rich it could buy a condo in Condado, hire a maid and still make a flan look like welfare dessert.

While her sisters prayed over asopao[52], she prayed no man would ruin her digestion.

She was the aunt with a roll of bills tucked in her ample bosom like a covert treasury. When we were cash-challenged, she'd pull a roll out — warm, perfumed — and hand it to my mother like a mob payoff.

Always laughing, always radiant.

She moved through life unbothered; maybe because she skipped the child-rearing apocalypse entirely.

While her husband, **Tío Ancieto**, demanded café negro and blasted Mozart as if salsa were a communist plot, Aurelia sipped Veuve Clicquot and did whatever the hell she wanted.

In a family ruled by *asopao* and chaos, she was liquidity and the legend.

Officially, the family whispered *matriz infantil* — a childish uterus.

Unofficially?

She married the parasite.

Ancieto was a Cuban exile who fled Havana with half-smoked Cohibas, linen shirts, and zero intention of ever working again.

He drank only imported café negro, and read *The San Juan Star*, [53] as if it were scripture.

---

[52] **Asopao:** Puerto Rico's miracle stew; a shapeshifting hybrid between soup and risotto. It absorbs everything in its path, chicken, shrimp, olives, gossip. Best served at 2 a.m. to cure heartbreak, hangovers or the consequences of both.

[53] **The San Juan Star**: Puerto Rico's only English-language daily, written for readers who wanted to feel cosmopolitan while still stuck in traffic on PR Route #2. My father read it like it was *The New York Times*; Maman read only the obituaries, her version of keeping up with neighbors. My mother read the horoscopes, then used the business section to polish silver. It folded in 2008,

When I asked him what he did for a living, he leaned back like an emperor, and announced, *"I owned a cinema in Morovis."*

I was dazzled.

A mogul! A tycoon of the silver screen!

Until my father, gossip assassin, detonated over his J&B:

"*Lo mantenía Titi Aurelia.*"

Translation: Aurelia paid for everything, his cigars, his arrogance, his dandruff.

In a family where women ruled with recipes, rosaries or bluffing, Aurelia chose bluffing.

She didn't cook, she didn't breed, she bankrolled a fraud. Somehow, that was survival too.

Now that Maman and the tías are gone, I understand her differently.

She modeled another way to exist; childless, unapologetic, solvent.

In her laughter, I hear defiance.

In her champagne, freedom.

Because salvation doesn't always come in wafers and recipes.

Sometimes it just looks happy.

And that, too, is salvation.

THE DECODER

Survival Law #15: *Spot the frauds, savor the recipes and never mistake a costume for a crown.*

---

taking with it the island's las reliable source of both classified ads and moral superiority.

EPISODE 16 – MALE NANNY & ALOE VERA REMEDIES

12/25 — 10:00 PM

Rating: PG

Episode Description: *Healing from unlikely hands, and questionable plants.*

The Unlikely Hero

Every telenovela has an unexpected character who changes everything. He wore work boots, smelled faintly of sweat and earth, and believed pain builds character.

Yes, dear reader, I had a male nanny.

While other children were raised by women named Consuelo who smelled of Fabuloso and resignation, I was raised by **Eduardo "Lolo" Cedeño**, a gentle soul from Jayuya, where the mountains were steep, the cows opinionated and childhood came with no warranties.

Lolo was one of twelve siblings, which meant he learned early that survival was competitive. His mother cleaned our house, and somewhere along the way, Lolo was promoted — or drafted — into the role of live-in nanny, maid, and unofficial third parent.

Forget gold stars and naptime. Lolo practiced the ancient Puerto Rican child-rearing philosophy of *you'll understand when it hurts.*

Our games? Oh, honey, not your coddled *Ring Around the Rosie* nonsense.

We would be chased around with a stick when we asked:

"¿Papá puedo ir al río?" "Dad, may I go to the river?"

"No — because it's swollen and you will die."

"¿Papá puedo ir a la montaña?" "Dad, may I go to the mountain?"

"No — because there's no cabin, and you will die."

Character building. Latino edition.

Neighborhood games were no safer. *La cebollita* involved clinging to a light pole while other children violently peeled you off like layers of an onion. Roller derby at Jennifer Holly's house was full contact because her *marquesina*[54] was smoother than our emotional traumas.

Who needed helmets when we had sheer stupidity?

Then there was the bike incident.

I barreled down Valencia Street; my ankle caught in the spokes and left a chunk of my heel like a receipt from childhood. My mother did not rush to comfort me. She leaned over the balcony and delivered her diagnosis:

"Eso te pasa por irte lejos."

That's what happens when you go too far.

No sympathy. No Band Aids. Just a life lesson served cold.

Enter Lolo.

---

[54] **Marquesina:** Puerto Rican driveway turned party palace, your social status was measured by the floor, not the car.

Calm. Precise. Unbothered. He walked into the yard, hacked off a thick aloe vera[55] leaf, split it open, and rubbed the slime directly into my open wound like he was marinating a *lechón*.

Was it FDA approved? Absolutely not.

Did it sting? Like hell.

Did it work? Enough to limp through the rest of childhood with both heels intact.

Survival Commentary: On Madrid Street, pain wasn't coddled. You got yelled at, then patched with a plant. Somehow, that combination worked.

As with all great characters, Lolo had a plot twist.

He found God. Or maybe God found him hiding behind a mop.

He left Puerto Rico, became a Franciscan monk, and rebranded himself as **Fray Domingo**. In the 1980s, being gay in Puerto Rico was more dangerous than blasphemy. Faith wasn't his calling — it was his shield.

Years later, I was studying acting in New York, at Circle in the Square when Lolo called. He was in town. He wanted to see me.

Reader, it was a trap.

The East Village apartment was full of strangers; the kind of crowd that looked like the rejected cast of a reality show. Lights dimmed. A slideshow flickered on the wall.

AMWAY. [56]

---

[55] **Aloe vera:** The Caribbean Neosporin. Always growing in a cracked pot by the porch. Applied raw and slimy to burns, cuts, and mosquito bites with the full faith of three generations of abuelas. FDA approval irrelevant. Efficacy: legendary.

[56] **Amway:** The only pyramid where the jewels were cubic zirconia dreams and bulk detergent.

A man named Blake, launched into a sermon on gospel bulk detergent and "final freedom." My childhood nanny, the monk, had lured me into a multi-level marketing ambush.

Puerto Rican superstition always warned us; si hay gato encerrado, there's a secret brewing. At the exact moment I suspected betrayal, I opened a door and an actual cat escaped. The metaphor literally purred into existence.

Lolo wasn't all aloe and pyramid schemes. He knew how to preserve magic, too.

One Christmas Eve, I caught him lugging presents into the living room at 2 a.m. Santa hat crooked. I said nothing the next morning. I wanted the lie to live.

Another time, at El Morro, Vero, Cata and I accidentally knocked over a life-size *Nacimiento.* Shepherds fell. Plastic Baby Jesus went flying. Lolo rebuilt Bethlehem under thirty seconds, and whispered, *milagros happen but clean up your mess.*

The Final Goodbye

Years later, he returned from Guatemala sick.

When I saw him again at the airport, he sat in a wheelchair — fragile, smiling, eyes still mischievous.

"Cha-hiiii-toooh," he called.

I answered, "¿Papá puedo ir al río?"

He laughed softly, "*No, porque está crecido.*"

That was our gospel: warnings disguised as love.

As I hugged him, people stared. They believed what they were taught — that his illness was contagious, shameful, earned. I knew better. Shame was the disease. Cruelty was the carrier.

Lolo didn't join the monastery because God called him. He joined because it was the only place where men like him were allowed to exist without explanation.

Standing there under fluorescent airport light, I realized the shame was never his. It was mine; for loving him quietly when I should've loved him loudly.

If there's an afterlife, I hope it looks like a *marquesina*—music playing, aloe plants on the porch, and Lolo laughing, finally free.

THE DECODER

Survival Law #16: *Not every savior wears wings. Some wear aprons, smear aloe on your wounds, and teach you that love can survive shame, laughter, and even bad pyramid schemes.*

EPISODE 17 — CARMINA & CARMELA: DOUBLE TROUBLE

12/25 — 11:00 p.m.

Rating: PG

Episode Description: *Because every telenovela needs rival queens, and Madrid Street had two.*

Every Neighborhood Has Its Dueling Divas

Two sisters, one disco decade, and a neighborhood that never forgave a good scandal.

On Madrid Street, gossip was both sport and survival.

The Calderonas

On Madrid Street, our divas arrived as a mismatched duet: **Carmina and Carmela, the Calderonas**.

Not twins, but close enough for San Juan to short-circuit trying to tell them apart; two green-eyed storms in a barometric pressure of gossip.

One: Carmina, voluptuous, perfumed, forever mid-dubi-dubi.

The other: Carmela, thin, tennis-toned, allergic to humility and humidity.

Together, they made the street feel like *Dynasty* dubbed in Spanish; sequins, suspense, and the faint smell of Aqua Net despair.

Prologue: Gossip Was Our Currency

Every driveway was a runway.

Every balcony, a confessional.

Bingo night? A blood sport.

Disco Decathlon

San Juan in the 1980s was not casual. It was competitive pageantry. Friday through Sundays meant a sequined marathon, with preparation as rigorous as Miss Universe: mani-pedis sharpened into weapons, Jordache vacuum-sealed into thighs, Bonnie Bell gloss thick enough to blind suitors.

Hair teased into skyscrapers of Aqua Net. Emerald eyeshadow stretched from lash to brow. Pearls whispered respectability while Benson & Hedges in a cigarette holder screamed tragic heiress; Vero's Boquilla: instant European art-film energy. [57]

Mami forbade smoking, which of course made it mandatory. Vero, ever the strategist, tried to disguise the smell by gargling with *Babe*,[58] yes, the Margaux Hemingway perfume, not mouthwash. She swore it neutralized nicotine; in reality, she smelled like a chain-smoking prom queen in a Sephora fire.

Did it work? Of course not. Our hair still reeked of disco sin, and Aqua Net. But in our minds, we were tragic Hemingway

---

[57] **Boquilla:** Spanish for cigarette holder. The ultimate accessory of tragic glamour, wielded by women who knew that smoke looked better with a frame. Think Audrey Hepburn in *Breakfast at Tiffany's*, Marlene Dietrich in *Morocco*, and even Cruella de Vil (the animated cautionary tale). In Puerto Rico a Benson & Hedges inside a boquilla turned any girl into a European art-film heroine; tragic backstory optional.

[58] **Babe**: Margaux Hemingway's 1970s perfume, jasmine, musk, and denial plotted like liberation. "You're like no other babe ever born. The commercial cooed, as if feminism could be applied behind the ears. It couldn't. It just made you smell like Studio 54 after last call.

women; eyebrows thick, lungs questionable, destined for subtitles.

Carmina presided as our glamorous chaperone; chauffeur, treasurer, firewall. Her job was to shepherd fifteen-year-olds through discos thick with cocaine and polyester mafiosos.

Without her, we'd have been headlines in *El Vocero*.[59] With Carmina, we learned how to walk into danger and exit alive.

The Weekend Disco Circuit

The weekends had choreography:

- Friday: *Isadora* at the Condado Plaza (sparkle + promises)
- Saturday: *Juliana's* at the Caribe Hilton, mink stoles mingling with martinis and whispers.
- Sunday: *The Flying Saucer* in Isla Verde, twirling inside a UFO-shaped dome, sequined survivors of an alien abduction.

But the finale came after the last call. Always.

El Hamburger,[60] in Puerta de Tierra: open till 5 a.m., neon lighthouse facing the ocean. Burgers dripped, gossip slurred, and survival was measured by who could keep their heels on until sunrise.

---

[59] **El Vocero**: Puerto Rico's tabloid of the 70s and 80s; a daily bloodbath wrapped in newsprint. The title screamed in bright, crime-scene red letters, usually above a full-color corpse. Think *The National Enquirer* meets *Narcos*, with the subtlety of a machete. If it bled, it led. And if it didn't, they'd find someone who did. Every barbershop and bodega had a copy, usually open to the goriest page.

[60] **El Hamburger**: Post disco sanctuary where grease met alcohol until 5 a.m. Survival tip: The real after-party was between the buns.

The discos tested your glamour. *El Hamburger* tested your stamina. Grease was our communion wafer. If your Jordache survived the burger juice, you were ready for Sunday Mass.

Carmina and Rocky Buenaventura

At *Isadora*, under mirror balls and polyester humidity, Carmina met Rocky Buenaventura; Condado's white pants mafioso. His chains interrupted the DJ's system. His Sharpie beard arrived before he did.

She didn't just fall; she *plummeted,* in heels and denial.

Roses, Condado mansions, weekends in St. Thomas. Watching her was like watching a *Televisa* heroine trip over the same lace hem, episode after episode; predictable, devastating, impossible to stop.

Rocky had a talent for romantic gestures and federal offenses. When he wasn't sending orchids, he was allegedly shipping *other things*.

Dad called it early: "*Ese tipo huele a cárcel,*" he muttered over his J&B… that man smells like prison.

And dad was right. Rocky didn't ghost her; he got arrested for cocaine trafficking. Which, on Madrid Street ranked just above tax evasion and slightly below bad highlights.

The Princess Cruise: Floating Madness & Maritime Love Affairs.

After Rocky's arrest, Carmina needed an exorcism. She didn't book therapy; she booked a cruise. A literal escape, powered by Cunard and denial; because heartbreak dissolves beautifully in deep sea and maritime "accidents."

When the sisters announced they were boarding the Princess, Madrid Street held a vigil.

Rumor said one was escaping heartbreak, the other hunting for it. Both packed like refugees from Studio 54; feathers, furs, and enough perfume to fumigate the Caribbean.

I was fourteen, seasick, and armed with Dramamine and judgment.

On opening night, Carmina volunteered for the hypnotist show, fainted mid-twirl and woke up flirting with an officer before the applause stopped.

By day two, both sisters had bagged one:

- Carmina's officer: Irish, poetic, teeth like hope.
- Carmela's officer: Italian-ish, gold watch, questionable paperwork.

Dinner turned cinematic when an officer calmly ate a wine glass; stem, rim, crunch. Then he smiled; blood glimmering like Chanel No. 666. I thought: *So, this is adulthood; people bleeding politely.*

By mid-voyage, the crew went on strike. This unfortunate event cut my cruise trip short, but Carmina got a chance to get engaged… to Officer Douglas.

Carmela was bored. The Italian was replaced by a Portuguese count who introduced himself as "Count de Saudade," as if loneliness were a title of nobility. He claimed to own "three vineyards, two hearts, and one unpaid Amex."

Carmela – The Chill

Carmela returned home claiming to be Countess Adjacent.

Her new suitor had the confidence of someone who once Googled "aristocracy" and never looked back. His constant companion: La Condesa, his mother, a woman who turned every dinner into a hostage situation with a single glance.

Rumors proliferated: Was he after her passport? Her patio furniture? A Netflix true crime docuseries? My father didn't blink. "He'll poison her," he said over J&B. "Or toss his pet python to distract her, then push. You'll read it on the cover of El Vocero."

He wasn't being metaphorical.

The prophecy almost checked out when Carmela found receipts from La Perla lingerie; not for her but for la Condesa.

Even Madrid Street, where scandal was oxygen, gasped.

Carmela handled betrayal the way women of her generation did: with retail therapy and real estate. No husband, no heirs, but jewelry, a hurricane-proof house, and the smug glow of someone who dodged both bankruptcy and reptilian homicide.

She chose survival on her terms. Maybe that was the bravest romance of all.

What I Learned from the Calderonas

Watching the Calderonas, I learned that heartbreak was just rehearsal; every bad romance warm-up for the moment you finally choose yourself.

Carmela thought she'd found a Count; what she really found was clarity. The illusion was fairytale. The reality check was freedom.

Latina Survival Closing Lesson

Marriage isn't the only ending. Sometimes survival looks like a Range Rover, gold chains, and perfect hair in the middle of a blackout. That's not loneliness; that's victory disguised as good lighting.

THE DECODER

Survival Law #17: *Never underestimate a diva; especially when she's heartbroken. Glamour fades, but survival always looks fabulous under pressure.*

EPISODE 18 – THE BARBARELLA SON INCIDENT

12/26 —12:00 a.m.

Rating: PG

Episode Description: *Because sometimes the ventana reveals what daylight politely ignored.*

In telenovelas, someone is always eavesdropping. Secrets aren't whispers; they are shares traded in a bizarre *Novela Stock Exchange* where gossip is the only currency that matters. (See LSG Decoder: Novela Stock Exchange)

Cliffhangers depended on it: a heroine crouching in a hallway, the villainess pressing her ear against a door, a gardener hiding in the bushes, falling in love with la patrona.

So, of course, I thought I was the one gathering secrets.

Until it wasn't.

Picture it: fourteen years old, in the shower, lathering like a Pantene commercial, when suddenly…

Two eyes. Black. Beady. Peering at me through the aluminum window.

I froze. He didn't. We locked stares for a full two seconds before I unleashed the scream of a thousand novenas.

How did he get up there? Past security? Past the electrified gates? Past Titi's rosaries guarding the door? To this day, it's a mystery.

My bet? **José**. Barbarella's son. My modeling agent's little disaster. The boy with black Converse, bad ideas and *ojos desorbitados* that said *arson is my love language*. Witty, reckless, always one dare away from juvenile detention.

Yet José wasn't the only neighborhood hazard. On Madrid Street, there was always that guy, the one in the white Celica who'd slow down, pretending to ask for directions. We were teenage girls in cutoff shorts, curious but cautious, until we saw it. He wasn't looking for Calle Madrid; he was performing his own one-man show, stark naked, engine humming, hand in motion.

We screamed and ran, which only seemed to delight him.

Until one day my sister **Vero**, never one to back down, marched right up to his car, knowing exactly what was coming. She waited for the grand reveal, tilted her head, and said, "*¿Eso es todo?"* Is that all you got?

He peeled away, and she just stood there, victorious, like the patron saint of unbothered women. Fabulous training for her future Wall Street career; when men show you their power, you negotiate up.

I wish that had been the last time a man tried to see what wasn't his to see.

Fast-forward a decade: same eyes, different window. Only now, the peeping Tom had a title — Network Executive — and a helicopter budget. He flew over my beach house *to check the weather*, sent a virus to my phone, and dispatched a private investigator… someone always found me at bars where a seat appeared like divine intervention.

At that time, I was dating a high-level weed dealer; a proud Blood with a soft spot for literature. He got shot soon after. In the balls. Karma or coincidence? Hard to say. Either way, the universe keeps receipts.

Maybe spying on me was these men's escape.

Maybe writing this is mine.

And if you're still reading, admit it: you're a voyeur too.

THE DECODER

Survival Law #18*: If you can survive chaos, heartbreak, and ghosts, you can survive anything. Just bring heels; the devil respects stilettos.*

EPISODE 19 – FIESTA DE REYES: THE EVENT OF THE SEASON

12/26 — 1:00 a.m.

Rating: PG

Episode Description: *A Christmas party bigger than some weddings and more chaotic.*

By the time Christmas ended, Madrid Street began its annual metamorphosis; from quiet suburb to televised spectacle.

Every telenovela has a showpiece: the party — a blowout where feuds, secrets, and forbidden glances collide under the guise of family bliss.

When the whole clan, neighbors, uninvited ex-lovers, and a few gun-wielding uncles are crammed together with music, rum, and unresolved grudges… anything can happen.

On Madrid Street, our showpiece was La Fiesta de Reyes.[61] Every January 5th, Epiphany's Eve, my parents threw the party of the year. *Dynasty* meets *Narcos* meets a Catholic exorcism with a live band.

This wasn't a backyard barbecue. It was social warfare disguised as a holiday. Lobsters the size of Chihuahuas, Dom Pérignon flowing like holy water at a Vatican cover-up, Iris Chacón in a mink coat despite the tropical humidity.

[61] **Fiesta de Reyes:** Jan. 5, Eve of the Epiphany or Víspera de Día de Reyes; Christmas but make it camel chic.

The Food: Puerto Rican Foreplay

Before gossip comes grease.

Pastelillitos de queso y carne, alcapurrias, surullitos —glorious, fried, cholesterol grenades, best eaten hot. (See LSG Decoder: Fried Cholesterol Death Appetizers)

And the pièce de résistance? An entire, red waxed Edam cheese, smuggled like contraband royalty; boiled, melted, and served with *pan de agua*,[62] our sacred carb.

You hovered by the frying station like it was the stock-market-floor, grabbing fritters while still lava-hot: *cómetelo rápido antes de que se efríen.*

Then came the *pasteles*[63]— not cake, but plantain-leaf couture filled with pork, raisins, and olives boiled until steaming. "*Pasteles fríos empachan a la gente*," the old Aguinaldo warned. Cold pasteles make people sick.

Childhood metaphor: hurry up, eat before it gets cold. Hurry up, get dressed. Hurry up, life won't wait. Puerto Ricans are not known for patience.

There were hams the size of suitcases, and *pernil*. Pork's shoulder marinated for weeks; its meat falling off the bone in garlicky surrender.

The dessert table glittered like a Puerto Rican Palacio Real: *arroz con dulce* and *tembleque* (Maman's), *dulce de papaya* (Tía Ramona's), *pastelillitos de guayaba* (from Panadería Pepín), and Titi Marina's *flan de coco* that could heal generational trauma.

---

[62] **Pan de agua:** The love child of French and Italian bread, but better. Crusty on the outside, soft and steamy inside, engineered to be eaten before you get home. Meant to be slathered with butter while still hot, preferably in the car with zero shame. A masterpiece of simplicity: golden, flaky and utterly incapable of surviving the drive from the panadería.

[63] **Pasteles**: The Puerto Rican hot pocket, plantain leaf couture edition.

And of course, *turrón de Alicante*, the Spanish nougat that broke more molars than family curses.

Petra & The Pilgrimage

Then came the coquito from Petra: condensed milk, hand grated coconut milk squeezed through a cheesecloth (or in the mountains, a pantyhose), sweetened and spiked with *pitorro,* Puerto Rican moonshine rum.

Fetching Petra's *coquito*[64] and *pasteles* in Gurabo was a pilgrimage. My mother always sent me with my father "to keep him from getting distracted by every bar with a *vellonera*[65] and bottle of *pitorro*."

Translation: to keep him from returning with more rum than resolutions.

Enter: My Father, the Pro Bono Country Lawyer

My father's clients rarely paid cash. Instead, he was compensated with sacks of yuca, homemade cheese wrapped like Tiffany's, and the occasional gallon of *pitorro,* strong enough to power a Cadillac.

His barter economy:

- One inheritance dispute = three dozen *pasteles*
- Two divorce consultations = one goat (alive, chewing my school shoes in the backseat)

---

[64] **Coquito**: Coconut and condensed milk, rum and poor decisions in a bottle

[65] **Vellonera**: Archaic word in PR for jukebox. From vellón, either a nickel in San Juan or a dime in Ponce, these tiny coins carried the weight of entire breakups. The more you cried, the more you played. Think of it as Puerto Rico's emotional vending machine.

- A will contest = crates of *quenepas*[66] and a handmade hammock

To the *jibaros,*[67] my father wasn't just a lawyer. He was a therapist-poet-priest-hybrid. Estranged couples arrived ready to kill each other and left kissing like a telenovela finale. Cousins fighting over deeds reconciled with a handshake and a shot of *pitorro.* Litigation denied; reconciliation served with *caldo de gallina.*[68]

Profitable? No. Karma points? Enough for a skybox in heaven.

Reflection: Kindness as Currency

As a child, I thought my father was naïve. Why settle for quenepas when you could get a check? But he taught me that kindness was its own currency.

Puerto Rican impatience made me hurry through life, but from him I learned that sometimes the richest payoff isn't money. It's leaving people better than you found them; even if what they hand you in return is a sweaty bag of root vegetables.

Even now, when people say, "it's not about money," I don't roll my eyes. I nod. Because I grew up watching a man live it and still come home with dignity and dinner.

The Party as Novela

---

[66] **Quenepas:** Puerto Rico's summer addiction, half fruit, half choking hazard. Green marble of temptation with slippery pulp and a pit the size of regret. You suck, chew, and pray not to die looking cute. Sweet-tart, sticky and sold in traffic by men who swear theirs are the juiciest.

[67] **Jíbaros:** Puerto Rican Mountain peasant, turned folk hero, from machete-wielding farmer to cultural icon and bad Bunny couture.

[68] **Caldo de gallina:** Not to be confused with caldo de pollo. Stronger, older, and capable of reviving a dead man, or ruining a childhood. (See LSG Decoder for trauma)

In the background, *aguinaldos* played; both live and from a D.J. *Saludos, Saludos. Si no me dan de beber, lloro*... and the island anthem of power outages: *Y venía la brisa y fuaaaa*... lights out. Still relevant, still mortifying.

Weddings shrunk in comparison.

And dressed immaculately was my legendary cousin: **Sabina Zambrana, The Blue-Eyed Amazon.**

Six feet tall. Volleyball arms. Disney princess hair. Blue eyes, the rarest Puerto Rican export. She was our family's trophy. Naturally, *la Fiesta* was her stage.

Here she met **Colo** (yes, that was his name: equal parts mafia snitch and failed salsa singer). They married; on the same day that our neighbor, **Carmina Calderona** married **Officer Douglas**, the doctor/officer she met on that ill-fated Princess Cruise.... *Yes, the same one that went on strike after her heartbreak from Rocky Buenaventura.*

My mother, ever the producer, decided both weddings should share one bridesmaid, me, and one dress.

I spent the day being shuttled between ceremonies like emotional luggage. "Efficiency" she called it. I called it trauma wrapped in lace. Two brides, one day, one dress, because apparently love, like wardrobe, was meant to be recycled.

The day played like a split-screen telenovela: on one side, Sabina, radiant and unbothered, marrying her salsa-singing Colo under a tent of chiffon and denial; on the other, Carmina, our cruise-ship romantic, clutching Officer Douglas, M.D., as if seasickness could be cured by matrimony.

I ran between ceremonies, lipstick fading, bouquet wilting, and faith in humanity circling the drain. My mother directed both productions like a general at war, one eye on the buffet, and one on the photographers. By nightfall, the heels blistered, the curls collapsed, and two sets of newlyweds posed under the same rented arch, as if efficiency were a sacrament.

Cut to: *La Fiesta de Reyes* The chaos picked up right where the vows left off; only louder, shinier and better catered. Dominican waiters sprinted across the terrace balancing trays of *pastelillos, pernil* and enough *coquito* to tranquilize a horse. My mother, in Valentino knockoff, orchestrated like a socialite Marie Antoinette who had discovered Groupon.

It was pure decadence, a fever dream of gluttony and glamour. Because every Puerto Rican party hides a subplot, I started wondering what the boy cousins were up to.

What Were the Boy Cousins Doing?

Locked in my bedroom. For what?

- Drugs?
- Playboy?
- Smelling my underwear like degenerates?

To this day, I don't know. Some mysteries are better unsolved.

The Guest List? Iconic

This wasn't just a party; it was the unofficial backstage lounge before the Grammys.

- **Tavín Pumarejo** – Puerto Rico's answer to Junior Samples meets Bad Bunny, the original jibaro rapper, cracking jokes between rum, his *pava,*[69] vibrating like a lie detector.

---

[69] **Pava**: Straw hat. From Jíbaro chic to Bad Bunny couture.

- **Iris Chacón**[70] – our national treasure in a white Rolls Royce and a white mink coat despite eighty-degree weather, glittering like divine punishment.
- **El Trio Los Barones** crooned boleros while topping off their own glasses.
- **Jerry Rivera, Sophy, Ednita Nazario, Luis Raul** – just casually hanging out like this was a random Thursday in Guaynabo.

And among them, floated Sabina, blue-eyed, volleyball-armed, smile flashing like a disco ball, our family's trophy.

Enter: My Father, the Poet

As if chaos needed more, my father would seize the microphone, not to sing, but to deliver a ten-minute, drunken, operatic poetry reading. Papi recited Neruda on crutches, scanning for men who might defile my virtue as if poetry itself were pepper spray.

Grown men shifted uncomfortably. Small children cried. The waitstaff froze mid-tray.

It was embarrassing then. Later, I'd understand poetry was the only language left when the rest of life spoke in bullets and unpaid bills.

My mother's jewelry clinked in disapproval. Somewhere in the distance: gunshots. My uncles had begun their annual pistol salute to the Magi.

Cue: The Midnight Meltdown

By midnight, my mother was seething. Why? Because she had become convinced that my father was flirting with an *artista*.

---

[70] **Iris Chacón**: A national treasure you couldn't claim at customs

Sometimes, this was paranoia. Other times… well, Puerto Rican men live by three words: *Negativo, negativo, negativo.*[71]

Meanwhile, my uncles, drunk and armed (because of course), fired their pistols into the night sky. Rumors swirled that a falling bullet took out an unlucky eye. I stood horrified — and fascinated — every year.

The Magic of the Three Kings

Before bed, we placed shoeboxes of grass under our beds for the Magi's camels. My father loved this ritual because it let him reject Santa Claus with gusto: "Ese Santi Claus no es *puertorriqueño.*" As if guzzling French champagne and eating Spanish nougat was.

The 3AM Cookie Sales Catastrophe

One year, at 3:00 a.m., I woke up fully convinced it was morning. I put on my Girl Scout uniform, sash and all, and marched into the still-raging party, prepared to sell cookies.

People lost their minds (*nothing unites Puerto Ricans like a public humiliation they didn't pay for*). Humiliated, I flew back to my room, swore I'd never show my face again, and collapsed under my Troop 12 sash.

Naturally, by the next Fiesta de Reyes, I was back in the madness; older, wiser, and slightly more aware that our version of "normal" was not normal.

In the end, *La Fiesta de Reyes* wasn't just a party; it was proof that chaos, love and good *pernil* could coexist on the same plate.

---

[71] **Negativo, negativo, negativo:** the Island's unofficial marriage insurance policy. See LSG Decoder for details.

Would I change it? Not for all the *turrón* in Spain.

THE DECODER

Survival Law #19: *If your family party doesn't require a helmet, elastic pants and a referee with poetry skills, was it even a fiesta?*

EPISODE 20 – KOTEX PORTFOLIO / PUBERTY LESSONS

12/26 — 2:00 a.m.

Rating: PG

Episode Description: *My body betrayed me, and my family had thoughts about it.*

Every telenovela heroine has a secret she guards with her own life.

Mine wasn't an affair, a love child, or even a hidden fortune in the Cayman Islands.

It was blood.

Literal blood.

The spirits had warned me of many things — visions, omens, and Doña Lucrecia's wheezing prophecies.

But not this.

Nobody had told me. Not my mother, not my sister, Vero, not even the Virgin Mary. And she usually handled these things.

And then it didn't stop.

I bled for six straight months.

Did I say anything?

Of course not.

I just stole Kotex pads like a kleptomaniac until Mami discovered her entire stockpile had vanished.

She stormed into my room like a general mid-coup.

"¿Por qué no dijiste NADA?!"[72]

"I thought it was normal!" I wailed, clutching my mattress like Joan Crawford in *Mildred Pierce.*

In our house, pain wasn't punishment.

It was a hobby.

Cue the doctor.

Cue the hormonal regime of doom: birth control pills, three a day, morning, noon, and night.

Enough to tranquilize a horse.

Mami, crossing herself furiously, added: "Just because you're on the pill doesn't mean you should be sleeping around."

Sleeping around?

I didn't even know what that was.

My most illicit activity was sneaking an extra *pastelillo.*

Meanwhile, I could no longer enjoy the beach.

Every time I pinned a bulk-sized Kotex pad to my underwear, there was a 50/50 chance it would betray me.

Would it shift?

Would it leak?

Would it detach mid-cha-cha?

Only God knew.

Madrid Street had trained me for chaos — pistols in the night, Lolo's imaginary river, Papito and his wannabe Ocean's Eleven crew — but Kotex pads?

---

[72] ***¿Por qué no dijiste nada?***: "Why didn't you say anything?" a.k.a. the national anthem of Latina girl puberty.

These were a new level of treachery.

The pad wasn't just an object.

It was a weapon of public humiliation — a scandal in waiting. The kind of thing that could destroy a *quinceañera* faster than a drunken uncle with a pistol.

Enter: Giselle Fontana (Telenovela Cameo)

Giselle was Vero's glamorous, cigarette-smoking friend who claimed to be a model.

She had teased hair, red manicures, and an aura of cheap perfume strong enough to kill mosquitoes — and possibly men.

One day, Giselle handed me her modeling portfolio.

"Show this to Barbarella," she said, meaning the Condado modeling agency.

I flipped it open, expecting Grace Jones, Jerry Hall, Studio 54 fabulousness.

Instead?

Giselle.

In a nylon leotard.

No tights.

Barefoot.

Striking exaggerated "fashion" poses that looked like interpretive dance meets constipation.

And in every single shot — clear as day — was the bulging, unmistakable outline of a Kotex Maxi Pad.

The Kotex Portfolio: A Tragedy in 8 x 10 Glossy

I couldn't breathe.

Who took these pictures?!

Was there no one on set to scream:

"¡Mija! Your Kotex is showing!"

Vero and I sat on her bed, flipping page after page, tears streaming down our faces — desperately avoiding eye contact because if we did, we'd combust.

When we got home, we collapsed on the floor in full hysterics.

What was she THINKING?!

WHO was the SICKO behind the camera?!

Mami took one look at the portfolio, pursed her lips and delivered the final blow:

"*¡¿Dónde estaba su madre?!*"

Where was her mother?!

And honestly?

That was the real question.

The thing about puberty is that it's all secrets.

The secret of the stain in your underwear.

The secret of the pills you don't understand.

The secret of a body you don't yet trust.

Madrid Street taught me how to survive pistols, gossip, and spirits.

But puberty was the first time I realized my own body could betray me — and worse, that everyone had an opinion about it.

In a novela, this is the cliffhanger: the heroine faints, the camera zooms on her diary, and the audience screams at the television.

My big reveal?

That adolescence wasn't about parties or gossip.

It was about the secrets we kept — the ones we guarded like treasure — until they slipped out in the most humiliating way possible.

Just don't forget: every heroine has a secret.

The trick is knowing when to reveal it… preferably not in an 8X10 glossy.

THE DECODER

Survival Law #20: *If you bleed long enough, you stop apologizing for the stain.*

EPISODE 21 – PAPI'S PEP TALK

12/26 — 3:00 a.m.

Rating: PG

Episode Description: *Believe in yourself when no one else does.*

The fan overhead went click-click, a metronome reminding me: this moment wouldn't come again. Every telenovela has that scene: the lights fade, cheesy violins swell, and the heroine steps into her confessional monologue.

This was mine. Except my cathedral was Papi's ErgoLuxe bed (courtesy of Don Sixto de la Siesta, mattress king and unsolicited philosopher), my balcony was a flickering TV, and my spotlight came from the glow of *Los Picapiedras.*[73]

It was one of those hot, sticky Torrimar afternoons when even the coquí frogs sounded too tired to sing. I'd just come from ballet, still sealed inside black tights and a leotard that held onto sweat like a grudge, my hair scraped back in a bun. I was about to shower when, by divine scheduling error, Papi came home early.

By 4:30 p.m. we were sprawled in front of the TV: Pedro Picapiedra and Pablo Mármol dubbing their way through existential Spanish *Yabba-Dabba-Doo.* The fan clicked in time with Fred's bowling feet, a beat steady enough to carry us both into the ritual.

[73] **Los Picapiedras:** The Flintstones, real but much harder to mute.

I sat cross-legged by Papi's head, black comb in hand, pretending to be Vidal Sassoon as I slicked back his hair. Occasionally, we flipped to Pacheco,[74] Puerto Rico's Mr. Rogers; if Mr. Rogers raided Gene Kelly's wardrobe and moonlighted at El San Juan Hotel.

Then, between Fred's brontosaurus burger and Pacheco's shuffle, I produced a crumpled piece of paper: my catalog of teenage self-hatred.

I delivered it like a doomed telenovela heroine.

"My legs are freakishly long. My mustache could rival Frida Kahlo's if not electrocuted weekly. My feet? Gigantic. Size ten: Clydesdale chic. No waist. No boobs. Buck teeth in a medieval metal cage. I'm terrible at math. No boy will ever love me."

It wasn't a list. It was an indictment. A glossy exposé worthy of *¡Hola! Magazine; Charo Toledo: The Adolescent Years, A Tragedy in Twelve Bullet Points.*

(Lights fade. Spotlight narrows. Violins swell.)

There I was, adolescent me — confessing every flaw as if the walls themselves were witnesses. My secret wasn't a forbidden lover or a bastard child. It was my own body. And in the logic of adolescence, that scandal was enough.

Papi's Sermon

Papi raised the ErgoLuxe upright like Moses about to deliver the tablets. He looked at me, deadpan.

"How many inferiority complexes should I have, Charito… but I don't?"

---

[74] **Pacheco**: Joaquín Monserrat, the unshakably cheerful Spanish born TV host who ruled Puerto Rican after-school television on El Show de Pacheco (WAPA-TV).

Then came the sermon. Not fire-and-brimstone, but steady, tender, annoyingly unarguable:

"You can walk, talk, laugh, and eat without help. You're beautiful, even if you don't see it. You're hilarious. You memorize stories like a camera. You recite poetry like a diva at the Ateneo. You speak French, Spanish, and English like you were born trilingual. And most importantly… we love you."

Then as if he'd hidden a stack of gilded cue cards inside his nightstand, Papi launched into the Five Commandments of Survival:

1. ***FOCUS***: "Like the sun hitting a magnifying glass to burn through a barrier, you must aim your intentions sharp enough to break anything in your way."
2. ***DELEGATE***: "Just because you cannot walk, doesn't mean you can't get there. Find someone who can walk for you and let them carry you past the obstacle."
3. ***LISTEN & LEARN***: "Rich or poor, educated or illiterate, kind or evil, everyone has something to teach you. Take the lesson, even if you don't like the teacher."
4. ***ENJOY LIFE***: "Make time for great food, music, poetry, and laughter with friends and family. Without those, even success tastes bitter."
5. ***BE BALANCED***: "Be a banker, a lawyer and a poet. Protect your money, defend your rights, but never stop writing verses."

Then, the closer, a line that silenced even the ceiling fans:

"Charito, if you live by these, nothing and no one can convince you your dreams don't matter."

I folded my list of flaws into a cootie catcher — one of those paper fortune-tellers that predicted whether you'd marry Brad Pitt or die with four cats — and slipped it into the sweaty pocket of my ballet leotard, close to my heart but out of sight.

In every telenovela, the heroine survives her confession not by hiding her flaws, but by turning them into weapons. That day, Papi gave me mine: faith in myself, faith in my ridiculousness, faith in survival.

THE DECODER

Survival Law #21: *Fold your insecurities into a cootie catcher and remember: you're the fortune, not the paper.*

EPISODE 22 – SURVIVAL IN MADRID STREET

12/26 — 4:00 a.m.

Rating: PG

Episode Description: *Because every barrio has a baptism, and hers came with palm trees, heartbreak, and an imaginary river.*

Childhood on Madrid Street was a paradox: extravagant parties and strict discipline, old money and blue-collar hustle, glamour and gunfire.

Papi declaimed Neruda on the *terraza* while my uncles fired pistols into the night like exclamation marks. Maman's bingo vendettas unfolded with the solemnity of a papal conclave — if conclaves served *Holsum*[75] donuts and shade.

Madrid Street was equal parts opera and sitcom, *Dynasty* and *Looney Tunes.* Carmina swooned over Rocky Buenaventura in pants so tight the seams qualified for worker's comp. Papito, and his crew turned the street into a rocket range, launching bottle rockets from soup cans and stealing mangoes like broke Robin Hoods.

[75]**Holsum**: Not just pastry; currency. Entemmann's with Catholic guilt and better packaging. The pastry that sanctified, baptisms, velorios, and neighborhood coups. A Holsum box on the tablecloth meant legitimacy, you'd tithed to the gossip economy, and your membership was valid for one evening only.

Lolo swore a river ran beneath the asphalt. Step in, you drowned. I once tripped on my Girl Scout sash and nearly died of dry-land drowning.

Every Fiesta de Reyes was a season finale: camels waiting for grass in shoeboxes, Sabina crooning boleros in sequins, and Barbarella's son peeking through the shutters — a barrio Phantom in training.

Maybe that's the secret to Latina survival: learning to be both:

- A Girl Scout at 3:00 a.m. and a bridesmaid at 3:00 p.m.
- A spy in a pleated skirt and a debutante with skinned knees
- A cousin who laughed too loudly and a daughter who kept quiet during Amway pitches
- A survivor of onions, pistols, and lingerie receipts

Because survival isn't about dodging ghosts. It's about learning their choreography.

Madrid Street taught me that luxury and scandal, tragedy and comedy, could share a plate. One night you ate lobster the size of a Chihuahua, the next morning you were picking grass for the Reyes Magos.

You could clap for Iris Chacón in mink and still duck from a stray bullet. You could sit through an Amway convention in New York and still feel Doña Jacinta's couch haunting the room like secondhand guilt.

The Final Bow of Madrid Street

Survival was an art, and Madrid Street was my conservatory. It trained me in melodrama, sharpened me in chaos, and humbled me in sequins.

Madrid Street was a stage, and everyone had their bow: bingo queens with vendettas, gossiping tías with binoculars, onion-fumed kitchens, poodles with better portfolios that Wall Street, Papito's *titeritos*[76] and their firecracker arsenal, Sabina's boleros bleeding heartbreak, and Barbarella's son — the Phantom rehearsing tragedy through aluminum shutters.

They were my first cast, my fiercest critics. Madrid Street wasn't a block; it was a telenovela stuck on "season finale." Tears, betrayals and that one neighbor allergic to poor people.

And mi amor… I was born to tell this story.

THE DECODER

Survival Law #22: *On Madrid Street, survival wasn't about picking tragedy or comedy; it was dancing both in sequins.*

Telenovela Flash Forward

(Music swells. Camera freezes. Push in. Classic novela tease.)

This isn't nostalgia. Every telenovela ends with a reveal, and mine is no different.

Madrid Street didn't end in childhood. It followed me into adolescence — to first loves, first betrayals, smoky marquesinas, and dances where onions weren't the only thing making me cry.

One day, Papi's Neruda verses gave way to my own poems about boys who didn't notice me. The pistols in the night turned into traffic accidents and the kind of losses you can't outrun.

If childhood was rehearsal, adolescence was opening night. Madrid Street was still whispering cues, daring me to step into my next act.

---

[76] **Titeritos:** miniature delinquents; pre-owned hoodlums; the training wheel edition of heartbreakers. Mami could spot them at 200 yards.

ACT III

FROM DISCO BALLS TO CHICKEN INN

(Episodes 23-30)

EPISODE 23 – SAINT JOSEPH, THE BEARD AND THE BUSTELO HEIR

12/26 — 5:00 a.m.

Rating: PG

Episode Description: *Faith, caffeine, and facial hair run in the family.*

Every Catholic school has its Christmas pageant, but Academia San José didn't just put on a pageant, we staged an extravaganza that could've been directed by Pedro Almodóvar after three martinis.

I was in second grade when my acting eminence arrived. My role? Saint Joseph. A boy. Destiny clearly had a sense of humor.

Virgin Mary went to Matilde Cruz, who looked like a living Pietà. Baby Jesus was a doll, though even the doll seemed vaguely traumatized under the choking incense haze.

The set was a fever dream: shepherds in polyester bathrobes, Magi in sequined caftans borrowed from their mothers' cocktail wardrobes, and angels with wire-hanger halos puncturing their scalps.

Me? Saint Joseph, in sackcloth, sandals, and a glued-on beard that made me look like a pint-sized Fidel Castro cast in *The Nativity Reloaded.*

The nuns directed the whole fiasco like tyrants with Broadway ambitions. Sister Mary Agnes barked "*Más sentimiento,* Joseph! Mary mira al niño with love, not like you're waiting for an enema!"

The audience was its own novela: Puerto Rican society mothers in Escada suits and dripping gold medallions fanned themselves with programs, whispering:

"Ay bendito! Matilde looks so virginal, un angel de Rubens."

"But Charito... so tall, legs like a giraffe. That poor girl must have been adopted."

"Her father is beaming. Claro, she's already the star of Villa Caparra."

My father was ecstatic. Finally, a production worthy of microphones. Enter Mercado, his friend with the aptly mercantile surname, driving on El Camino packed with loudspeakers the size of refrigerators. The church became less *Silent Night* and more *Bad Bunny preshow.*

That night sealed my fate. My father decided I had the gift. He told anyone who'd listen that his daughter was born for the stage.

Years later, I'd end up on *El Show de Don Cholito*[77] with José Miguel Agrelot himself. Don Cholito — portly, brilliant, biting, sometimes in a pava hat — Puerto Rico's comedic patriarch, compared me on live radio, to Anjelica Houston. One day, Saint Joseph, the next Morticia Addams.

Back at the pageant, destiny brewed stronger than espresso. In the pews, sat José Bustelo — yes, heir to the Bustelo Coffee empire.[78]

When I pulled off my beard and revealed I was, in fact, a girl in a T-shirt and shorts, he fell hopelessly in love. From that day until sixth grade, he shadowed me through recess like a lovesick novela villain — appearing in hallways, lurking in stockrooms, caffeinated by obsession.

Mami warned me: "Nunca, Charito — never give a boy hope if you don't mean it. One smile, and he'll be naming your children before dessert."

---

[77] **Don Cholito:** Our morning man and the only comedian with an arena named after him. See LSG Decoder.

[78] **Bustelo Coffee**: East-Harlem born, Cuban-style espresso by a Spanish founder; beloved in Boricua and Cuban kitchens alike.

So, I did what every well-trained Catholic schoolgirl knew how to do: I ducked, dodged and disappeared… evading Bustelo like a tax exile avoiding Hacienda.

Looking back, I could've been queen of the Bustelo coffee empire, my face on yellow cans in every bodega from San Juan to the Bronx. But no — my destiny wasn't espresso; it was drama.

I didn't know it then, but that beard would be my first disguise, and every role after would be a search for the girl underneath it.

THE DECODER

Survival Law #23: *When life casts you as Saint Joseph at eight, wear the beard and own the role. Dynasties fade; destiny does not.*

EPISODE 24 – THE LUGGAGE HEIST OF '78

12/26 — 6:00 a.m.

Rating: PG

Episode Description: *What only Troop 12 could have prepared me for.*

Other families went camping for kumbayas, canoeing, and mosquito bites.

In my family? Even a Girl Scout trip had the production values of a Televisa primetime drama. Because in my life, there are no simple plotlines — only betrayals, humiliations, and cliffhangers shot under bad lighting.

At Academia San José, the rich girls joined the glamorous Troop #2. They sold cookies with cashmere socks while their fathers — senators, judges, tycoons, signed checks for the whole box.

Me?

"Too *comemierdas*!"[79] My father scoffed.

"You need to be with real people." My mother said.

So instead of country-club camping, I was packed off to Troop 12, where cookie sales happened in front of gas stations and "team building" meant learning which girl's cousin was already in prison.

---

[79] Comemierdas: Lit. Shit eaters. Puerto Rican for snob, but dumber and in better shoes.

By the time I was chosen for the Saint Lawrence University summer camp, I thought: "At last! The moment when the poor-but-plucky heroine finds her destiny."

I packed like I was opening for Bianca Jagger at Studio 54 — minus the budget, cocaine or actual invitation. Satin skirt. Perfume samples. Eyeliner sharp enough to cut glass.

Then… novela lightning strike.

The airline lost my luggage.

Villain close-up: the airline clerk, mustache worthy of an evil hacendado, shrugged as he stamped my boarding pass.

"Señorita, the bags are… desaparecidas."

Somewhere in Syracuse, his mistress was already strutting in my linen skirt, whispering my lines in bad Spanish — "Si, mi amor."— while smelling faintly of Bonnie Bell Strawberry Kiwi.

Day one: no clothes, no toiletries, no dignity. Just me and a borrowed Walmart T-shirt that reeked of wet Doritos and adolescent despair.

But here's the twist within the twist: Troop 12 had trained me for this episode. While the Academia girls camped in pearls and bug-spray atomizers, we lit fires with Bic lighters and sheer rage.

Troop 12 taught me what *Siempre listas* really meant — not ready for marshmallows, but for betrayal, humiliation, and the inevitable plot twist.

So, I survived.

I hand-washed my underwear in the sink with soap strong enough to peel paint. I wore my camp uniform like couture in a *Dynasty* spin-off. I walked into flag ceremony in gym shorts so stiff they deserved their own SAG card.

The rich girls rotated wardrobes like novela villains in an opening-credits montage. I rotated shame, polyester, and borrowed deodorant from Willow who clearly had a contract clause against using deodorant.

But the greatest twist? That camp was only foreshadowing.

Years later, when my ex slashed my tires, cut every appliance cord, stole my mother's jewelry, and left me $100K in debt, did I faint like a weak side character?

Por favor. I'd already learned how to make dignity out of borrowed deodorant.

Cue swelling violins.

Cue eyeliner in perfect close-up.

Cue my lips, trembling with righteous fury:

"*Yo sobreviví cabrones*!"

Troop 12 revealed the secret script note behind the Girls Scout motto. "Always prepared," was never about flashlights or matching luggage. It meant resilience, discipline, and a survival kit you pack in your chest — not your Samsonite.

THE DECODER

Survival Law #24: *In my novela, villains plot, fortunes collapse, but the heroine? She survives.*

EPISODE 25 – THE FIRST TIME I SAW SNOW

12/26 — 7:00 a.m.

Rating: PG

Episode Description: *Dreams crushed by suede.*

Every telenovela heroine eventually gets whisked from her natural habitat by a *galán* and dropped into some fantasy wonderland: Cancún, Paris, at least a seaside resort with a yacht in the background.

Me?

I got Lake Placid.

No galán, no yacht… just my mother, her Aqua Net helmet and the wrong boots.

Christmas in Puerto Rico was its own fever dream of decadence:

- A whole pig spinning on a spit in our patio, basted like it was a Fabergé egg. My uncle stood shirtless, sweat dripping, auditioning for *Magic Mike: Lechón Edition.*
- Mountains of pasteles steaming while the women of the house argued like a Senate subcommittee.
- Coquito so sweet and boozy it could seduce and anesthetize a small country.
- Neighbors showing up uninvited with trays of flan glistening like designer handbags under floodlights.

And of course, the occasional blackout — because nothing says "holiday magic" like roasting pork over a bonfire made from broken rocking chairs while your mother shouts death threats at the electric company.

It was operatic. Excessive. Fabulous. Very Kevin Kwan, if Kevin Kwan had been raised in the Caribbean, surrounded by pigs and patio furniture set aflame.

Snow, meanwhile, was imported fantasy: pumped through Hallmark movies or faked at *Plaza Las Américas*[80] with a plastic snow machine while Mariah screeched in the food court.

So, when my parents announced, "We're going to Lake Placid for Christmas!" Vero and I fainted like we'd just won a condo on *The Price is Right.*

At last, snow angels, sleigh rides, mistletoe kisses; maybe even a spontaneous proposal from a Kennedy.

The Footwear Apocalypse

Let me tell you about my mother.

Mami curates. She accessorizes. She will die on the hill of elegance. She believes Crocs are a moral failing; silk blouses are armor, and dressing for the weather is for peasants.

So instead of buying us practical snow boots, she outfitted us in... **suede**.

That's right. Suede boots for Lake Placid.

The fashion equivalent of:

- Bringing a Birkin to a flood.
- Wearing chiffon to a volcanic eruption.
- Fighting climate change with a Dyptique candle.

The first time I stepped into real snow, my joy lasted three seconds. Then came the wet. The cold. The pain. My toes froze instantly — entombed in designer leather coffins.

---

[80] **Plaza Las Américas:** Puerto Rico's mall of malls. Air conditioning, handbags, judgment, and parking-lot warfare included. See LSG decoder.

While local kids frolicked like Coke-commercial extras, I hobbled through Lake Placid like a frostbitten peasant in *Les Misérables.*

The soundtrack wasn't Mariah Carey anymore; it was my internal monologue screaming, "Amputation. Amputation now."

Horse-drawn sleighs? Erased. Ice skating? Blocked out.

All I recall is plunging my blue toes into scalding water, convinced I'd discovered a new form of medieval torture.

So that was my "White Christmas":

- Frozen
- Miserable
- And to this day, suede triggers me like a bad ex.

Telenovelas end with revelations, slaps, and fainting spells. Mine ended with the realization that snow is just cold water dressed up for Instagram—and that my mother's definition of elegance, could, in fact, kill me in style.

THE DECODER

Survival Law #25: *Snow looks magical until it soaks your socks. Choose survival over suede.*

EPISODE 26 – THE ART OF THE DISCO PARTY

12/26 — 8:00 a.m.

Rating PG

Episode Description: *Platform shoes, disco lies, and chaperones.*

In every soap, the ingénue hovers at the edge of the party — invisible, mocked, ignored, until fate intervenes. For me, that party was a marquesina in San Juan in 1978.

It was the age of disco balls, polyester so flammable we were one Bic lighter away from mass casualties. Bee Gees' lyrics were treated like scripture.

At fourteen, your entire social worth hinged on whether a Jesuit schoolboy asked you to slow dance. It was Darwinism in glitter.

Every weekend, some poor parents surrendered their carport for the sacred rite: the marquesina party — a teenage bacchanal of Pepsi, warm Medalla, and outfits that could ignite on contact.

Meanwhile, in the adult zone, a coven of doñas nursed *cidra*, ate *mantecaditos*, and surveilled the dance floor like undercover Vatican agents.

Their mission? Prevent *traqueteo.*[81] One slip of a hand and you were exiled to all-girls-school Siberia.

The rules were brutal:

- Girls on one side. Boys on the other.
- You could not ask them to dance.
- You could not dance alone.

[81] **Traqueteo**: From groping to drug running, same energy, forbidden.

- You could not dance with each other.

Because apparently, disco was invented to teach us Catholic shame.

The Ingenue Moment

I stood there like a wax figure of Madam Tussauds— tall, brace-faced, praying someone, anyone, would pick me.

Then it happened…

Serra.

Not even his first name, just the name on his basketball jersey. But he was tall, handsome, and carried the social power of John Travolta in *Saturday Night Fever.* And that night, to the divine orchestration of Donna Summer— or maybe sheer boredom— he asked me to dance.

Cue: *How Deep Is Your Love.*

There I was, floating—braces reflecting the disco ball, heart pounding in Morse code.

Then, disaster.

His hand slid to my lower back.

Catholic reflex kicked in. I grabbed it, shoved it north, and delivered a mid-slow-dance sermon on virtue, chastity, and God's eternal surveillance system.

Serra never asked me to dance again.

Let's be honest. I was fourteen, five foot eight, all legs, no boobs, no waist, acne, braces and… a mustache.

A full-blown mustache.

If my life were a novela, this was the humiliating cold open before the commercial break — the moment designed to make viewers scream, "*¡Dios mío! ¿Cómo sobrevivirá esta criatura?*" My God! How will this child survive?

Looking back, the disco wasn't about dancing. It was survival: a test of whether you could enter adolescence armed with sequins, Catholic guilt, and a shaky sense of rhythm.

Spoiler: I couldn't.

But humiliation has its uses. That mustache? It sent me straight to Hato Rey and the sadistic Russian aesthetician who introduced me to electrolysis — and pain as a lifestyle choice.

THE DECODER

Survival Law #26*: At fourteen, sequins and borrowed choreography count as confidence. The mustache comes off; the shame never does.*

EPISODE 27 – ELECTROLYSIS: THE PAIN OLYMPICS OF 1978

12/26 — 9:00 a.m.

Rating: PG

Episode Description: *Because being Latina means fighting your genes, one follicle at a time.*

In any decent telenovela, there comes the makeover episode. The humble, innocent ingénue endures her transformation — tweezed, waxed, bronzed, hair-sprayed — until she emerges looking less like a butterfly and more like a freshly shellacked baboon.

Mine was no different.

Only my transformation wasn't sequins and soft lighting.

It was a medieval torture chamber in Hato Rey.

Electrolysis[82] in the late '70s was not beauty; it was barbarism disguised as self-care.

The clinic sat between a tennis club and a hair salon, as if proximity to leisure could soften the horror. My mother would head next door for her blow-out while I was sacrificed to a Russian aesthetician with false eyelashes thick enough to swat dragonflies.

The waiting room was decorated with a single terrifying poster: a 300-pound bearded lady beaming under the caption —

[82] **Electrolysis:** Beauty via electrocution.

Electrolysis Changed My Life

My mother studied the poster.

Then my face.

Then the poster again.

Decision made.

The Procedure

The Russian flipped on her magnifying lamp, leaned close, and hissed: "*You have been shaving. You vant to look like man? You vant to look like picture?"*

And then she jabbed.

An electrified needle pierced each follicle.

Zap.

Zap.

Zap.

She played *Space Invaders* with my upper lip.

I screamed. She zapped harder.

"You vill come back next week," she barked, unmoved by my agony.

I stumbled out red and swollen, my lip coated in "healing cream" that looked exactly like a milk mustache. A glamorous telenovela heroine? More like a Humpty Dumpty with Noxzema.

Electrolysis wasn't progress. It was punishment.

Each appointment was a morality play: *sin dolor, no hay belleza.* No pain, no beauty — which really meant we will hurt you into acceptability.

Looking back, the makeover wasn't about vanity; it was about survival.

To be Latina in the late '70s meant you were expected to fight your genes like a gladiator. We weren't taught to embrace our wild, glorious hair; we were taught to electrocute it into extinction.

THE DECODER

Survival Law #27: *Beauty fades, but electrolysis pain is eternal. Choose your battles; some scars are invisible but still burn.*

EPISODE 28 – THE BLONDE AMBITION EXPERIMENT

12/26 — 10:00 a.m.

Rating: PG

Episode Description: *Spoiler — It all went as badly as you think.*

As required by telenovela code, there comes a moment of reinvention. The ingénue gets amnesia and wakes up with bangs. The betrayed wife dyes her hair to look like the mistress. The villainess disguises herself to frame the innocent *estúpida.*

While my upper lip was being electrocuted weekly at the electrolysis clinic, the rest of me staged a coup. I grew three inches in one summer. Suddenly, I was "model material."

Our neighbor, who ran a Condado modeling agency called Barbarella (because nothing says elegance like naming yourself after Jane Fonda in a space bikini), spotted me and declared: "She should be a model."

Next thing I knew, Saturdays were consumed by "modeling school." We were taught to walk the runway, drink soup without slurping and sit like heiresses waiting to inherit haciendas.

The grand finale: a runway fashion show for Primitivo. He was Puerto Rico's own Valentino — five-foot-two, chain smoked like Sartre, and waved a cigarette while declaring, "She will be my muse.:

But first, he said, "I needed a look."

The Makeover

Enter: the bleaching cap of 1978.

A rubber cap was suctioned onto my scalp, and a sadistic stylist yanked strands of hair through tiny holes with what looked like medieval dental tools.

Hours later, I emerged with "TIPS" — the 1978 version of highlights. I didn't look like a muse. I looked like a recently divorced 25-year-old with a fake ID.

Still, mascara and bravado were enough to sneak me into San Juan's disco underworld: Juliana's, Isadora, The Flying Saucer. There, polyester met polyester and lies were the dress code.

In Puerto Rico, *la rubia* wasn't just a look; it was an identity upgrade. Blonde, equaled status, desirability, social currency. Blue contacts sealed the fantasy. Suddenly, you were part-time Swedish, full time aspirational.

A Puerto Rican woman with blonde hair and blue contacts wasn't just a woman. She was a Siberian husky prowling the dance floor, worshipped and ridiculed in equal measure. To be blonde was to be reborn, even if your roots betrayed you within a week.

Looking back, the bleach wasn't about hair; it was about escape. About wanting to look like anyone else — anyone who didn't carry the weight of family expectations, electrolysis appointments, and whispered gossip about too-long legs.

Becoming blonde was survival cosplay: a temporary passport into glamour, desirability, and the lie that you could be someone else if you just fried your hair enough.

THE DECODER

Survival Law #28: *Hair bleach is temporary. Polaroids are forever.*

EPISODE 29 – THE TRAGICOMEDY FALL OF CRYSTAL FONTAINE

12/26 — 11:00 a.m.

Rating: PG

Episode Description: *How tight jazz pants predicted a future.*

Every telenovela has its pivot — that inevitable moment when the heroine must reveal her gift. Maybe she sings. Maybe she scrubs. Maybe she weeps prettier than anyone else. The galán falls for her because of that shimmer of purpose.

My supposed gift? Ballet.

The Torture Chamber

At Academia San José, we were trained into "ladies," polite, obedient, chronically anxious. School began at seven sharp, allowed one brittle recess at 10:30, and no food until 2:30 p.m.

Why? Because the Dominican nuns invented intermittent fasting long before Goop monetized hunger.

By dismissal, I drifted home like a Dickens orphan, only to find Mami had turned our dining room into Versailles.

- Steak Diane — *bistec encebollado* with delusions of grandeur
- Coq au Vin — *fricasé de pollo* in a French accent.
- Lobster Thermidor — because *mariscos criollos* were vulgar.

The silverware gleamed, the ceiling fan wheezed, and my mother performed gentility as if our Guaynabo house were the Ritz, and the neighbor's laundry flapping outside were simply stage décor.

Then came ballet class.

Madame Claudine & Crystal Fontaine.

Madame Claudine's Dance Studio was a converted garage with a cracked mirror and a whiff of mildew that smelled faintly of crushed dreams. Yet, she had once danced with American Ballet Theater, and that was enough to grant her divine license to terrorize generations of Puerto Rican girls.

Her daughter, **Crystal Fontaine**, was the chosen one.

Crystal was everything I was not: tall, blonde, leg-shaver, rumored to have lost her virginity at fourteen — which in Catholic Puerto Rico was the social equivalent of joining a Satanic sect.

She glided in each day wearing vacuum-sealed jazz pants and halter tops that began where faith ended. Her lids shimmered turquoise; her lashes could have swept off the floor if she ever deigned to plié.

Meanwhile, I resembled a Siberian goat herder preparing for the long winter. My mother, terrified of my "premature sexuality" forbade shaving. Result: legs so furred the Bolshoi could have cast me as Wolf #2 without an audition.

"*Para que nadie te vaya a estar tocando,*" she warned.

So, no one touches you.

Effective birth control. I give her that.

The Ballet Hierarchy

Naturally, Crystal was Swanhilda.

Me? Coppélia.

Not the ballerina.

The doll.

My entire role was to sit motionless on a gilded chair, clutching a prop book, while others fluttered around me in tulle. A decorative object. A metaphor for Catholic girlhood if there ever was one.

Because in traditional novelas, the ideal woman isn't fierce or flawed; she's porcelain — admired for stillness, not for movement.

And there I was, literally cast in that role.

The Supporting Cast

My sister Vero danced in the corps with her best friend, **Lourdes Quiles** — a girl perpetually in a liquid diet and the verge of fainting.

Lourdes worshipped fabric. She could identify polyester by touch, like a psychic reading a palm. If I wore anything synthetic, she'd pinch my sleeve, squint though Coke-bottle lenses, and hiss, "*¿Esto es seda?*" If I said no, she looked at me as though I'd confessed to murder.

At discos, she ditched her glasses and peered at men like Rorschach blots: "*¿Ese tipo es lindo o feo?*" As if Prince Charming versus frog were a matter of interpretation.

Onstage, her blindness turned ballet into slapstick. Every other count, she body-checked my sister with linebacker grace.

From my chair — frozen as Coppélia — I shook with silent laughter. Dolls weren't supposed to move, but watching Lourdes ricochet off Vero like a human pinball was divine comedy.

Soy una muñeca.

Then came the cruelest twist. My classmates from Academia San José attended the recital. They leaned forward, transfixed — not by Crystal's pirouettes, but by me.

By me doing nothing.

Still.

Silent.

Perfect.

Afterward, they whispered that I looked "so elegant, so mysterious."

Humiliating? Absolutely. But also intoxicating — to be praised for absence. To be adored precisely because I was immobile.

Cue the spotlight.

Cue the single tear.

Soy una muñeca.

Only years later did I realize being a doll wasn't punishment; it was prophecy. The fate of every "good girl." To be admired not for what she does, but for how gracefully she waits.

The Fall of Crystal Fontaine

Decades later, curiosity, and a dash of *schadenfreude*, sent me Googling Crystal Fontaine.

She has a PornHub account.

Same eyeliner. Same defiant stare. Now paired with a belly-dancing costume and a PayPal link. The prima ballerina had become the prima fetish model.

And the final pirouette of fate? Crystal is fat.

Not "curvy."

Not "soft."

Fat — expanded by time, tragedy, and every bad decision her jazz pants once foretold.

If you ask Mami, she just sighs and says, "*Sobrada,*[83] it was bound to happen."

Coda: The Doll Grows Up

Years later, I understood that the doll never leaves you. She just learns new poses.

In the boardroom and waiting rooms, in love and in loss, I've caught myself holding that same stillness — chin lifted spine straight — silence mistaken for grace. The world rewards composure, not truth; poise, not protest.

But inside, the doll is cracking. Not from age, but from awakening.

She's learning that motion isn't rebellion; it's resurrection. That breaking her porcelain smile is not ruin, but release. That a woman who finally stands, speaks, dances off her pedestal, doesn't lose her beauty.

She reclaims it.

THE DECODER

Survival Law #29: *Grace won't save you from gravity, or bad taste in boys. Dolls may be fragile, but they endure.*

---

[83] **Sobrada**: PR code for girl who's too much, too flirty, too eager, too pleased to please. Half insult, half prophecy, what good girls call the ones who dare to want.

EPISODE 30 — LUCA BELLINI & THE FIRST KISS DEBACLE

12/26 — 12:00 p.m.

Rating: PG

Episode Description: *Because every great romance begins with bad lighting and good gossip.*

If you were raised on telenovelas, as any properly supervised Latina child was, then you knew that girlhood revolved around three milestones: your *Quinceañera*, your first attempt at heels (feeling like a newborn giraffe on roller skates). And, of course, *The Kiss.*

Not a kiss.

The Kiss.

Capitalized. Italicized. Underscored. The one that could either crown you as a heroine or condemn you to spinsterhood in a house full of unsolicited advice from Titi Marina and her army of incontinent Pomeranians.

Naturally, Mami fortified my adolescence like a Pentagon operation:

- Chaperones[84] — Rotating titis and family-approved gay men. No heterosexual male within ten miles was safe.
- Cousin Quarantine — Because in telenovela logic, people fall in love with cousins all the time. Disturbing — but historically accurate.

[84] **Chaperones:** Because nothing says romance like your aunt breathing down your neck.

- Religious Fearmongering — Daily Virgin Mary reminders: She managed it — why can't you, Charito? Never mind that I was on birth-control pills for "biblical hemorrhaging," Mami remained unconvinced.

Yet, though the cracks in the fortress slipped ***Luca Bellini***.

Enter Luca Bellini

Luca was the son of an architect, which in Puerto Rican society meant his family wasn't just rich; they had taste. He loved jazz, which sounded intellectual at the time, though in hindsight it was just Chuck Mangione.

Somehow, he got my landline: 783-1013. This was the Dark Ages — no caller ID, no voicemail. Waiting for a boy to call was like waiting for Godot... if Godot were hormonal and enrolled at a Jesuit school.

Luca passed Mami's final test. If a boy didn't introduce himself with dignity and proper enunciation, she hung up mid-sentence. No regrets.

Luca cleared the bar.

The First Date

Dinner at Old San Juan's *Cosa Nostra*[85] followed by dancing at Juliana's in the Caribe Hilton.

Juliana's wasn't just a nightclub; it was a stage. Sons of fallen TV dynasties leaned against the bar, rum-drunk, and radiant. Menudo and Los Chicos appeared to deafening shrieks. Peter Frampton looked sunburned; Madonna allegedly drifted though on her way to scandal, and Milli Vanilli whispered conspiracies over cocktails. George Michael glided in pastel linen; Elizabeth Peña laughed too loud at a joke too small for the room.

---

[85] **Cosa Nostra:** the only bar where you order a Negroni and get loyalty points and plausible deniability.

Everyone was watching everyone. And apparently, everyone was watching *me.*

After dinner, Luca led me into the Atlantic moonlight. He leaned in, grabbed my waist, and —

Tongue.

All of it.

¡¿Qué carajo?!

I shoved him off like a scandalized nun. Tears in my eyes, I blurted, "I've never been kissed before."

He froze, softened, tried again — just lips this time.

And reader, that I liked.

Training for Greatness

Determined never to be ambushed again, I sought my older sister Vero, veteran of one illicit beach kiss. She became my Obi-Wan.

In front of the mirror, she commanded, "Watch and learn."

We kissed our reflections. With tongue. Mortifying.

Then, for the finale she popped a maraschino cherry into her mouth, chewed, and pulled out the stem tied in a perfect knot.

¿Qué clase de brujería es esa?

She refused to explain. To this day, I remain mystified.

Redemption at The Rocky Horror Picture Show

Despite the fiasco, Luca called back. He invited me to see *The Rocky Horror Picture Show*,[86] a cult classic he'd discovered in the States. He described it like a party — drag queens, corsets, toast flying, chaos in the aisles.

---

[86] **The Rocky Horror Picture Show**: America's camp revolution; Puerto Rico's "¿Y eso que es?

We arrived in Santurce, braced for decadence.

The theater was empty.

No costumes.

No shouting.

No toast.

No rice.

Just me, Luca, and Tim Curry in heels performing for an audience of two while coquís croaked outside in perfect rhythm.

It was mortifying.

Luca glanced over, panicked — as if to say, *I swear this was wild in New York*. Meanwhile, I sat frozen in the sticky vinyl seat, convinced we'd stumbled into a government experiment in humiliation.

And yet, through weirdness, we bonded. We held hands. We shared popcorn. We laughed at the silence — the flop, ourselves.

And when the kiss came — soft, tentative, real — it was better than any toast-flinging bacchanal.

Because it was ours.

That night taught me something: sometimes, the flop is the gift. When spectacle fails, intimacy sneaks in. When the show collapses, life improvises.

A failed revolution can still end in a kiss.

THE DECODER

Survival Law #30: *A bad first kiss is a blessing. It lowers expectations for everything after.*

EPISODE 31 – LA CUEVA DEL CHICKEN INN

12/26 — 1:00 p.m.

Rating: PG

Episode Description: *Secrets revealed in pizza.*

Every telenovela follows the same sacred script: finale scandal first, then the reset, new location, new villain, darker stakes. If Academia San José was repression, La Cueva del Chicken Inn was temptation.

The place was a novela set: white stucco walls shaped like a cave, dim lighting made for infidelity, booths designed for clandestine affairs. Married doctors, crooked bankers, divorce-happy lawyers, all sat under fake stalactites, slicing pizza while slicing their marriages.

Mami, naturally loved it.

"The good times," she'd sigh.

For whom exactly? We'll never know.

Polyester Purgatory vs. Pizza Salvation

First Friday Mass at ASJ was Catholic cosplay: blinding white uniforms, suffocating sermons, fainting girls. We looked like an army of polyester postulants on a forced march to salvation.

But the reward was lunch with Mami at La Cueva del Chicken Inn.

One minute, I was choking on incense, the next inhaling garlic bread beneath neon roosters and plastic saints. It was my own split-screen telenovela: purity on one side, sin on the other — and me, in the middle, eating mozzarella sticks.

The Death of My Modeling Career

La Cueva was also the scene of another plot twist: the death of my modeling career.

After one night out with the Barbarella models, Mami returned home furious.

"That industry is a cesspool of heroin and Mazola injections," she declared.

One look at those women, veins collapsed, cheeks puffed with cooking oil, and she slammed her manicured fist on the table.

"You're not wasting your life in that world of addicts and oil!"

And just like that, my future as Primitivo's muse dissolved under the fluorescent cave lights of La Cueva del Chicken Inn.

Lady Sings the Blues, and So Did I

The darkest survival lesson didn't happen at La Cueva del Chicken Inn.

It happened the night Mami took me to see *Lady Sings the Blues* at the Astor Theater.[87]

With Papi, even a movie was a production — lost keys, wrong turns, impatient humming like static. By the time we arrived, the lights had dimmed.

---

[87] **Astor Theater:** formerly Kresto-Denia, the only cinema brave enough to show *Grease* and *Thank God Is Friday* at 10 a.m.

Mami stayed behind to help Papi find his seat. I went ahead, a little girl swallowed by velvet darkness and the scent of popcorn and perfume.

Onscreen, Diana Ross was shooting heroin; the trumpet wailed.

Beside me, a man who belonged in hell slid his hand under my panties.

I was six.

I didn't scream.

I didn't move.

I just disappeared inside myself — learned, in an instant, that silence could be armor.

I never told anyone. Not Mami. Not my titis who would've hunted him down with gold-plated letter openers.

Mami thought she was teaching me about jazz, heartbreak, and addiction.

Instead, I learned about shame, survival, and how to keep singing with a broken voice.

The Latina Survival Guide Lesson

Here's the paradox, dear reader: one moment you're laughing about polyester uniforms and secretaries having affairs over pizza; the next, you're learning to live with a truth so dark it bends your spine.

That's survival.

Sometimes it's laughing at Puerto Rican logic ("Why is this place called *La Cueva del Chicken Inn* if it serves pizza?").

Other times, it's holding your pain so tight it becomes another uniform you wear.

And maybe — just maybe, that's why Mami built her fortress. Why every rule, every sermon, every *no*, came laced with tremor. She never said it, but sometimes I wonder if she knew.

If she saw the fear behind my silence and decided that protection — even prison — was the only mercy left.

Maybe Mami knew.

Maybe that's why she guarded me like a secret.

Protection was her prayer.

And I was the unanswered one.

THE DECODER

Survival Law #31: *You can survive polyester, pizza caves, and Catholic guilt. What breaks you is always the thing no one sees.*

ACT IV

PREP SCHOOL PUBERTY & OTHER NATURAL DISASTERS

(Episodes 32-39)

EPISODE 32 – UNIFORMS & CODES: SADDLE SHOES, SLAMBOOKS, AND THE BOSSU

12/26 — 2:00 p.m.

Rating: PG-13 (For spiritual repression and tragic grooming choices)

Episode Description*: Catholic school as surveillance — what you wear, what you confess, and who you pretend not to want.*

There are many ways to ruin a child. Lock them in a basement. Feed them carob instead of chocolate. Raise them in a cult.

Or send them to Academia San José.

Uniforms were our corsets; the shame came pre-ironed.

The nuns ran the place like mob bosses in polyester. They carried rulers like switchblades, slapped desks like they were auditioning for *West Side Story* and could sniff out impure thoughts at twenty paces.

Sister Mary Agnes, vice principal and my astrological twin, called our shared Leo birthday, "divine kinship."

I called it Stockholm Syndrome with rosaries.

From the outside, I sparkled — Honor Society president, trophies clanking like a one-woman marching band. Inside, I was a bonsai: trimmed, wired, and spiritually compact enough to fit on a guidance counselor's desk.

Catholic school wasn't about God. It was about *props.* The pleated skirt, the crisp blouse, the navy vest — costumes in a morality play where the real show happened at our feet.

You could predict a girl's future by the sound of her saddle shoes in the hallway.

Royals clicked like destiny.

Novus clicked like ambition.

Mail-orders shuffled like an apology.

The light at the end of the tunnel was loafers — the emancipation papers disguised as footwear. Not everyone made it.

Wanda Ivette's skirt crept two inches north; her vest fit like a confession booth, and somehow, she sexualized orthopedic saddle shoes. Pregnant at sixteen, gone before finals. The nuns gasped. The *tías* murmured, *"Pues claro."*

Still, even in a surveillance state, I had my cell: girls who made repression survivable.

My tribe: a goddess who made kindness look illegal; a mystery wife-in-witness protection, a caffeinated disaster the height of a Doberman on espresso, and me, "*Bamber,*" forever mispronouncing horror titles.

Friendship, like Catholic guilt, is forever.

At 10:30 a.m. the convent bells tolled for Recess — our Eucharist of neon Cheeto dust, contraband Coca-Cola and *mallorcas,*[88] sugared within an inch of medical intervention.

Presiding over it all: **Jacks.**[89]

---

[88] **Mallorcas**: Bread so divine it made butter a sacrament.

[89] **Jacks:** Proof that children once entertained themselves with sharp objects.

Ten metal stars, one rubber ball, and enough competitiveness to summon Satan. My mother had been a champion, which I assumed meant heredity would handle it.

Spoiler: it did not.

Jacks was merely foreplay.

The main event was the **Slambook** — a spiral notebook disguised as stationery but actually the CIA's teenage division. Have you kissed? Who do you like? Initials only. Primitive cryptology. Devastating accuracy.

Which brings me to the **SHY** scandal.

A cute boy, tragically named Shy, confessed he liked someone in Madrid Street whose initial could be V or M. Veronica (my sister) of Matilde[90] (me)?

A telenovela without the wardrobe budget.

Naturally, I staged my femme-fatale debut: shaved one calf in secret. The next morning, I unveiled its gleam like a Fabergé egg. In my mind, Claudette Colbert. In reality — razor burn, Mercurochrome and two weeks grounded.

Shy remained unmoved. Vero and I remained friends. The Slambook stayed inconclusive.

Catholicism 1, Seduction 0.

Then came **The Bossu**.

We crashed a basketball tournament in Ponce. Miss Rosé, my goddess friend, landed Jason — green-eyed and mythic. I was paired with the Bossu; nickname literal, back curved, fate cruel.

We were even reading *Notre Dame de Paris* in French class; so of course, he felt like homework — tragic, laborious and assigned without my consent.

---

[90] **Matilde:** Literally, mighty in battle which honestly, explains everything.

Rosé frolicked.

I deflected lunges like a matador facing a bull with scoliosis.

Thus began the omen of my love life. gods for my friends, *Bossus* for me.

- The guitarist with a "bad back" who lived in a basement and distrusted deodorant.
- The grad student with "bad posture" who quoted Nietzsche and paid rent never.
- The film editor with "bad vibes," three cats, and no bed frame.
- The man with a literal hump; emotional, financial, or metaphysical.

Bossus all of them.

Because in our world, intimacy was a code; what you wore, what you wrote, what you could bear without speaking.

School taught us the first lesson: if you can't win the game, mock the uniform and fake the scoreboard.

THE DECODER

Survival Law #32: *Life's a pair of saddle shoes — squeaky, stiff, humiliating. Learn the code, play along, and graduate with your dignity intact. The rules don't change; only the uniforms.*

EPISODE 33 – THE PISICORRE CHRONICLES / DON VI'S VAN & THE GOSPEL OF TELENOVELAS

12/26 — 3:00 p.m.

Rating: PG

Episode Description: *Salvation arrives in a van with a portable TV and telenovelas.*

Growing up in Torrimar and attending Academia San José meant we were spared the indignity of a yellow school bus. No, querida, we were chauffeured in a gleaming, white *pisicorre*;[91] a kind of traveling VIP lounge on wheels.

Picture it: a dozen hyper-intellectual, hormone-fueled teenagers crammed into polyester uniforms that clung like industrial-strength Saran Wrap. Infernal pleated skirts. Saddle shoes for the underclassmen, dignified loafers for the seniors.

Each of us lugging faux-leather briefcases heavy enough to cause lifelong scoliosis. The lockers? Decorative — good only for hiding contraband *merienditas*,[92] sweating *sandwichitos de mezcla* in ninety-degree heat because refrigeration was apparently for the public-school proletariat.

[91] **Pisicorre**: From pisa y corre, ('step and run'); school van, but with salsa and fear.

[92] **Merienditas**: The sacred Puerto Rican ritual of snacking between lunch and dinner, usually involving café con leche, galletas and whatever your abuela pulled out of the bottomless tin of Danish butter cookies (that contained sewing supplies).

Those vinyl seats were hot, blue, and sticky. Sit down without slipping and you'd leave half your thigh behind, like *chuletas*[93] sizzling on a griddle.

Enter Don Vi — short for Don Vidal — a portly man with the patience of a saint and the aura of someone resigned to chauffeuring Puerto Rico's overbred aristocracy.

We were insufferable: teenagers demanding Elton John, Donna Summer, and Menudo at full blast while he longed for bachata. But Don Vi was clever. How do you silence a van full of hormonally deranged honor students?

The answer: **Telenovelas.**

This was the 80's and somehow, Don Vi managed to install a tiny battery-powered TV with an antenna that looked capable of picking up signals from Mars.

Between cerulean thighs welded to vinyl and briefcases cutting off circulation, we watched Venezuelan soap operas and Brazilian period dramas fetishizing slavery, at three in the afternoon, on the way home from school.

It worked like pharmaceutical magic. Silence. Peace. Hypnosis. We sat spellbound as actresses slapped their rivals, cried mascara tears, and swore vengeance between commercials for *Café Yaucono.*[94]

---

[93] **Chuletas:** Pork chops fried in oil and family tears. Maman would cry while she fried them, whispering, "*ese pobre hombre*" while my mother made my dad sleep in the car.

[94] **Café Yaucono:** P.R. sacred brew, dripped through a cloth filter, before artisanal was a thing. Famous for being better than Café Rico, and infamous for his cringe jingle, "*Todos los negros tomamos Café Yaucono.*" Colonial baggage never tasted so smooth.

Years later, over Thanksgiving turkey, my friend Cata resurrected the mystery: Was it *Infamia* [95]or *La Heredera*[96] that tamed us? Did Don Vi prefer reruns *of Escrava Isaura*[97], that Brazilian masterpiece where colonial trauma wore hoop skirts? We may never know.

What we do know is this: that sticky van became our first moving cathedral of melodrama, where salvation smelled like vinyl, sweat and pork chops.

THE DECODER

Survival Law #33: *Trapped with hormone-crazed teens? Forget logic. Play a telenovela; puberty bows to a dramatic slap.*

---

[95] **Infamia**: (1981) Televisa classic where betrayal was the plot, the mood, and the dress code.

[96] **La Heredera**: (1982) Venezuelan novel proving that inheriting millions only guarantees daily tears and at least one evil aunt in shoulder pads.

[97] **Escrava Isaura**: (1976) Brazilian novela about slavery; basically, colonial trauma in 100 episodes, hair always on point.

EPISODE 34 — THE SCIENCE FAIR THAT WASN'T ABOUT SCIENCE AT ALL

12/25 — 4:00 p.m.

Rating: PG

Episode Description: *Because sometimes the experiment isn't chemistry — it's chemistry.*

In true telenovela fashion, the daughter may be the reason for the party, the audition, the contest, but it's always the **mother** who steals the scene.

She arrives demure, pearls polished, allegedly just there to chaperone. She leaves with a suitor and a plot twist.

So, when Academia San José announced its annual science fair, I should've known the real experiment wouldn't involve Bunsen burners.

It would involve **Mami.**

The rules were strict:

- No volcanoes.
- No baking soda.
- No "my hamster runs in circles" projects.

It had to be serious science — the kind that made Dominican nuns feel they were presiding over the birth of Puerto Rico's next Nobel laureate.

Papi, ever the strategist, declared, "Go to the University. Find a scientist."

So off we went, Mami and I, into the sticky jungle of Río Piedras, where a weary man named **Sr. Figueroa** was testing natural pineapple pesticides in a greenhouse that smelled like mildew, ambition, and failed air-conditioning.

He lectured about *ananas comosus* while I scribbled nonsense like "photosynthetic enzymes = yes?" But his gaze?

Fixed on Mami.

Linen slacks. Pearl studs. The faint scent of Ralph Lauren and superiority. Mami didn't flirt; she *gleamed.*

By the third visit she laughed too loud at his fungus jokes. She adjusted her hair like humidity was foreplay. She stood among the *piñas* like an heiress inspecting her tropical estate.

"Charito, take notes," she ordered without breaking eye contact.

Notes on what? Botany or seduction?

When I teased her later — "Mami, are you really that interested in pesticides?"— She looked scandalized.

"¡Charito! I would never disrespect your father."

And yet, her eyes sparkled like test tubes catching fire.

For the first time in years, she wasn't just a caretaker, martyr, or martyr-in-training. She was radiant. Desired. A woman rediscovering her tropical voltage in a greenhouse full of spiky fruit.

For one humid summer, the only thing more potent than the pesticide was Mami.

Because sometimes the daughter's project is just the pretext. The real experiment is chemistry.

On Science Fair Day, I presented my "groundbreaking" project with the gravitas of a future Harvard fellow: long words I couldn't pronounce, charts I didn't make, gestures worthy of Miss Universe.

Naturally, I won first prize. The nuns applauded. Papi beamed. Sr. Figueroa clapped politely.

But I knew the truth.

That science fair wasn't about science at all.
The real winner was Mami, who — for one humid summer — rediscovered her forbidden piña.

THE DECODER

Survival Law #34: *Science may impress the judges, but chemistry always steals the novela.*

EPISODE 35 – BRIBES, BAD DRIVERS & THE ROAD TO SURVIVAL

12/26 — 5:00 p.m.

Rating: PG

Episode Description: *Because in my family, driving was less skill and more scandal.*

In my family, driving wasn't a rite of passage.

It was a moral hazard.

A social betrayal.

A telenovela plotline on four wheels.

We had drivers, of course — not because we were busy or important (though laziness helped), but because the women in my family firmly believed that driving was for *poor people… or prostitutes.*

Maman, my grandmother, sat in the back seat like a dethroned European monarch, clutching her rosary and muttering, "Women who drive end up in scandals." She wasn't wrong.

The last woman she'd seen behind the wheel was La Gata, my grandfather's mistress, rewarded for her services with a Cadillac that gleamed like sin itself. From that day on, Maman decided that steering wheels were instruments of moral decay.

So naturally, the women of my family outsourced the sin.

If you're going to outsource driving, outsource it badly.

There was **Cundo Flechazo,** my father's valet, who could inhale a platter of *arroz con pulpo* drenched in *pique*[98] and then shed a single cinematic tear, as if mourning the octopus personally.

Then came **Don Jonás**, a Vietnam vet turned family chauffeur. His PTSD smelled like Johnny Walker Red. My father, sentimental to a fault, refused to fire him because, "*¡Ay bendito!*[99] *El hombre ha sufrido demasiado.*" Which is fine — until the man who's suffered too much is the one driving your children home from ballet lessons.

The Mercedes Incident

So, when it came time for me to learn to drive, Papi announced that he — and only he, would teach me.

"Bonding," he called it.

"Attempted homicide," I would later call it.

He placed me behind the wheel of his beloved Mercedes, a car worth more than most Puerto Rican homes, and instructed, "Accelerate with confidence."

I did.

Within seconds:

- Two fender benders behind us.
- Three taxi drivers crossed themselves.
- One father gripping the passenger seat like a man awaiting last rites.

When we finally stopped, smoke curling from the tires, he turned to me in a whisper so calm it was terrifying:

---

[98] **Pique**: Fermented chaos in a rum bottle. My dad swore it cured sadness, Cundo Flechazo swore it caused it. Both were right.

[99] **¡Ay bendito!:** The Swiss Army knife of Puerto Rican expressions. A hug, a dagger or a one-way ticket to jódete category, depending on tone. See LSG Decoder.

"Maybe we hire a professional."

Señor Martinez, the Legend

Every ASJ girl learned with **Señor Martinez Driving School**. His Toyota had dual controls because trust was not his love language.

Legend said that while you practiced parallel parking, his hand might "guide" your thigh — a euphemism straight from hell. The miracle wasn't that girls got licenses. It's that we survived the lessons.

Martinez was "connected," whispered to bribe the DMV examiners, so every trembling convent girl passed. Harassment. Nepotism. Corruption. The holy trinity of the Puerto Rican learner's permit.

Why He Never Tried It with Me

For reasons still unknown, Señor Martinez never laid a finger on me.

Theories include:

- I had braces.
- I radiated abstinence energy.
- My convent-girl body screamed "taser."
- I was taller than him.

Whatever the reason, I was spared — and I learned to drive.

And scandal or not, the man taught me two survival lessons that outlasted his Toyota:

1. Count to three at a stop sign or risk fiery death.
2. Parallel park like a sociopath — get close enough to graze the other car, then crank the wheel like you're breaking into Fort Knox.

Reader, I can parallel park better than most men can fake an orgasm.

The Latina Survival Guide Lesson

- Rich families always have help, and the help will always be insane.
- Driving is rebellion disguised as progress.
- Even predators can teach you something useful.
- Bribes aren't corruption— they're tradition.

And that's how I survived learning to drive: with nerves of steel, a killer turn radius, and Maman spinning in her grave every time I start the engine.

THE DECODER

Survival Law #35: *In Puerto Rico, survival isn't defensive driving… it's strategic bribery.*

EPISODE 36 – SCANDAL, SEDUCTION & A NEUROSURGEON'S TONGUE

12/26 — 6:00 p.m.

Rating: PG

Episode Description: *Mami meets Olivia Pope, Boricua edition.*

Every telenovela follows the same choreography: forbidden love arrives by the pool. At Cerromar or Caparra, you'd see the married politician sneaking glances at the babysitter; the socialite's husband "teaching" synchronized swimming to someone not his wife.

Pools were chlorinated confessionals — baptismal fonts for sin.

But in my life, scandal didn't wait for summer. It strutted straight into Academia San José, in the form of a Catholic school girl with perfect hair, falling for a married man.

Not just any man, but a distinguished neurosurgeon — old enough to have personally watched the moon landing and smug enough to believe his tongue was a medical instrument.

At Academia San José, where nuns ruled with iron fists and hypocrisy was the unofficial extracurricular, scandals were as common as monogrammed schoolbags.

Still, this one felt like it could bring down the Puerto Rican Medical Association *and* the Archdiocese in one fell swoop.

Her name was **Emma Santillán** — breathtaking, magnetic, Afro-Latina goddess. Her father? A world-famous brain surgeon, the kind of man who had socialites faking aneurysms just to book a consultation.

One afternoon, Emma pulled me aside, eyes wide with lust and Catholic guilt.

"I'm having an affair with a married man."

WHAT?!

This was not a "my boyfriend didn't call me back" problem. This was, "I'm dating a fifty-year-old neurosurgeon who billed in dollars and whatever existential dread he caused" problem.

And who was I, a braces-wearing fifteen-year-old, supposed to call? *Ghostbusters*? Vatican hotline?

There was one solution.

Enter: Mami, Mafia Fixer

My mother had the instincts of a mafia lawyer and the moral rigidity of a nun. The second she heard the words "affair" and "neurosurgeon," her eyes narrowed like she was about to take down Watergate.

"We'll go to her house under the pretext of reviewing French lessons," she declared. "And then we'll launch the attack."

Reader, I barely had time to grab my *Larousse* dictionary, before I found myself in Emma's living room, clutching a French textbook while my mother — in full *Televisa* mode, cut through small talk like a machete.

"So, Emma, querida… who is he?"

Out it spilled, like a badly kept society secret. The man? **Dr. Angelo Vargas**. Neurosurgeon. Respected. Married. Colleague of Emma's father.

SHAKESPEARE.

SOAP OPERA.

SCANDAL.

Emma sighed dreamily: "I love him. He does things to me I never thought possible, his tongue..."

"STOP." Mami barked, in the exact tone you'd use to stop a child from running into traffic. "No details... just give me his address."

The Confrontation

The next day, Mami faked a neurological emergency and demanded an appointment with Dr. Vargas.

Picture it: a woman with zero headaches, no migraines and the constitution of an ox, storming into the most prestigious neurosurgeon's office, clutching her head like she was about to faint into the arms of St. Jude himself.

I waited outside while she disappeared into the consultation room.

To this day, I don't know what happened in there. Did she threaten him with the wrath of the Puerto Rican legal system? Did she casually mention she knew every judge, priest, and hairdresser in San Juan? Did she hypnotize him with the sheer force of Catholic maternal rage?

All I know is that she walked out headache-free, lipstick immaculate, and smiling like a woman who had just won the lottery.

By the following week, Dr. Vargas had ghosted Emma completely.

Emma's Novela Meltdown

Emma was devastated. She clutched her diary like it was scripture.

"He won't call me back… I still love him!"

And me? I wanted to scream: "GIRL, HE'S FIFTY. HE IS MARRIED. HE IS BASICALLY MEDICARE-ELIGIBLE. MOVE ON."

But instead, I lied through my braces. "I didn't say anything."

She hugged me, overwhelmed with gratitude, while I silently wondered if she'd ever realized my mother had just carried out a surgical strike on her love life.

The Aftermath & Moral

Emma eventually became a psychiatrist. Ironically, she now specializes in love addiction. Because of course she does.

As for Dr. Vargas? He vanished from San Juan society gossip, only to resurface six months later in the San Juan Star: "*Local Neurosurgeon Joins Doctors Without Borders.*"

The irony was delicious. The man who once seduced teenagers in Condado now saving lives in war zones —trading caviar and mistresses for malaria pills and humility.

And Mami? She turned the fiasco into a lifelong lecture series:

- Men will always try to take advantage of young girls.
- Never date anyone more than two years older than you.
- In fact, younger is better. *("Cougars have more fun, Charito.")*

Honestly?

She was right.

Because sometimes the real scandal isn't the affair itself — it's witnessing a Puerto Rican *mother* on a mission.

THE DECODER

Survival Law #36: *A medical degree can't save you from gossip. Family scandal spreads faster than malpractice suits.*

EPISODE 37 – THE STAGE & THE CZARINA

12/26 — 7:00 p.m.

Rating: PG-13 (For colonial traumas, delusions of grandeur, and accidental cousin crushes)

Episode Description: *Nothing says "talent" like reciting abortion poetry while your art teacher claims to be a Romanov.*

In every Puerto Rican girl's coming-of-age story, there's a moment when performance stops being extracurricular and becomes survival.

Mine began with ***Oratoria***,[100] Catholic public speaking as blood sport.

At Academia San José, *Oratoria* wasn't about eloquence. It was about domination. Think *The Hunger Games* meets *Miss Universe* produced by the archdiocese.

Categories included:

- *Poetry*: Cry until they hand you a trophy.
- *Comedy*: Louder = holier.
- *Essay*: Mock trial for teenagers.
- *Original Writing*: Melodrama with footnotes.

All of it delivered in Spanish, English and French, because nothing heals colonial wounds like trilingual trauma.

[100] **Oratoria:** Alumni of Oratoria went to fill San Juan's courtrooms, anchor desks and cocktail parties, reminding everyone that in P.R., survival has always been a performance.

Our coach, **Doña Mercedes Villalobos,** ruled like a pearl-clad dictator. She barked verses until our tongues bled consonants.

My mother, sensing opportunity, conscripted me into family-party performances.

"¡*Recítame la poesía, Charito*!" she'd command, sherry in hand, as if I were Edith Piaf resurrected to entertain tipsy lawyers.

Refusal meant exile from the buffet.

So, there I was — fifteen, braces glinting under fluorescent light — declaiming poetry about teenage pregnancy in front of cousins who hadn't even hit puberty.

Mid-monologue, I locked eyes with **Julián Marcano;** my second cousin, Puerto Rican Robert De Niro. Cologne of rebellion.

He handed me a *screwdriver* — vodka and orange juice. Liquid permission.

The burn hit my throat. The shame dissolved. And for one glorious second, I wasn't a girl forced into public speaking hell.

I was María Félix in a close-up: luminous, tragic and possibly in love with her cousin.

Then the applause ended. The titis whispered. Reality returned — sticky, judgmental, and citrus scented.

If *Oratoria* taught me to perform for survival, **art class** taught me to hallucinate my way through it.

Enter **Sra. Anastasia Vladimirovna Romanova-Orlovsky** — art teacher, nicotine oracle, and self-proclaimed last surviving Romanov.

In Puerto Rico.

Let that sink in.

According to her, she was the lost duchess of Russia, forced into exile and condemned to teach watercolor fruit to sweaty teenagers who smelled of Jean Naté, chalk dust, and despair.

Her "palace" was a Borinquen Towers one-bedroom overlooking a Walgreens.

Her "Fabergé eggs" were Avon bottles shaped like swans.

We called the Walgreens *the Winter Palace* and got on with our colonized lives.

Two island rules kept her employed:

1. Never disrespect your elders.
2. Never anger a lunatic — *la fuerza de los locos*[101] is supernatural.

So, we bowed to the Dutchess of Tempera.

"ART IS PAIN!" she'd hiss, fumigating us with Virginia Slims like holy incense.

I painted a banana.

She exhaled tragedy.

"This," she sighed, "is why Russia fell."

Ma'am, we are in Guaynabo.

Disbelief felt dangerous. She referred to Sister Mary Agnes as "the Grand Inquisitor of the West." Every class was a séance— chalk instead of candles.

Her exit was pure telenovela.

---

[101] ***La fuerza de los locos***: Mami swore the insane had Hulk-level strength; could lift cars, break doors, or throw you across the room when possessed. Moral: never anger a lunatic; madness is its own superpower.

She dropped her cigarette into rinse water, removed her glasses, and declared,

"History betrayed me."

Then she left.

No purse.

No attendance sheet.

Only smoke and pirated Chanel No. 5.

Years later, I checked:

- The eggs were Avon.
- Russia stayed fallen.
- My banana never rose to the occasion.

I think of her whenever I remember that cousin's smirk, that family stage, those fluorescent lights.

Performance saved us both.

She faked royalty. I faked confidence.

Call it mixed media survival.

Because in Puerto Rico — or Hollywood — survival requires one skill: Turning humiliation into theater and calling it heritage.

THE DECODER

Survival Law #37: *When life demands a talent show, crown yourself and perform. Delusion is just confidence with better lighting.*

EPISODE 38 – THE DARK DAY OF ACADEMIA SAN JOSÉ

12/26 — 8:00 p.m.

Rating: PG -13 (For incense, hysteria, and minor lesbian panic)

Episode Description: *A day that lives in infamy… mine.*

Every telenovela saves its juiciest scandal for the finale.

Ours involved no miracles, no saints — just two teachers and one rumor that could've brought down the Vatican Wi-Fi.

The Set-Up

Imagine a school with:

- **All nuns:** Women who could smell sin before you committed it.
- **All girls:** Hormones compressed into cerulean pleats.
- **No boys**: Because apparently the mere sight of a male wrist led straight to conception.

Into this pressure cooker walked **Mme. Marchand**, the French teacher— half Givenchy, half baguette — and **Doña Mercedes Villalobos**, our Oratoria/Spanish instructor and self-proclaimed descendant of Isabel la Católica.

They despised each other with the precision of rival monarchs.

The Cultural Cold War

"Paris is civilization!" declared Mme. Marchand.

"Madrid built it and sent it in galleons!" snapped Doña Mercedes.

Every staff meeting felt like a Treaty of the Pyrenees re-enactment; minus the choreography, plus menopause.

Then came the whisper.

They're in love.

The Assembly That Broke a Nun

Joint presentation: "Great Cultural Capitals of Europe."

Mme. Marchand swept onstage in silk. Doña Mercedes followed, ruffles weaponized.

"Paris, city of light!"

"Madrid the empire of soul!"

Gasps.

A scarf flew.

A bun trembled.

The stare locked; half duel, half foreplay.

Sister Mary Agnes clutched her rosary until it drew blood. Sister Teresa fainted like it was cardio.

For three eternal seconds, time stopped.

Then the microphone screeched — miracle by feedback — and the moment dissolved.

The tension between Mme. Marchand and Doña Mercedes spread through the school like cheap perfume.

By recess, half the girls were whispering about "forbidden love," and the other half were deciding which teacher they hated more.

Somehow, poor **Srta. Diciembre**, the English teacher everyone feared, got swept into the narrative.

She'd been spotted near the auditorium, clutching her gradebook like a shield, and rumor did the rest.

Whether it was misplaced hysteria or divine retribution, by sundown the gossip had evolved.

If there was sin in the air, surely, she was *part of it.*

The Graffiti

By dawn, crimson letters screamed across the front wall.

"SRTA. DICIEMBRE COME CHOCH."

Translation unnecessary.

The paint ran out before the final vowel, divine mercy by aerosol.

The Aftermath

Lockdown.

Nuns barricaded the doors like the Inquisition was trending. Girls sobbed, rosaries tangled, and even the Virgin Mary seemed to roll her plaster eyes.

By noon:

- The wall was repainted.
- Srta. Diciembre had "resigned for personal reasons."
- The air reeked of Paco Rabanne pour Homme and panic — the holy trinity of forbidden faculty love.

The funniest part?

I missed the entire apocalypse.

I'd called in sick — safely at home with my *Corn Flakes*, *Tiger Beat*, and a zit the size of the Sacred Heart — when Vero phoned, shrieking:

"¡Charo! The nuns are having a nervous breakdown, and someone wrote *choch* on the wall!"

It was the first — and last — time I ever regretted perfect attendance.

When the dust (and bleach fumes) finally settled, the scandal took a life of its own.

The nuns never mentioned it again.

The students whispered it like scripture.

I returned to school a reluctant celebrity — known not for my grades but for surviving the *Great Choch Incident of '84*.

By then, gossip had cooled into folklore.

That's when the real confession arrived.

Weeks later, Doña Mercedes confessed — over coffee, and Catholic guilt — that Mme. Marchand was *not* having an affair with her at all…

…but with her unemployed husband: the actual Duque de Bilbao, currently "consulting in wines," which apparently meant drinking them professionally.

Yes.

A real Spanish duke.

Imported like a problematic Rioja.

Both women had spoken to my mother — allegedly about my "academic progress" — while secretly using me as their mutual courier of concern.

Only years later did I realize I had been the unwilling *Celestina*:[102] the messenger girl between a bored aristocrat and two dueling pedagogues.

And poor Srta. Diciembre?

She was the meanest English teacher alive — corrected your grammar mid-sob — but also a lifelong spinster in a country that treats unmarried women like unsolved crimes.

Maybe the graffiti was revenge from a failed student.

Maybe it was true.

Or maybe it was just the island's favorite pastime: Punishing any woman who lived alone and wore sensible shoes.

Her real crime wasn't desire.

It was dangling modifiers.

Because that's the thing about Catholic school:

Facts never mattered.

Only the story.

And mi amor — we told it like scripture; with better lighting and worse dialogue.

Cue theme song.

Freeze-frame on a trembling nun clutching a mop.

Roll rosaries across the credits.

---

[102] **Celestina:** The original go-between from 1499 Spanish classic *La Celestina*, a bawdy proto-novela disguised as literature, a former madam turned, "messenger of love," arranged secret trysts for star crossed nobles, mostly for profit and occasionally for sport. Every Latina with a phone, chisme, and questionable boundaries eventually becomes one. I apparently did it at 15, minus the commission.

Cut to me at home circling Leif Garrett's face in *Tiger Beat*, blissfully unaware I'd just been collateral damage in European diplomacy.

THE DECODER

Survival Law #38*: Repression always leaks — sometimes in graffiti. Bring rosaries, Wite-Out and a plausible alibi.*

EPISODE 39 — SURVIVAL LESSONS FROM ASJ: FASHION, FAMINE & F*CKED-UP CONDITIONING

12/26 — 9:00 p.m.

Rating: PG

Episode Description: *High School was warfare; Aqua Net was artillery.*

As tradition dictates in telenovelas, there's a Cinderella ball.

The heroine arrives in ruffles.

The rival sister sweeps in with scandal.

And the best friend barges in wearing something so outrageous it steals the entire subplot.

At Academia San José, our masked ball was **UNICEF World Day** — proof that even charity could be weaponized for applause.

Instead of chandeliers, we had folding chairs. Instead of masks, we had "ethnic costumes" — a colonial masquerade for starving children.

I, of course, played the ingénue.

Flamenco ruffles. Polka dots. Castanets imported from Spain. Miss Universe meets Miss Misguided Patriotism.

Vero stormed in as *Princess Leia* — polyester robe, twin buns, plastic blaster from K-Mart.

The nuns weren't sure if *Star Wars* counted as "heritage," but they also weren't about to take on the Rebel Alliance.

And then came **Estrella**.

While we all played along with the global charity kabuki, Estrella arrived as *Pac-Man*:[103]a giant cardboard circle painted yellow, with a triangle cut out for her mouth.

She shuffled through the courtyard, gobbling air, chased by a classmate in a blue bedsheet pretending to be a ghost.

The nuns clutched their rosaries.

The parents whispered about sacrilege.

The children roared in delight.

I didn't know whether to clap, hide, or apply for a transfer.

Pac-Man didn't just crash UNICEF World Day.

She devoured it.

My dignity included.

Charity, Guilt and the Catholic School Diet Plan

Before the parade, Mami staged her annual guilt ritual.

She brandished UNICEF pamphlets of skeletal children with flies orbiting them like saintly halos.

"Mira," she said. "You see this child? He is dying because he wasted food. Now eat everything on your plate."

So, I ate.

And ate.

And still eat like Armageddon has a confirmed RSVP.

Until the plot flipped at Caparra Country Club:

"¡*Ay no, Charo*! A true lady never finishes her food. *Para las apariencias*."

---

[103] **Pac-Man**: (1980s) In P.R. Pac-Man was the original wellness program: eat everything before your sister, the ghosts, or the patriarchy gets it. A cardboard prophecy that foretold every diet, deadline, and dysfunctional family dinner to come. See LSG Decoder for early arcade trauma and inherited carb guilt.

So:

If you didn't eat, children would starve.

If you did eat, you were tacky.

Welcome to the Catholic School Girl Diet Plan: Sanctified starvation, accessorized with lace socks and a smile sharp enough to floss with.

Vero ignored the sermon, inhaled her flan, and muttered, "May the Force be with You."

Estrella — still encased in her Pac-Man armor — bit into a *pastelillo* and pretended to chomp a nun.

The Fashion Show Hunger Games

If UNICEF was our masked ball, the *Annual Fashion Show* was our grand finale.

Staged at Caparra Country Club.

Choreographed by haute couture priestess Carlota Alfaro.[104]

Part runway. Part coronation. Part social death match.

The year before, Vero had ruled the catwalk — Leia by day, disco diva by night.

Polyester sparkle. Teased hair so high it required FAA clearance. The Brooke Shields of Guaynabo — if Brooke rolled her eyes and ate more *pastelillos.*

When my turn came, I committed patriotic suicide.

"Let's do Puerto Rico!" I suggested.

---

[104] **Carlota Alfaro**: Puerto Rico's undisputed queen of couture; part designer, part drill sergeant, part secular saint of satin. Her models didn't walk; they genuflected in chiffon. Every society girl's dream was to be touched by Carlota," though her touch often involved pins, critique and the faint scent of Aqua Net and judgment.

Applause worthy of Miss Universe.

Until the soundtrack began.

No Madonna.

No Lauper.

Just Rafael Hernández.

Try strutting to *Preciosa.*

It's like breakdancing to *Ave María.*

Carlota, naturally, selected me for every outfit.

Every. Single. One.

Apparently, I was her muse. Or her cautionary tale.

The girls erupted:

"Why does SHE get Carlota's touch?"

"Why does SHE get all the clothes?"

"Why does SHE get to be the Virgin Mary of prêt-à-porter?"

Mami, ever charitable, whispered:

"Mi amor, let the short, fat one's model too."

So, I stepped aside for the masses and kept only the Bridal Collection.

Satin gown.

Veil.

Dove arms.

Carlota instructed me to flail like a bird.

Thanks to Barbarella Modeling School — and electrolysis — I became an electrocuted dove in satin.

The Caparra crowd clapped politely, pearls rattling like castanets.

Vero, heckled from the cheap seats: "Use the Force, Charo."

Estrella — still half Pac-Man — waddled down the aisle going: *waka waka waka.*

I nearly died on the runway.

(The dove did too.)

The Survival Lesson

As I floated offstage, whispers followed:

"*Qué linda…*"

"Qué novia perfecta..."

I smiled.

But inside, something clicked — the sound of a lock turning on a door I never planned to open.

Which is why I vowed, on that runway, never to marry.

Years later, I understood: Academia San José wasn't about fashion.

Or famine.

Or couture starvation.

It was about performance.

Eat just enough to look grateful, never hungry.

Let others win — but make sure they know you let them. Save starving children in flamenco ruffles, but only if your castanets were imported.

And above all:

Keep your Leia sister and your Pac-Man friend close.

They'll remind you it's all theater.

And survival comes from mocking the script.

Telenovela Epilogue

Every novela ends with a twist.

The bridal dove gets the applause.

But the rebel Leia and the anarchist Pac-Man get the reruns.

Years later, people still whispered about La Princesa Leia de Caparra and Pac-Man de Santurce — the sidekicks who turned a Catholic couture runway into an intergalactic arcade, and proved that survival isn't about fitting in.

It's about stealing the scene.

THE DECODER

Survival Law #39*: Every masked ball crowns a Cinderella. But survival belongs to the rebels and the weirdos.*

ACT V

CATS, CURSES & OTHER INHERITANCES

(Episodes 40-49)

EPISODE 40 – LESBIAN PANIC, MARIPOSITAS & OTHER FAMILY EMERGENCIES

12/26 — 10:00 p.m.

Rating: PG -13 (for airborne sapphism, fried wontons & maternal hysteria)

Episode Description: *Because nothing terrifies a Puerto Rican mother more than lesbianism or running out of soy sauce.*

The Aftermath of the Great Choch Crisis

After the Dark Day of Academia San José — when someone graffiti tagged COME CHOCH on the convent wall and nuns started twitching like exorcism extras — my mother decided vigilance was the only vaccine.

She began scanning the horizon for signs of deviance: short haircuts, sensible shoes, women laughing too freely at salad bars.

In her theology, lesbianism wasn't a possibility; it was a communicable disease — spread through eye contact and Judy Garland songs.

If I so much as admired another girl's handwriting, she'd squint and whisper, "Careful, Charito; *eso se pega*." I didn't know what *eso* was, but it sounded like something you could catch from a contaminated *Trapper Keeper*.[105]

[105] **Trapper Keeper:** a plastic vault for homework, secrets, and the crushed souls of kids who forgot their dividers.

The Forbidden Feast

To distract herself from sapphic outbreaks, Mami staged weekly pilgrimages to Chung King, the Chinese restaurant by Borinquen Towers.

We entered like royalty sneaking into exile. The waiters wore polyester Mandarin jackets that screamed *Forbidden City* meets Woolworth's. We ordered in whispers: *arroz chino*, sweet and sour pork, and *mariposita*s.[106] The smell of soy sauce clung to our lace dresses; the glamour was MSG-based and deeply spiritual.

Afterward came dessert diplomacy: *pana*[107] ice cream for patriots, Baskin-Robbins vanilla for colonizers. Then church, to confess the sodium.

Cinema of Repression

Sundays ended at the movies, which doubled as my mother's anti-lesbian boot camp. When Angie Dickinson removed her blouse in *Dressed to Kill*, Mami launched herself across the aisle like Kevin Costner in *The Bodyguard*, shielding my eyes with such force I saw the Virgin Mary in IMAX.

She never flinched at male nudity, probably because it didn't exist, but a single glimpse of a woman's nipple could apparently cancel my heterosexual future.

Her panic only made breasts fascinating. Forbidden fruit, but underwired.

---

[106] **Mariposita**s: Fried wontons rebranded as "little butterflies." Flutter directly into your arteries and land softly on your regrets.

[107] **Pana:** Breadfruit. Tropical starch disguised as vegetable nobility. PR slang for buddy; one feeds you, the other asks you to borrow 5 bucks and a charger.

Enter Estrella: My Pac-Man with Eyeliner

My salvation was Estrella, adopted from Spain by my Madrina Magnolia — the Catholic Angelina Jolie of 1979. Estrella flunked math but majored in eyeliner and chaos.

Together we were a two-girl telenovela:

- Boat episodes: baby-oiled and sun poisoned on her dad's yacht.
- Blackout episodes: exploring my mother's *Closet of Death,*[108] a storage abyss where wreaths and tangled extension cords plotted homicide.
- Sleepwalking episodes: I karate-chopped her Coca-Cola in my sleep; she framed the stain like forensic evidence from *Juicio Final.*

At matinees, we invented the sandwich de papa: a KFC bun stuffed with French fries and existential despair.

When the screen flashed cleavage, Mami dove again, shrieking, "¡No mires!" While Estrella calmly asked for extra ketchup.

I saw more drama in my mother's blocking than in Brian de Palma's entire filmography.

Lesbianism: The Family Inheritance (Allegedly)

Years later, Mami's paranoia matured into folklore. She swore lesbianism ran in the Nazario line like diabetes.

There was Cousin **Selene,** a born tomboy, crop-haired, tragic only to those allergic to confidence. According to family science, she wasn't gay, she'd just suffered a heartbreak so severe it bent her orientation like rebar in a hurricane.

Selene fled to New York, returning once in red Bermuda shorts and hair cropped like a rebellious altar boy. She became *Patient*

---

[108] **Closet of Death**: Every Puerto Rican house has one. A storage pasillo closet with live wires, expired wreaths and moral danger. Opening it required, faith, a flashlight and sometimes a will. See the LSG Decoder for contents.

Zero. Afraid of contagion, my cousins refused to sit beside her in the Caprice. I did.

She mentioned her "*amiga*," the euphemism every lesbian in the 1980s was required to use. No one asked questions. Everyone feared answers.

At Luquillo kiosks, we drowned the tension in *bacalaítos*[109] and Medalla beer. Because in Puerto Rico, nothing smothers panic like fried cod and denial.

Avoidance as Love Language

Our clan believed silence could sanitize anything:

- Drinking problem? Say nothing.
- Illegitimate child? Smile tighter.
- Mistress named La Gata? Buy her a Cadillac and move on.

Control the story, and you controlled reality — at least until the commercial break. So, we performed, ate, and pretended. Selene didn't pretend. She just was. And in a family that worshipped denial, existing authentically was the boldest sin of all.

Revelation by Soy Sauce

That Sunday, at Chung King, between the wontons and the whispers, I realized that Mami's panic wasn't about sin. It was about survival. To her, being a good woman was just staying heterosexual enough to stay safe.

She wasn't protecting me from being lesbian. She was protecting me from becoming free.

---

[109] **Bacalaítos**: Fried codfish fritters; proof than in PR no one has solved trauma with a salad.

Epilogue

Years later, when I kissed a girl under a disco ball in San Francisco. I half-expected Mami to appear from the shadows, wielding a rosary and a fire extinguisher.

Instead, I just smiled, ordered Chinese take-out, and whispered to the *maripositas*, "We've come full circle."

THE DECODER

Survival Law #40: *Parents can block cleavage and dodge truth, but repression always reruns. The sequel's called real life.*

EPISODE 41 – AGUA, DRAMA, Y PUNTOS DE MARIPOSA

12/26 — 11:00 p.m.

Rating: PG

Episode Description: *In telenovelas, pools are not just pools.*

After the Panic, the Pool

After months of my mother policing cleavage like the Vatican's regional manager for Lust Prevention, a pool felt downright liberating.

Chlorine instead of guilt. Skin instead of sin.

Every true telenovela requires a pool, perfect eyeliner, and at least one dramatic plunge.

Soraya Montenegro screams. *María la del Barrio* disappears beneath the surface. Paola from *La Usurpadora* fake-drowns until a shirtless man flexes her back to life.

Estrella and I strutted in, like synchronized sirens; matching swimsuits, zero coordination, and enough baby oil to deep-fry a seagull. We were "twins," though I was 5'8" and she was 5'3" on tiptoe and ambition.

Together we looked like an optical illusion: Cher and Charo in a discount Vegas revue. Estrella carried her transistor radio like a torch of rebellion, blasting Willie Colón and Rubén Blades', "Plástico."[110]

The brass blared across the pool deck, the salsa of vanity; those plastic boys and girls sweating "Chanel No.3" and chasing status, while we strutted in our borrowed glamour, too young to know he was singing about us.

She winked at me. "Let them stare," she said, lip-gloss gleaming like armor. We were waterproof, flammable, and tragically self-serious.

The Fall (Featuring Gravity and Poor Judgment)

At *Cerromar*,[111] surrounded by cousins and competitive swans, I decided to rise — literally. I hoisted myself out of the pool using my arms, channeling Bond-girl energy and forgetting physics.

Slip.

Chin.

Edge.

Blood.

Cut to ambulance.

Estrella ran behind, wailing, "¡*Mi gemela artística!*" like an understudy auditioning for *Evita*.

---

[110] **Plástico**: Hit song from Colón's and Blades iconic album, *Siembra* (1978), the best-selling salsa record in history. A disco-salsa warning about fake people, which I danced to more times than I've healed from.

[111] **Cerromar**: (Dorado, PR) In its Hyatt-era glory, Cerromar was PR idea of Hollywood; Coquí disco thumping like Studio 54 in guayaberas, hamburgers that somehow tasted like money, and water so blue it could've been unionized. Now sits abandoned; an overchlorinated ghost of luxury, proof that even paradise fades and survival sometimes means carrying the story after the lights go out.

Six butterfly stitches later, I looked like Frankenstein's niece at a *quinceañera*. Estrella signed my bandage like it was a cast and whispered, "At least, now you have character."

My Mother's Spin (Classic Nazario PR Strategy)

Mami was unbothered. "It's under your chin, *mi amor*. The only man who'll ever see it will already love you or be trapped under furniture."

Translation: Disfigurement was fine, as long as it photographed well.

To her, scars were fine, cellulite was the apocalypse. Passing ugly still counted as passing.

Theology of Chlorine

Coach Melba, prophet of near-drowning shouted, "*¡Siempre listas*!" before tossing a literal baby into the pool. The baby swam. Effortlessly. Probably unionized later.

Years later, sinking in heartbreak, debt, or the emotional deep end of a creative career, I'd remember that Pampers baby, that scar. That day I bled at the Hyatt like a saint of overachievement.

Cue — close up: fogged goggles, chlorine tears, me whispering to the ghost of Melba, "*Si el bebé sobrevivió, yo también*."

The swans glided.

The baby swam.

Soraya shrieked.

Estrella filmed it on a disposable Kodak and sold tickets.

And I survived; chin scar and pride dented, ego chlorinated but intact.

Because survival, darling, isn't graceful; it's just dry enough to clap before the next act.

Final Button – Willie Colón/Rubén Blades Coda

Estrella's radio crackling with "*Plástico.*"

They warned that all that glitter peels, that someday we'd have to shed our sequins and swim naked in the truth.

But we were too busy posing, plastic girls, waterproof dreams, melting under the Caribbean sun.

Now I hear it differently.

The disco is gone.

The pool is drained.

The butterflies have scars.

And still…

They fly.

THE DECODER

Survival Law #41: *Survival is the only medal that never tarnishes.*

EPISODE 42 – CERRO GORDO:

HOOK-NOSED HEARTTHROBS, TIFFANY LAMPS AND THE SUMMER THE OCEAN TRIED TO KILL US

12/27 — 12:00 a.m.

Rating: PG

Episode Description: *Because every first love deserves a little salt, scandal, and property damage.*

The Great Migration

Every summer, we fled Guaynabo like fading aristocrats escaping a coup; caravans loaded with *pastelón*[112] trays, mosquito repellent, and the Nazario women's collective vanity.

Destination: **Cerro Gordo, Vega Alta**, a stretch of coastline my mother's family colonized like the Puerto Rican Bourbons on timeshares.

Beach hierarchy, island edition:

- **Dorado Beach**: foreign investors who said "gracias" with guilt.
- **Cerro Gordo:** nouveau riche, diesel perfume, and rented speedboats.

[112] **Pastelón:** Puerto Rican lasagna made with plantains instead of pasta, proving carbs can be both sweet and deceitful. One bite and you'll forgive your entire family… until cleanup.

- **Public beaches**: peasants and soft coolers.

The Titi Cabal

Our matriarchs were a Televisa ensemble with better jewelry:

- **Titi Mirra Sol**, casino boss, Bacardi in one hand, lighter in the other.
- **Titi Marina Luz**, rebel accountant who ended an engagement mid-rosary.
- **Titi Lía**, pharmacist to the stars, two-for-one secrets with every Valium.
- **Titi Ofelia**, who exiled a cousin for mispronouncing Hermès.
- **Titi Estela**, queen of the marble mansion, where humidity went to die.
- **Tio Ernesto** (**"Don Neto"**), businessman of undefined legality.

And among them shimmered **Alejandro Cabrera**, the senator's son; tan, yacht-equipped, and so beautiful it made Catholicism feel redundant.

Alejandro Cabrera: My Hook-Nosed Heartthrob

Tall, bronzed, tragic... his profile suggested both nobility and mild sinus congestion. He was my first telenovela crush: a *galán* with just enough trauma to qualify as deep.

One dusky evening, he beckoned me toward his yacht. The ocean blushed pink; I blushed crimson. My cousin's hand-me-down swimsuit clung like regret. I tried to hoist myself aboard gracefully, slipped, swallowed seawater, and kneed him in the ribs.

Reader, *I was in love.*

The Tiffany Lamp Incident

Days later, Alejandro invited me to play pool at his family's palace. The table gleamed; mahogany, Vatican-polished, overseen by a Tiffany lamp worth my father's annual salary.

He lined up at a perfect shot, sunk it effortlessly. I took aim, swung, and…

CRASH.

The lamp exploded in a rain of stained-glass confetti. I froze, bladder trembling, and ready for banishment.

Alejandro just laughed — a warm, reckless laugh — and said the lamp symbolized his mother's neglect. "You liberated me," he added, as if I'd performed emotional exorcisms with a cue stick.

That night, I learned the first rule of love among the privileged; they don't crave perfection. They crave chaos; preferably imported.

The Posita of Doom

The next afternoon, our family gathered at a *posita,* a natural rock pool that looked saintly until the ocean decided otherwise.

WHAM.

A rogue wave smacked up like divine payback for generations of melodrama. One aunt vanished; rosaries flew like confetti.

Enter cousin **Sabina**, our resident heroine, who dove in full eyeliner and rescued the woman by her hair; not her hand. Because in my family, dignity was optional, survival mandatory.

Meanwhile, on the Yacht of the Gods

As we coughed up salt water, Alejandro Jr. cruised past on his yacht, sipping something citrusy, hair blowing like a shampoo commercial.

I had staged myself for this very shot; half reclined in the shallows, channeling *Coralito*[113] from Telemundo.

Instead, a wave sucker-punched me, plastered seaweed to my forehead, and filled my bikini with half the Atlantic. Alejandro didn't glance. The soundtrack died. My starring role drowned.

Don Neto vs. The Atlantic

Every morning, our mysterious uncle swam past the breakers like he was auditioning for martyrdom. One day, the current dragged him under. He flipped onto his back and began to pray, calm as a saint on a float.

A fisherman appeared, hauled him to shore, and delivered him home in time for dinner. That night, over filet mignon, Don Neto shrugged. "When it's your time, it's your time."

As if almost drowning were a scheduling conflict.

Survival Commentary

That summer taught me everything about class, chaos, and choreography.

- Wealthy men forgive broken lamps, not visible sweat.
- The ocean doesn't care about your lineage.
- Humiliation, like salt, preserves better than pride.

By September, the lamp was replaced, the bruises faded, and Alejandro had found a blonder disaster.

---

[113] **Coralito:** The 1983 Telemundo telenovela about a sweet but resilient girl whose life was basically a masterclass in tragic pauses, longing looks, and beachside tears.

But I still carry that summer, the laughter, the salt, the faint glass glitter in memory; proof that love and the ocean both demand sacrifice.

THE DECODER

Survival Law #42: *First love and the sea share a talent for wreckage. If you're lucky, all you lose is a lamp.*

EPISODE 43 – JULY 22, 1981: THE DAY I LOST MY HAIR (AND MY WILL TO LIVE)

12/27 — 1:00 a.m.

Rating: PG

Episode Description: *Scissors cut more than hair.*

Every heroine has a breaking point. Mine involved a belt, a beach, and a pair of rusty scissors.

In novelas, when the heroine cuts her hair, it's never about split ends. It's about betrayal, rebirth, or revenge.

In *Cristal* (Venevisión, 1985), Lupita Ferrer as Victoria Ascanio famously chopped off her mane in a fit of defiance, signaling Act Two.

At sixteen, I staged my own Act Two.

The Beach Confrontation

It was my mother's birthday party, and I was late. I had been hiking with the neighborhood kids, stumbling from Cerro Gordo to Vega Baja like dehydrated stray dogs. We returned sunburnt, sweaty, smelling of salt and mud.

Mami stood waiting in a caftan, wrath of God disguised as resort wear. Her paso fino ankles trembled like the horses she worshipped, ready to stomp and perform their melodrama on command.

And then came the punishment.

She beat me in public. With my **father's belt.**

That was the real mindfuck. Papi, disabled, couldn't lift his arm against us. But she swung his belt as if channeling his authority through her rage.

And when she was tired of it, she grabbed **his shoe**; his shoe, not hers, and struck with that too. As though she wanted us to believe he was present in every blow, even when he wasn't. She looked like an exorcist possessed by Emilio Pucci.

Tourists froze mid-piña colada. A pelican witnessed the entire beating. Even the crabs scuttled away in solidarity. All of it unfolded in front of cousins, crushes, and every potential Televisa extra within a two-mile radius. If there had been a camera, we'd have been wrapped by sunset and premiered on Channel 4 (WAPA TV).

Why? Because in her paranoia, she was convinced I'd been having sex in the woods with **Tutim,** the black neighborhood boy far more interested in water skis than me.

But here's what I didn't fully understand until much later: the paranoia didn't start with me.

Virginia Shadows

Generational trauma didn't just get passed down; it was accessorized and given a caftan.

Back in the 1950s, before the Civil Rights Act, my grandfather sent Mami to school in Richmond, Virginia. The idea was that she would forget my dad and marry a strapping American doctor: "*Para mejorar la raza.*"[114]

They placed her in the white dorms. The Southern girls slammed doors in her face. Even her New England roommate warned: never admit to having a Black relative, or she'd be reassigned to the Black dorm.

---

[114] **Para mejorar la raza**: Puerto Rican expression meaning, "to better the race," i.e. to marry or have children with someone whiter. A colonial hangover disguised as a compliment. Abuelas said it with pride: we unpack it with therapy.

So, my mother ate alone. A lot. She learned silence as survival. She learned that one rumor could exile you. That humiliation calcified into terror, and that terror warped into rage.

By the time she was back in Puerto Rico, raising daughters, it came sideways: in Tutim, in belts and shoes, in the obsession that her children could not; must not, be marked the way she had been.

She brought home a degree and a terror of rumors, both *summa cum laude.*

The Scissors

That night, seething with shame, I stormed into the bathroom. The mirror caught my red eyes, salt-stiff hair, and trembling hands. I grabbed the scissors.

Snip.

Chunks fell to the tile like deleted scenes from *Terms of Endearment.* Only with less Shirley MacLaine and more hormonal fury.

With each cut, I shed not just hair but the illusion of obedience.

The sound was jagged, metallic, final.

My scalp prickled under the humid night, my neck suddenly naked and vulnerable.

And I thought of that Tiffany lamp I'd shattered weeks earlier, glass raining like assassinated royalty. Alejandro laughing as though destruction could be liberation. But this wasn't a lamp. This was me, splintering. And no one was laughing.

My Mother's Horror

Mami was horrified. She hadn't raised a delinquent, a drug addict, or a sex fiend.

But now? She had raised…

A short-haired girl. Might as well have joined a cult or, worse, journalism.

And in her world, that was almost worse.

Survival Commentary

That haircut was my first rebellion. Not glamorous, not cinematic, just ragged chunks on a bathroom floor. But it taught me something telenovelas never showed: rebirth doesn't come with violins.

It comes with paso fino rage — a father's belt and shoe wielded by the wrong hands; glass lamps exploding in other people's mansions, and the invisible waves of Virginia that still broke against our shore.

And here's the cruel echo: my mother ate alone in Richmond to survive.

I cut my hair alone in a bathroom for the same reason.

Different acts; same exile.

THE DECODER

Survival Law #43: *A bad haircut is temporary. Learning to live with yourself takes longer to grow back.*

EPISODE 44 – EL COQUÍ: FAKE ID FOLLIES & THE BUDÍN / GALLO EXCHANGE

12/27 — 2:00 a.m.

Rating: PG

Episode Description: *Sometimes survival means saying yes to the wrong dance.*

At fourteen, I didn't want trouble. I wanted shoes that didn't squeak, lip gloss that survived one slow dance, and a song I could twirl to without knowing whose drink tinted their polyester.

El Coquí[115] was my curriculum: disco, salsa, merengue, and, if the older *primas* let me, one desperate bolero at the end of the night.

We slipped into Cerromar's disco with fake IDs that fooled absolutely no one. But the bouncer, probably paid in rum and cynicism, waved us through. Because the ID wasn't the costume. The music was.

The Dance Economy

There was a kind of market logic at play:

- Say yes to the short, awkward boy=you proved you weren't too *comemierda.*
- Say no, and the good-looking guys would brand you as stuck-up forever.

[115] **El Coquí**: Officially a frog. Unofficially, the disco where I learned lip gloss and fake ID could get you farther than biology ever did. See LSG Decoder.

So, I said yes. And sometimes, that yes, lit a match. The short boy became my shadow, circling like a devoted satellite.

Meanwhile, the *galanes* smirked, watching the joke they thought would humiliate me turn into a loyalty contract I hadn't signed.

It was *piscinita* all over again: one slip, one laugh, and suddenly you had a nickname or shadow you couldn't shake.

Survival by Rhythm

But here's the truth: none of it was sinister to me. I was fourteen with a fake ID and an appetite for rhythm. I didn't crave conquest. I wanted to disappear into the mirrored wall, to lose myself in basslines and perfume clouds.

Perfume, sweat, hairspray, Medalla beer spilled on tile. The air was so thick it felt like we were swimming again, but this time in sequins instead of salt water.

And still, the real danger wasn't the boys. It was politeness. Saying yes, because silence had been written into my family's constitution. Yes, to dances, yes to gossip, yes to surviving humiliation with a smile.

By Dawn

By dawn, eyeliner smeared, sweater borrowed, I understood something adult for the first time: innocence doesn't protect you from misunderstanding.

That short boy with prayer in his eyes thought my yes meant forever. Alejandro Cabrera Jr., bronzed yacht god, never even looked in my direction.

And me? I was stuck between devotion I hadn't asked for and indifference I couldn't escape.

Survival Commentary

What El Coquí really taught me was this: saying yes is easy. Living with the fallout is harder — especially when "yes" felt safer than silence.

And sometimes, politeness is another way of being trapped.

THE DECODER

Survival Law #44: *One dance isn't a marriage. A "yes" isn't forever. And silence will betray you faster than a fake ID ever could.*

EPISODE 45 – LATIN ALZHEIMER'S & THE GHOST LANDLORD

12/27 — 3:00 a.m.

Rating: PG

Episode Description: A family saga of grudges, bigamy, and butts.

Ah, Latino Alzheimer's, the mystical condition where we forget absolutely everything except a grudge. Miss a birthday? You're erased from the family Bible. Forget a saint's day? You might as well defect to Siberia.

But that one insult whispered by your great-aunt's second husband's mistress's nephew in 1973? Engraved in marble, embroidered on throw pillows, and repeated every baptism, funeral, and *quinceañera* until the end of time.

The cure, of course, is impossible. The condition thrives on rosaries and repetition. It was the background music of my childhood: resentments layered over trumpets, grudges in counterpoint with bongos.

The Party That Launched a Thousand Side-Eyes

Mayagüez in full regalia: a party that looked less like a family gathering and more like the opening reception for the UN.

- Mountains of *arroz can gandules*[116] gleaming like 24-carat gold

[116] **Arroz con gandules:** Rice, pigeon peas, and the reason your aunt side-eyes anyone who brings quinoa to a Christmas party.

- Pasteles stacked like a precarious domino tower
- A whole *lechón* displayed on a silver tray so large it could've been borrowed from Imelda Marcos

RSVP optional. Judgment mandatory.

Its mouth was stuffed with a Red Delicious apple.[117] The lace *manteles* weren't tablecloths; they were heirlooms. Cut crystal goblets so heavy they could double as murder weapons.

And beneath this glitz? A Cold War. My mother hadn't spoken to two of her brothers for decades.

Enter The Ghost Landlord

- Tio Ernesto "Neto" Nazario, forever infantilized by a toddler's mispronunciation.
- Tio Mauro, the Ghost Landlord, capable of collecting rent without ever appearing in the flesh.

Their crime? When my grandfather died, the sons inherited haciendas, land, businesses, entire blocks of downtown property. The six daughters each got *five hundred dollars.*[118] Not five thousand. Not even a battered Buick Skylark with one working door. Five hundred. Just enough for a rocking chair and maybe a lace mantilla if you haggled.

My mother clutched that injustice like other women clutched Hermès Kelly bags in hurricanes: white-knuckled, immovable, daring anyone to pry it from their grip.

Enter the Bigamist Uncle

But the inheritance was only one storyline. Tio Mauro was too ambitious for a single arc. While lawyers divvied up assets, he

---

[117]**Red Delicious Apple**: the 1980s supermarket status fruit, waxy, flavorless, bizarrely incongruent in tropical Puerto Rico where mangos, guavas and quenepas grew in scandalous abundance.

[118] **Five hundred dollars:** The kind of inheritance amount that makes you say "gracias" out loud and "¿en serio?" in your soul.

was starring in his own novela: *The Bigamist Uncle and the Fine Art of Juggling Two Wives.*

One wife in Mayagüez and one in Aguadilla.[119] Two parishes, two fully functioning households, and two groups of neighbors pretending not to notice.

No GPS. No WhatsApp. Just pure, analog duplicity: powered by charisma, Catholic guilt and a pocket calendar. Everyone knew.

But Rule #1 of *Puerto Rican Fight Club* was always the same: we do not talk about Tio Mauro's second family.

Echoes of Silence

Mauro didn't invent duplicity. He inherited it.

Before his two wives, there was El General, with Maman at home and La Gata on the side. Two women, two lives, separated not by honesty but by silence. Everyone knew. Nobody said a word.

That same silence shadowed my mother in the Deep South years later. She carried silence forward into his solution. Why whisper? Why hide? His trauma logic said: marry them both. Legalize the duplicity. Put the silence in writing. Because in our family, silence wasn't just golden. It was cement. The only thing hurricane-proof.

Mauro on the Road

He commuted east to west, west to east, like some tragic telenovela Odysseus. Always in a white Cadillac with red leather seats, crisp guayabera, Panama hat tilted just so.

The road would pass sugarcane, *flamboyanes*, scattering blossoms across his hood like confetti for a parade he didn't deserve. And still, no matter where he landed, Mayagüez or

---

[119] **Mayagûez vs. Aguadilla**: Think New York vs. Los Angeles but crammed into 110 miles of tropical coastline. The rivalry was just as inflated, the egos just as big, and the traffic about the same.

Aguadilla, he was protected by the same thing that had kept the Nazarios standing for generations: **silence**. Our cement. Poured thick over scandal until the cracks no longer showed.

The Women

One wife was a Taína goddess: tall, copper-skinned, with the posture of an earthquake survivor.

The other was fairer, softer, and owner of a derriere so legendary it had nicknames depending on your level of decorum: *El Culo* if you were drunk, *El Fundillo* if vulgar and *La Pantalla* ("the Screen") if you wanted to sound poetic about its sheer surface area.

Both swore they were the only Señora Mauro. And both were, technically, right.

Shaula

Shaula, one of Mauro's daughters, was unforgettable. She had the thickest jibaro accent this side of a 1950s radio drama. Every vowel rolled like it was carved in mountain stone. Every consonant curled like sugarcane leaves. And we, spoiled little monsters, mocked her endlessly:

We parodied her "Arrrroooh!"

We turned her "Chacho!" into Broadway finales.

We stretched "¡Pa' lllaaaa!" into comedy routines that brought down the house.

My mother seethed. Because mocking an accent isn't just mocking sound; it's mocking where someone comes from. And she knew we weren't as far removed from it as we wanted to pretend.

The Real Curse

The curse wasn't Mauro's duplicity. It wasn't even the inheritance fiasco.

The curse was the fiction we were raised on that some Puerto Ricans were "better" than others. That skin tone, accent, and class dictated your worth. That polishing your R's and flattening *íibara* vowels somehow made you closer to Spain.

Looking back, Shaula had it right.

She was gorgeous, funny, and ferociously herself. While we were cosplaying as elite socialites, she was living loudly, *jíbara* accent and all. That was the real aristocracy.

Complication of a Villain

Yet I can't write Tio Mauro off completely. Because yes, he was chaos personified, but he also taught me how to dance salsa and merengue.

At that very party, when I choked on an ice cube and collapsed like a Televisa heroine mid-betrayal. He was the only one sober enough to notice. He Heimlich-ed me across the dance floor. The ice cube shot out like a champagne cork.

My uncle, the bigamist, grudge holder, rescuer. A villain with impeccable rhythm and surprisingly reliable CPR.

Survival Commentary – Echoes of Silence

So yes, our family was a novela of grudges, secrets, and scandal. But even villains occasionally moonlight as heroes. Because trauma doesn't just echo. It replicates.

If El General rehearsed duplicity with Maman and La Gata, Mauro staged it in full production with wives and paperwork. Same novela. New season. Bigger budget.

Silence? That was the cement. The binding agent stronger than truth.

Because in Puerto Rico, only cement houses survive hurricanes.

Ours wasn't built of honesty or forgiveness.

It was built of silence; layered, reinforced, and unbreakable.

THE DECODER

Survival Law #45: *Echoes of Silence: Secrets don't stay buried. They wait for the worst moment to resurface, usually mid-salsa. And silence, like cement, keeps the whole cracked structure standing, until the day it doesn't.*

EPISODE 46 – VILLALBA: AJO, LIMÓN Y CEBOLLA[120]

12/27 — 4:00 a.m.

Rating: PG

Episode Description: *How my abuelo cured everything with vegetables.*

By day, **Don Bonifacio Oliviano** was pure gravitas; guayabera so crisp it could slice bread, Panama hat at a holy angle, surveying his coffee plantation like a Sicilian Pape in exile.

By night, he became Puerto Rico's first wellness influencer; part monk, part moonshine messiah.

The Gospel According to Don Bonifacio

Forget Father, Son, and Holy Spirit. The real Holy Trinity: garlic, lemon, and onion.

- Garlic to ward off demons and neighbors
- Lemon to bleach polyester sins and guilty consciences.
- Onion to cure heartbreak, repel mosquitoes, and double as budget therapy.

Doctors? Charlatans.

Hospitals? Theme parks for weaklings.

Antibiotics? CIA spyware in pill form.

[120] **Ajo, Limón y Cebolla:** Don Bonifacio Oliviano's DIY gospel: garlic for demons, lemon for detox, and onions to cry out your trauma. Who needs doctors when you have condiments?

Science was optional. Faith was mandatory as long as it came with garlic breath and good coffee.

The Don Bonifacio Health Plan™

- Flu? Swallow garlic like communion
- Guilt? Lemon shot + primal scream
- Heartbreak? Cry into an onion until you forget his name or at least lose your sense of smell.

Maybe that's the real cure he left us: not garlic or lemon, but the stubborn belief that survival could be homegrown.

Chanel Nº Cafecito

The true sacrament, though, was coffee. Beans roasted in the open air until the mountain smelled like Chanel Nº Cafecito; burnt sugar, soil, forgiveness. Brewed with river water so holy, it tasted like liquid obstruction.

Steam rose from the pot and clung to your lashes, a perfume of earth and devotion. And because this was Puerto Rico, toddlers were handed bottles of coffee *en biberón.*[121]

Forget milk. Our bottles came pre-loaded with caffeine and Catholic guilt. Which explains everything about our collective impatience, dramatics, and inability to stand in line quietly.

Distinguished Coffee Baron by Day, Pitorro Messiah by Night

When coffee failed, there was always *pitorro*, moonshine so feral it could run an airplane or reset the entire year of 1947. The Governor himself sent convoys to fetch gallons.

Don Bonifacio's alleged "secret ingredient"? Urine.

---

[121] **Biberón:** bottle, a.k.a. bibi, usually referred to baby bottle but sometimes to a bottle of rum.

"For fermentation balance," he insisted; though everyone knew he lived for the chaos of making the elite drink his biochemistry.

Customer Reviews (c. 1950s)

★★★★★ "Pairs well with pork, ammonia notes." *Governor's driver*

★★★★☆ "Cured my sciatica, erased my marriage." *Small town judge.*

★☆☆☆☆ "Definitely pee!" *Anonymous nun*

Villalba: The Real Housewives of Onions

Every telenovela has its *escondido;* the hidden twin, the secret heir, the cousin with a mysterious limp. Ours was no different. And trust me: moonshine was nothing compared to our family drama.

- Abuela Sofia (4'9", Sicilian, and rumored to have "accidentally" bombed a fascist building.)
- Tia Lucinda (could plan a funeral faster than most people boil rice; had a punch card at the florist.)
- Danubio (the family *escondido*[122] trotted out for portraits like a soap-opera extra, then whisked off stage before Act Two, to prevent questions or plot development.)

Because in our family:

- Nobody gets abandoned.
- Everybody gets folded in like mismatched Tupperware lids.

---

[122] **Escondido:** The relative you present for family photos, then stash away like contraband. May be a cousin, a child, or a suspicious wad of mattress money. See LSG Decoder.

- Explanations optional. Gossip mandatory.

Villalba itself was a telenovela: fainting spells, forbidden romances, artisanal moonshine occasionally spiked with urine, toddlers hyped on espresso and uncles who swore their side hustles were "government adjacent."

Villalba: *The Real Housewives of Onions.*

Same drama. Cheaper jewelry. Better morals.

The Grandfather I Remember

I wish I'd been older, old enough for *sobremesa* talks with Don Bonifacio, my one loving grandfather and unofficial patriarch of all things caffeinated.

The other, El General, died electrocuted in a family tragedy so dramatic it could've won a telenovela Emmy. He'd opposed my parents' marriage, which means if he'd lived, I'd be an unwritten plot twist.

So yes, Don Bonifacio was it; my sole abuelo, my novela patriarch, gone when I was six. When I think of him now, it isn't scandal I hear; it's the sound of his coffee grinder, steady as a heartbeat.

Sometimes when I open a bag of coffee, I swear the scent carries laughter, old tobacco and the faint sound of someone blessing the morning.

He manually grounded those beans like he was keeping time for the island. That rhythm lives in me still.

Maybe that's why I write, to keep the rhythm going, to grind memory into something strong enough to sip, bitter enough to remember.

I am the granddaughter of a coffee farmer and a *pitorro* maker, and both liquids run through my vein: one to wake me up, the other to mellow me down. These days, I just keep coffee. *Pitorro* had too much truth in it.

Because honestly, survival was never elegant; it just had good flavor. You work, you love, you forgive the family ghosts, you add milk and sugar to the chaos.

Some people inherit real estate or jewelry.

I inherited caffeine, rum and a high tolerance for melodrama.

It's not glamorous but it's legacy.

And somewhere between the grinder's hum and the *pitorro*'s kick, I can still hear Abuelo Bonifacio; laughing, blessing, saying…

"Charito, drink life strong, but never forget to savor it."

THE DECODER

Survival Law #46: *If your family recipe involves urine, call it artisanal, and remember: every generation ferments its own cure. Some heal with prayer, some with pitorro and some with laughter disguised as memory.*

EPISODE 47 – TITI FIERA: THE WOMAN WHO BUILT HER OWN DAMN LIFE (AND POOL)

12/27 — 5:00 a.m.

Rating: PG

Episode Description: *Boss energy before it was a hashtag.*

What's more "do it yourself" than building an IKEA chair? Building an entire swimming pool, by hand, in a tropical pueblo, armed with a hammer, a cigarette, and generational fury.

Every telenovela pueblo has its *La Dueña*, the iron-willed landowner, feared and respected, hardened by betrayal but never defeated.

Villalba had ours too.

Except she wasn't a scripted character.

She was my aunt.

The impossible, unstoppable Titi Fiera.[123]

She wasn't just family; she was a cautionary tale rewritten as a blueprint.

---

[123] **Titi Fiera**: Vero and I adored her. To us, she was Puerto Rico's Beth Dutton meets Clint Eastwood; minus the ranch, plus a DIY swimming pool.

DIY Before It Was a Hashtag

Here's the paradox: our titis modeled the kind of woman Mami never raised us to be, a do-it-yourself woman in a world where you had staff.

And yet, when I moved to the United States, I discovered the *American Dream* comes with *terms and conditions*, and buried in paragraph 47, subsection C, it says: if you don't do it yourself, it will never get done.

In fact, the fastest way to get it done *is* to do it yourself.

I've carried that lesson everywhere: from painting houses, to baking cakes, to even driving a semi-truck (but that's another book).

But the prototype? The ur-model? It was Titi Fiera.

Every time I doubt myself, I hear her voice: "*Mija, stop waiting for the cavalry. You are the cavalry.*"

The Widow Who Refused the Script

According to my father, she killed her American husband; not with poison, not with rage, but with neglect.

"*Lo mató de hambre,*" he'd say with a smirk as if starvation were an act of feminism.

Where most widows wilted, she built.

Widowed early, she chose not tragedy but reinvention.

She built her own queendom:

- A house fortified with locks, tarps, and stubbornness.
- A shotgun leaned casually by the *greca*,[124] because in Villalba, caffeine and self-defense share counter space.

---

[124] **Greca:** The heroine of every Puerto Rican morning. A stovetop espresso maker that hisses, steams and delivers drama in liquid form.

- A yard crawling with feral cats, mangy dogs, and one rooster named Pancho who strutted like the villain of a 200-episode arc.

The pueblo christened her *La Dueña de Villalba*,[125] not because she owned the land but because she owned the narrative.

The Pool, the Reputation, the Almost-Romance

- **The Hacienda**: She didn't inherit a ranch; she carved a swimming pool out of stubbornness and volcanic rock. No permits, no engineers, no men. Just sheer willpower, sweat, and spite. It became Villalba's Versailles; a miracle people gossiped about more than the weather. Neighbors come to gawk. The priest came to bless it. The government came to fine her.
- **The Reputation**: Regina Villarreal was called *Víbora*. Titi was *bruja, loca, Viuda Negra*. And yet, the same people who whispered in church came knocking when their roofs leaked, or their pigs ran loose.
- **The Forbidden Romance (Almost):** In novelas, a man sneaks past the armor. In Titi's story? A Jehovah's Witness once offered to fix her gutter. She leveled her shotgun and deadpanned: "The only thing you're fixing is your watch. Vete." Curtain down. Faith restored. Gutter unfixed.
- **La Venganza**: In soap land, vengeance is against the jilting fiancé. Titi's vengeance was against the very sentence *una mujer sola no puede*. She rewrote it every day, hammer in hand.

On Televisa, La Dueña redeems herself through love, marriage, and reconciliation with the pueblo.

But this was Villalba.

---

[125] **La Dueña de Villalba**: Every novela heroine has her title, *La Patrona, La Vibora.* Ours was simply "Fiera". She didn't inherit power; she constructed it, brick by stubborn brick.

And Titi Fiera was no script.

The Woman We Watched

At dusk, she'd sit beside her outlaw pool; cigarette in hand, Pancho crowing at ghosts, shotgun propped by the greca. She looked like rebellion in curlers, the kind of woman men feared and little girls memorized.

The smoke from her cigarette curled like punctuation to a story only she knew how to tell.

The town whispered. But Vero and I didn't whisper. We stared at her like kids watching a superhero.

Because if there was one woman who proved you don't wait for permission, applause, or a man to hand you your life… it was Titi Fiera.

Because if you can survive IKEA instructions, you can survive anything, even a life built from scratch.

THE DECODER

Survival Law #47: *If they call you fiera? Wear it. Claws out, heart steady. Survival isn't handed down; it's hand built.*

EPISODE 48 – MARÍA DE LOS MILAGROS: THE GREEN-EYESHADOW ENTHUSIAST & PRE-INTERNET CATFISH

12/27 — 6:00 a.m.

Rating: PG

Episode Description: *Because miracles come in palettes, and filters were manual.*

Every telenovela needs its naïve *jíbara* heroine: the country girl with big dreams, questionable make up choices, and faith stronger than foundation primer. Ours was **María de los Milagros.**

Adopted in spirit by Titi Fiera, armed with stubbornness and smudged ambition, she was Villalba's own María la del Barrio; except with worse contouring and better stationery.

Her signature beauty trick was blending electric-green eyeshadow into the corners of her eyes "to open them up." In theory, glamour. In practice, a radioactive parrot auditioning for Studio 54.

Once, she tried this on me. My mother recoiled as if I'd returned from war with face paint. "¡Charito! You look like you went to church for Ash Wednesday, and the priest missed your forehead!"

María, however, was unshaken. She had bigger ambitions than perfecting her toxic-green aesthetic. She was orchestrating a romance with an American Army pen pal stationed who-knows-where, convinced she was writing to a Caribbean goddess.

I, eleven years old and terminally bored, was her official translator. Which meant her letters, breathless epics about longing, destiny, and eternal love, passed through my hands before reaching Army Guy.

Her version:

"My darling, I long to run into your arms and never let you go."

My version:

"Hey, what's up? Hope you're good. Can't wait to see you."

Translation services provided by an eleven-year-old cynic with zero interest in eternal love.

Somehow, the Army Guy didn't notice the tonal shift. He wrote back nightly, declaring his devotion, claiming he missed her every second, that he stared at her photo as if she were Ava Gardner in sepia.

And because telenovela demands it, all this epistolary passion led inevitably to *el gran encuentro;* the romantic showdown, the day fantasy met polyester reality.

The Safari Park Incident

We drove three sticky hours to Vega Alta, my legs clued to the vinyl seats, Vero and I giggled in the back, imagining the melodrama about to unfold.

The chosen rendezvous?

Safari Park,[126] Puerto Rico's bold but doomed attempt at an African safari, where lions sunbathed in resignation and giraffes looked one counseling session away from escape.

And right there, in this humidity-soaked zoo of despair, María met her "true love."

---

[126] **Safari Park**: Puerto Rico's African Safari in Dorado. Complete with confused giraffes, an underfed hippo and a stunt donkey diving into a pool.

He was not tall, dark, or handsome. He was polite. Nervous. Sweating through his discount polyester shirt. Instead of sweeping her into his arms, he presented her with a tiny paper-mâché tiger.

On its belly, in shaky handwriting, one word: friendship. Nothing says passion like recycled craft supplies and a platonic noun.

María froze. Then, with all the gravitas of a *Televisa* star betrayed at the altar, she turned to me, eyes wide with panic.

"*¿Qué significa esto*?" She hissed, clutching the tragic tiger like it contained state secrets. Without Google Translate or the benefit of mercy, I delivered the truth.

"It means… he sees you as a friend."

The Aftermath

Her face collapsed like a set after the finale. Three hours on the road, a parade of wilted animals, and all she got was a friendship tiger.

In a proper novela, there'd be thunder, mascara running in the rain, a slow zoom on betrayal. We just trudged to the car, no soundtrack, just disappointment and humidity.

Years later, after my divorce, I understood María in a way I hadn't before. Because I too ended up in my own Safari Park of disappointment: speed-dating.

Where the lions were replaced by **The Persian Bear**. The giraffes by **The Transylvanian Karate Master**. The Zebras by **The BMW Guy**.

And the cages were full of others:

- Mr. Crypto, who spoke only in Bitcoin metaphors.
- The Amateur Magician, who tried to pull a coin from my ear.
- The Salsa Dentist, who bragged about root canals between songs.

- The Life-Coach-In-Training, who asked for my birth time before my name.
- The Miami Prophet who claimed to see my aura… and said it was "chartreuse".

Different decade, same humiliation.

María walked away with a friendship tiger.

I walked away with the zoo.

Lesson

If María taught me anything, it's that disappointment travels well.

From the green eyeshadow to the polyester soldier, to my own tragic carousel of suitors, romance always delivers a plot twist.

At least María only wasted gas money.

I wasted Uber fare, good eyeliner, and, worse, a perfectly decent sense of optimism.

THE DECODER

Survival Law #48: *Be suspicious of anyone who calls green eyeshadow "natural." They're hiding bigger lies and probably own a friendship tiger.*

EPISODE 49 – THE CATS WHO CARRIED OUR SILENCE: A NOVELA IN THREE LIVES

12/27 — 7:00 a.m.

Rating: PG

Episode Description: *Because some survivors walk on four legs.*

Part I – La Gata Diva (Queen of Fur and Fury)

In every self-respecting telenovela, when a woman is nicknamed, La Gata, trouble is already staging its entrance. She's scrappy, underestimated, destined to claw her way from the alley to the altar.

We didn't just watch those women in Guaynabo. We lived with them; on our sofas, in our bathrooms, and occasionally on our chests at 3 a.m.

Other families inherited pearls. We inherited Persians with trauma.

Diva, our Himalayan-Persian heiress, was Versailles in fur: cheekbones sharp enough to cut polyester, temperament of an underpaid diva on her closing night.

My cousin Lourdes treated her like a celebrity, top down on the Mustang. Diva's coat rippling like a Pantene ad. Pedestrians gasped. Other cats hissed. Diva purred like destiny itself.

But novela logic is cruel. Lourdes left for Harvard Med, abandoning her starlet. Diva stayed behind with my parents, who had as much interest in pampering her as they did in joining a boy band.

When Lourdes returned, she brought rivals: Lucifer, a velvet-robed villain, and Chili, a red stray with reggaetón swagger.

This was Diva's La Gata moment. From pampered socialite, she became avenging fury: scratching, biting, reclaiming the narrative. For twenty-seven years she reigned, our feline Rosaura Ríos, mocked for her origins but impossible to ignore.

In a house thick with human feuds, it wasn't politics that dictated peace. It was Diva.

When she finally died, my parents whispered, "She's just sleeping." But we all felt it: the house emptier; the plotline ended; the dynasty closed.

Cats, like women branded gatas, survive by refusing to be tamed.

Part II – El Galán Penny (The Cat Who Lived and Died Like an Aristocrat)

Every telenovela galán has his spirit animal. Some ride stallions. Some strum guitars. My father's alter ego wore a tuxedo; fur, not fabric.

Penny, christened Penelope in a tragic misgendering, morphed into a swaggering Casanova with the libido of Wilt Chamberlain and the nine lives of Keith Richards. Think Fernando Colunga in *La Usurpadora,* but neuter-averse and covered in hair.

We begged to have him fixed. My father was appalled. "Take away his manhood?" "¡Jamás!" So, Penny prowled the nights of Torrimar like a soap opera playboy, returning home reeking of bad decisions and distant perfumes.

My mother muttered, "*Ese gato no tiene vergüenza.*"[127]

My father beamed with paternal pride.

"Penny is my friend," he'd declare, crutches gleaming like props. Every morning, he'd limp to the door and bellow, "Peeennnyyy" as if calling a co-star for the next scene.

---

[127] **Ese gato no tiene vergüenza:** Said of cats who steal food and people who steal lives shameless, bold, and usually purring about it.

The tuxedo hero always appeared, tail high, eyes bloodshot, charisma intact.

Then, one day, silence.

Day 1: No Penny.

Day 3: Grief.

We, the women, knew the truth. Penny had met Sr. Martinez's cursed Toyota Corolla and lost. But how do you tell a galán his mirror image died unglamorously on asphalt?

We didn't. We lied.

We said Penny ran off to Bayamón with a younger girlfriend; maybe fled to Miami to seduce heiresses.

Every morning, my father still called, "Peeeeeennnyy!"

And we still raised our orange-juice glasses in solidarity with the legend. Because in our family, love often survived through fiction.

Penny didn't perish; he ascended.

Like every Televisa hero, he left at the peak of his powers, reputation intact, libido undefeated. Some myths you protect, not because they're true, but because they keep the story going.

Part III – Coda: The Cats Who Carried Our Silence

We always joked that the cats ran the house. The truth: they ran the novela of our lives. They said what we couldn't. They fought when we bit our tongues. They filled the air when grief followed it out.

When people died, we went quiet; paperwork, wills, polite sobs. When the cats died, we wailed like the chorus of a Greek tragedy performed in Spanglish.

Cats weren't pets. They were stand-ins, saints, and witnesses. They absorbed the resentment, the unspoken cruelties, the laughter that saved us. And sometimes, like my tabby Papi... They absorbed too much.

Papi lived long enough to see me free of a man who confused control with love. Only then, cancer-ridden, did he let go. I don't believe that was a coincidence. He carried my pain until I could carry it myself.

That's the cruel magic of cats; they save us in silence. And when they go, they take whole storylines with them.

THE DECODER

Survival Law #49: *Survive like a cat; claws out, eyes open, landing on your feet every time. Protect the secret. Guard the heart. And when silence comes, purr louder than fear.*

ACT VI

SEQUINS, SURVIVAL & LEGACY

(Episodes 50–55)

EPISODE 50 – THE ATTEMPTED KIDNAPPING IN MY FATHER'S LAW OFFICE

12/27 — 8:00 a.m.

Rating: PG

Episode Description: *An actual crime starring my family.*

Because no proper Puerto Rican childhood is complete without an FBI raid, a mobster's girlfriend, a mistaken-identity scandal so stupid it could only have been plotted by a drunk *Señor de los Cielos* intern. That was Tuesday for us.

The Most Chaotic Office on Avenida Ponce del León

My father, Don Leopoldo Santos Oliviano de Vizcaya, Esq., ran a law office in Hato Rey that smelled like cigars, whiskey, and moderately felonious paperwork. The kind of place where:

- A senator signed documents at 11:00.
- And by 11:30 someone was swearing on the Virgin Mary they were "just there for coffee."

Enter the FBI, who somehow decided this was a hostage situation.

Mistaken Identity: The FBI's Dumbest Day?

Picture it: the Bureau, armed with satellites, wiretaps, and budgets bigger than Puerto Rico's GDP, decided my father, a man who:

- Walked with crutches,

- Wore La Esquina Famosa suits sharp enough to double as weapons,
- And considered "extra lechón" an act of treason... had been kidnapped by ***Filiberto Ojeda Ríos.***[128]

Yes, Filiberto: leader of *Los Macheteros*, Wells Fargo heist legend, revolutionary trumpet player. And the FBI thought he stormed into Ponce de León... to smoke cigars with my dad and dictate manifestos on an *IBM Selectric*?[129]

Leading the raid? My cousin **Ricardo**, Police chief, FBI darling, and a man who could turn a parking ticket into a Greek tragedy. He showed up like *Bad Boys 3: Boricua Reckoning.*

- Flak jackets,
- Assault rifles,
- SWAT extras fresh out of Sicario: San Juan

All to "rescue" my father who, spoiler, was drinking café con leche with his secretary.

Mami vs. The FBI

Meanwhile, in Guaynabo, my mother was mid-merienda in her orchid-filled solarium, *pastelillitos de guayaba* on china, *Justino Díaz*[130] singing Verdi. Then the call came:

"Titi, we're about to storm Tio's office. Hostage situation. Terrorist!"

---

[128] **Filiberto Ojeda Ríos**: Puerto Rican nationalist, trumpet player, and alleged mastermind of the 1983 $7M Wells Fargo heist. FBI headache, island legend.

[129] **IBM Selectric**: The diva of typewriters; a 1960s "golf-ball" goddess that made secretaries fast, executives insufferable and writers believe genius came standard. Now retired to vintage shops and writer Instagrams, where she poses like she still has a book deal.

[130] **Justino Díaz**: Puerto Rico's velvet cannon of a voice, the bass-baritone who went from San Juan to the world's grandest opera houses and made it look as easy as humming in the shower.

She didn't panic. She slammed down her pastelillo, grabbed us, and tore down Ponce de León like *Fast & Furious 12-Merienda Drift.*

Because if there's one thing Mami taught me, it's this: when danger shows up, we don't hide. We go toward it. Like heroines.

The Aftermath: FBI FAIL

No terrorists. No Filiberto. No hostages. Just my father, sipping coffee, annoyed that his cup had gone cold, while Ricardo and his SWAT team stood there like mall Santas in tactical cosplay.

Puerto Rican taxpayers: fleeced.

The FBI: humiliated.

My father: untouchable.

Marisela: La Jefa de HR Violations

Then there was **Marisela**, the real star. Waist-length hair. Blood-red nails. Miniskirts that violated both HR rules and the Geneva Convention.

She typed like a flamenco dancer and eventually ran off with **Riquelme**, a mafioso developer built like Danny DeVito playing *Scarface* in polyester. Naturally, she adored him.

Soundtrack: El Milagro del Amor

Here's the detail that only makes sense decades later: my mother adored the Spanish theme of *The Godfather*, *El Milagro del Amor*, crooned by Gianni Morandi. That night the song was on repeat. She swayed in the kitchen, mouthing: *Nosotros somos el Milagro del amor...*

She recognized the story we were living; half narconovela, half Scorsese, and met it without blinking. The theme wasn't just her favorite song. It was her code, her compass.

Epilogue: Narco-Soap, Scorsese Flick… or Villalba Coda?

Was that day a narconovela (*El Señor de los Cielos*, but humid), a Scorsese flick (with worse tailoring), or just another Tuesday on Ponce de León?

I know this: Mami understood the script. She wasn't reckless. She was prepared. Survival means stepping into the chaos, not shrinking from it.

Last I heard, Marisela resurfaced as all novela characters do. Not dead, just relocated; taking over Titi Fiera's finca in Villalba.

One dynasty of unruly women handing the torch to another.

THE DECODER

Survival Law #50: *Never fear a SWAT team. Fear an interrupted merienda.*

EPISODE 51 – MATH, MOBS AND LAWYERS

12/27 — 9:00 a.m.

Rating: PG

Episode Description: Wiretaps, division problems, and mental blocks.

Every telenovela needs a sadist. Not the tragic antihero; the pure sadist. Think Soraya Montenegro shrieking, "¡*Maldita lisiada*!" or Catalina Creel weaponizing an eye patch.

Mine was **Señora Calcetín**. Instead of stilettos, she wielded multiplication tables.

Señora Calcetín, La Villana Matemática

Imagine a woman cryogenically frozen in 1952, thawed solely to terrorize children with long division and mothballs. That was my fifth-grade math teacher.

- She hated fun.
- She especially hated me.

Get one answer wrong?

WHACK.

Wooden ruler to the knuckles like she was conducting the Vienna Boys' Choir on my hands. I froze like a hostage; convinced I'd die in that Catholic school and spend eternity counting on my fingers while Soraya cackled.

Everywhere else I was a prodigy:

- History: recited colonial injustices like indictments.
- Literature: monologues on tap.

- Religious Studies: verses delivered like *Jesus Christ Superstar.*
- Math? An abyss. A ruler-filled abyss.

One day she sent me home with a Warning Card that basically read: "Your daughter is too dumb for polite society. Plan accordingly."

The Sadist Hall of Fame

- Soraya Montenegro (María la del Barrio) memeable queen of cruelty.
- Catalina Creel (Cuna de Lobos): eyeliner, eye patch, empire.
- Señora Calcetín (Academia San José) fractions, mothballs, and cuticle scars.

Doña Chicharrón – The Math Angel

Enter Doña Chicharrón, tutor: eighty, orthopedic shoes, a halo of Vicks. Under her care, I scraped out an A-.

Did I learn math? No. Did I survive math? Barely.

To this day, when I glance at a budget, I feel her ghost whisper, "*¿Otra vez contando con los dedos ridícula?*"

Adulthood, or Math with Mafia Accessories

Salvation arrived via **Gina la Cobradora**, who re-taught me arithmetic without a ruler, but with repo-man tenderness. Not even Gina prepared me for the real math of my childhood.

When Your Allowance Arrives in a FedEx Envelope of Cash

Some kids got checks.

Some got wires.

I got crisp, untraceable bills, FedEx like holy communion.

Where did it come from? Don't ask.

Family Rule #1: Don't ask. Just spend.

Don Billy El Joyero: The Trunk-Show Mafioso

Shopping meant Don Billy: slicked-back red hair, cowboy boots: a gun tucked in one like a festive piñata.

He'd pop the Lincoln LTD trunk and… voilà!

Tiffany & Co. exploded inside. Diamonds, rubies, emeralds. Normal, right? I have follow-ups now.

The FBI Was Listening to Our Calls

Our house phone had clicks. Not static. CLICK-click. CLICK. The percussion of a federal wiretap. Why?

Mami swore J. Edgar Hoover himself had a dossier on my father for his *Partido Independentista Puertorriqueño (P.I.P.)*[131] voting record and friendship with its president, **Rubén Berríos Martinez**.

But looking back now, my dad wasn't just *independentista.* He was also a civil litigator, a bail bond broker, and an occasional philosopher of bad timing.

He ran bonds with his buddy, **Cundo Flechazo** and half their clients came straight from **Federal Correctional Institution, Tallahassee.**

Let's do the math (triggering!):

Lawyer + bail bonds + federal clients + wiretaps = this math doesn't even math.

Even Sra. Calcetín would've failed the arrangement ruler raised high, calling us *burras.*

---

[131] **Partido Independentista Puertorriqueño (P.I.P.)**: Puerto Rico's Independence party led by Rubén Berrios Martinez, a law professor turned protest icon. My father called him, "el abogado que actually did something."

The Real Lesson

Señora Calcetín wasn't just a bad teacher; she was my first sadist. Her favorite torture device wasn't the ruler; it was the *word problem.*[132]

If you have ten dollars and your friend borrows five, and caramels cost ten cents each, how many can you buy with twenty?

None, *señora.* Because math never made sense, and neither did life.

Compared to long division with Señora Calcetín, the FBI was light work. You don't forget your first tyrant. She carved equations into my bones: how to brace, how to listen for danger, how to disappear in plain sight.

In the end, the only equation that held was the one she never meant to teach me.

I was not the *variable* to be solved.

I was the *constant* that endured.

THE DECODER

Survival Law #51*: If life's equations never add up, trust your instinct, not the numbers. The answer is never in the math; it's in the survival.*

---

[132] **Word problems**: Early cognitive grooming for gaslighting.

EPISODE 52 – THE ERGOLUXE EMPIRE: BEDS, BLOW & BAD TOUPEES

12/27 — 10:00 a.m.

Rating: PG

Episode Description: *The Venn diagram you didn't know you needed.*

If you cross *The Godfather* with a vibrating-bed infomercial and sprinkle in Puerto Rican disco, you get my childhood.

Before the sequins and the beds that hummed like samba drums, there was gratitude: **Don Sixto de la Siesta**, founder of ErgoLuxe Adjustable Comfort Systems; mattresses for every mood swing.

He was my father's best friend.

My dad bent the Law's edges to keep him out of handcuffs; Don Sixto made sure my dad had a hospital bed with a dignity setting. Loyalty like that seeped into your memory foam.

Don Sixto: The Mobster Who Believed in Back Support

Whispers said he owned *gentlemen's spas* from Newark to Negril. When I met him, he was the Caribbean CEO of ErgoLuxe: suspiciously luxurious adjustable beds designed equally for geriatrics, gigolos, and creative accountants.

He wore a blond toupee so tragic it deserved its own therapist; discount Robert Redford meets offshore James Dean. Gold pinky rings screamed *tax-free account,* and his suits could redirect air traffic.

His son Lucio? A walking telenovela: white pants tighter than moral boundaries, silk shirts to the navel (chest hair as generational wealth), sunglasses indoors *and spiritually.*

Inevitably, Lucio was caught "transporting medical samples," fifty kilos' worth.

Strip clubs + cocaine + vibrating beds = vertical integration, baby.

Felino: The Diva Consigliere

The scene-stealer was his godson, **Felino de Rumba,** a weather event in silk. Shirts loud enough to trigger seismic alerts, jewelry bright enough to tan your retinas, cologne that lingered longer than regret.

He was our fairy godmother in heels; hips defying gravity, laughter cracking glassware at the Caribe Hilton. Beyond spectacle, Felino was family: fashion advice, sharpest gossip, secrets before they hit *El Nuevo Día.*[133]

Years later we danced at *Bachelor's*, San Juan's legendary gay disco, where no one cared who was who. With him, everything stayed fabulous.

The UFOs: Unidentified Flying Hombres

In those days, Felino and his circle from San Ignacio, the Jesuit prep school that produced half the island's politicians and all its best dancers, were part of what my mother and Cata's mom called the *UFOs*: **Unidentified Flying (H)Ombres.**

Their code for gay men who flew like saucers *voladores,* radiant, untethered, and suspiciously good at merengue.

They were our brothers, our crushes, our prom dates who showed up on time. Most of all, they gave our mothers peace of mind; proof that a girl could go dancing, come home glittered, and still graduate a lady.

---

133 **El Nuevo Día**: Puerto Rico's paper of record and national pastime. If it wasn't printed there, it didn't happen, or it happened quietly. Years later, I'd write for it myself, covering **Benicio del Toro**, **Chayanne** and **Ricky Martin's** *La Vida Loca*, back when my cousin was VP and the newsroom buzzed like a telenovela set; ink stained, over-caffeinated and fabulous.

"They won't ruin your reputation, *mija:* just your rhythm;" Mami said, handing me over like a debutante at Studio 54. She was right. Those San Ignacio UFOs taught me grace, glitter, and how to survive a room full of men who underestimate you.

Clubman: The Temple of Shoes & Sin

Felino's holiest sacrament was footwear. In the 1980s there was one cathedral: *Clubman.*[134]

Not a store; a shrine. Gucci. Ferragamo. Loafers sharp enough to cut tembleque, or men. The stockroom was his confessional, the shoehorn, his scepter.

Narconovela Archetype Roll Call

Don Sixto: Padrino of posture.

Lucio: Doomed narco-*galán.*

Felino: Fabulous consigliere turned saint.

If Telemundo had adapted my childhood, this was the pilot. Mob movie with sequins. *Goodfellas* with glitter. *Casino* with cologne.

Because allowance came in FedEx cash, jewelry from trunks, and our guardian angel wore heels.

Later, I'd work at the DEA, chasing the same kind of men I grew up around; men who believed loyalty, flash, and rules were written in perfume and fear.

The difference? I understood them. I spoke their language.

Maybe that's what the UFOs taught me all along: how to read power, how to dance with danger, and how to survive both the mafia and the *magia,* by never forgetting to sparkle.

---

[134] **Clubman:** Puerto Rico's cathedral of men's fashion; half boutique, half social experiment. The suits were tailored; the gossip bespoke. You went in for a blazer, left baptized in cologne and rumor.

THE DECODER

Survival Law #52: *If your bed shakes, pray it's the motor; not the money laundering.*

EPISODE 53 – EL DANDY'S BARBERSHOP: WHERE GROOMING MEETS MAXIMUM SECURITY AND HIGH SOCIETY MEETS LOW-GRADE FELONY

12/27 — 11:00 a.m.

Rating: PG-13

Episode Description: *Where confessionals came with a fade.*

In hacienda telenovelas, there's always that scene where the hacendado leaves his mansion to "mingle with the common folk," stroking his mustache and dispensing wisdom.

For other families, that was a metaphor.

For us, it was Saturday — and haircuts.

Because every week, my father strutted into *El Dandy's Barbershop,* Buckingham Palace with clippers, conveniently parked beside *El Oso Blanco,*[135] Puerto Rico's Alcatraz.

Naturally, the best place to get your fade tightened was within spitting distance of men who stabbed each other over karaoke disputes.

Daddy's Dangerous Spa Day

[135] **El Oso Blanco**: Part penitentiary, part cautionary bedtime story. See LSG Decoder

He could've gone anywhere:

- The Ritz-Carlton salon,
- Condado's Swarovski-scissor barber,
- Even a humble Supercuts

But no. My father, patron saint of reckless loyalty programs, swore by *El Dandy.*

Inside: velvet chairs, gold-framed mirrors, and a salsa soundtrack occasionally interrupted by riot rehearsals next door. He'd emerge freshly shaved, smelling like talcum powder, *Brillantina*,[136] and a lightly redacted indictment.

Meanwhile, my mother, queen of pearls, melodrama and recreational fainting, insisted I go along. "You must learn to survive anywhere, Charito," she declared, clutching her Chanel clutch like a rosary.

Forget ballet. Forget piano. My extracurricular was sipping a Malta in a barbershop where the men carried machetes and the gossip carried indictments.

Perrier with a Side of Felony

El Dandy's clientele was curated like a Netflix pitch deck:

- A narco in Gucci slides.
- A bishop moonlighting as a poker buddy.
- Two senators arguing over mistress stipends.
- One ex-Miss Universe runner-up pretending to be a receptionist.

---

[136] **Brillantina:** That slick, shiny hair gel of the 1980s; equal parts gladiator armor and disco glitter glue. On a rainy San Juan morning, Brillantina meant: "I came prepared for the apocalypse and the party."

My father's ritual? The combo: razor shave, *empanadilla de carne,* and a Perrier. Because hydration matters even when your barber is notarizing cartel property deeds on the side.

This was where I became a professional eavesdropper. I learned that:

- Imported whisky prices made the stock market look stable.
- Mistress money always stayed liquid (usually stuffed in **Louis Vuitton**).
- "In Miami" was code for laundering, hiding, or both.

Enter Mai Maravilla: Patron Saint of Prison Chic

Before *Oso Blanco,* she was a Condado shampoo girl massaging the scalps of San Juan's elite. Behind bars? She rebranded as the Beyoncé of Block C — with the organizational hustle of Kris Jenner.

Rule #1: Find a husband in three days. Like Amazon Prime, but with more shanks.

She married a *Ñeta*[137] kingpin and secured:

- VIP cafeteria seating (Nobu, but with trays).
- Priority cigarette access (the AmEx Black Card of prison currency).
- A chicas-only bathroom enforced with paddle diplomacy.

Naturally, they had a wedding: officiated by an inmate chaplain in a Versace knockoff stole. Guests in red bandanas. Cake smuggled in a laundry cart. Honeymoon suite: Cell Block C,

---

[137] **La Asociación Ñeta**: Puerto Rico's homegrown cartel-slash brotherhood-part revolution, part HR department for felons. Founded in Oso Blanco, it ran on loyalty, machetes, and excellent branding.

with "room service" by bribed cafeteria staff. The "It" Event of the season.

The Rituals (Because This Story Needed More WTF)

Her philosopher-husband even got a government grant (yes, taxpayer money) to write his memoirs revealing the Ñeta rituals.

My personal favorite?
Every 30th at exactly 8:00 p.m., the prison counted down:

10... 9... 8...

At one? A synchronized, full-volume, mass-masturbation in honor of fallen leader *Carlos "La Sombra."* [138]

Imagine New Year's Eve at Times Square, if the ball drop were sponsored by Trojan and monitored by parole officers.

Freedom, Haircuts, and Sequins

Mai Maravilla eventually left prison. The marriage dissolved (tragic). The kingpin returned to his other wife (predictable). And Mai reemerged declaring, "Freedom is everything." And freedom, apparently, comes with sequins.

Last I heard, Mai was up for *RuPaul's Drag Race: All Stars.* Proving, once again, that in life, as in prison, survival isn't about who you marry, it's about how well you accessorize.

Looking back, El Dandy's wasn't just a barbershop. It was education in power, spectacle, and survival.

---

[138] **Carlos "La Sombra":** Proof that in Puerto Rico even prison gangs have better branding than most tech startups.

My father, the hacendado, surveyed his pueblo.

Mai, the prison queen, was reborn as a diva.

Senators, *narcos*, bishops; all waiting under fluorescent lights for a shave, a secret, and absolution.

If church was where you confessed your sins, *El Dandy's* was where you got them lined up and faded.

THE DECODER

Survival Law #53: *Barbershops are confessionals. Tip well; your secrets depend on it.*

EPISODE 54 – THE CATHOLIC RETREAT THAT WAS SUPPOSED TO BE REFLECTIVE BUT TURNED INTO A CONFESSIONAL BREAKDOWN

12/27 — 12:00 p.m.

Rating: PG

Episode Description: *Where faith, privilege and waterproof mascara met their tragic unfolding.*

There's always a church scene in a telenovela. A heaving heroine, mascara surrendering, ready to derail a wedding in the name of truth. Our version? Same drama, better catering.

It was senior-year retreat season, and our "spiritual journey" at *El Conquistador*[139] in Fajardo had more to do with buffet schedules than salvation.

The Setup: Catholic Girls Gone Wild (Emotionally)

Before we scattered to colleges where our Puerto Rican accents would be treated like exotic accessories…

- Miss Rosé to NYU,
- Kerimina to Georgetown,
- La Venecia to Tufts,
- Estrella to Sagrado Corazón

[139] **El Conquistador:** Puerto Rico's Palacio Real-on-a-cliff; private island, chandeliered excess, and a bill that could ruin you before the Holy Spirit can save you.

- Me to Swarthmore (which my mother was 90% sure was a ski resort in Switzerland)

...we did what all well-bred Catholic girls did: booked a luxury retreat. Because nothing says *repent* like an infinity pool and a priest with a clipboard.

We meditated by the ocean, nodded at sermons while planning our "first day" looks, and held hands in prayer waiting for gossip to break like communion. Then the retreat leader pressed play on **Bette Midler's *The Rose.***

How Bette Midler Emotionally Wrecked a Room of Catholic Overachievers

There are two kinds of people:

- Those who hear *The Rose* and think, "Aw what sweet song."
- And those who hear it and feel compelled to confess every sin since the womb.

We were the second kind.

A sniffle. A wail. A domino collapse of hysteria.

Mascara ran like a Dali painting.

Pearls were ripped out, "because they felt heavy with sin."

By the second chorus, the ballroom looked like Sephora after a hurricane.

My Fatal Confession

Then came the priest's mistake: "Share what you're ashamed of."

I could've said:

- I cheated on a quiz.
- I skipped P.E.

- I fake-fasted during Lent.

Instead, I said the one thing I swore I never would: "I was ashamed of my father."

I kept going:

- I hated the stares when we walked into a room.
- I hated the whispers: ¿Fue polio? Was it war?
- I hated how his disability made me feel… different.

And worse…

I was ashamed of being ashamed.

Even Soraya Montenegro would've dropped her martini.

The Breakdown Heard 'Round Fajardo

Then Miss Rosé, ever the debutante, dabbed her eyes and whispered… "You know what's worse? Pretending you don't feel that way."

And that broke the dam.

Generational curses. Forbidden crushes. Every Catholic secret we'd lacquered under pastel cardigans came pouring out between snot and Ave Marías.

Emma Santillán admitted she'd developed a "spiritual" on her family's neurologist; specifically, his tongue, which described as "a divine instrument of healing."

The room gasped.

The priest crossed himself.

Kerimina muttered, "Girl, that's not how reflex tests work."

The varsity tennis prodigy confessed a crush on Kerimina and asked if that meant eternal damnation of just therapy.

And then… Estrella. My childhood partner in pranks and pop quizzes, shaking under the chandelier light.

She sobbed over *The Choch Incident,*[140] the infamous spray-painted masterpiece, "*Srta. Diciembre come choch,*" scrawled across the convent wall before she ran out of paint and nerve. It almost cost her graduation, and the nuns' last shred of innocence.

I stood; crossed the room and hugged her so hard our pearl bracelets clicked like rosaries. It wasn't forgiveness. It was survival in its purest form; two girls who'd grown up in some chaos, finally saying the quiet parts out loud.

By the final note, we weren't schoolgirls anymore. We were absolved telenovela extras with trust funds and runny mascara.

The Realization

I remember staring out at the Atlantic, Bette still wailing, realizing:

I wasn't built for normal.

I wasn't built for quiet.

I was built for spectacle; sequined, emotional, uncontainable.

Because I wasn't a wilted rose.

I was the whole damn bouquet: thorns, glitter, and a brunch reservation.

That night cracked me open. It made me ridiculous, and therefore, real.

---

[140] **The Choch Incident**: A legendary act of feminist vandalism that began as protest and ended when the spray-paint ran out. Both a scandal and a rite of passage; proof that divine intervention occasionally takes the form of a dying aerosol can.

Decades later, I recognize it as the rehearsal for every showbiz breakdown that followed.

The Finale

As the night ended, we floated out of that ballroom; barefoot, mascara-streaked, clutching each other's hand like survivors of our melodrama.

Outside, the ocean shimmered like liquid absolution. We were ridiculous, privileged, over-emotional, and holy in our way.

Girls who'd been taught to behave, now laughing too loud, praying too softly, and finally, finally, learning that survival wasn't sainthood.

It was spectacle.

And it was ours.

THE DECODER

Survival Law #54*: Fold your insecurities into a cootie catcher, slip them in your pocket, and remember: you're the fortune, not the paper.*

EPISODE 55 – THE MYTH OF SUCCESS & THE CHECKLIST THAT'S SUPPOSED TO MAKE YOU HAPPY

12/27 — 1:00 p.m.

Rating: PG

Episode Description: *Spoiler: It doesn't. But it will make you look good in a Christmas card photo.*

Every telenovela ends with a wedding, a will, or a yacht explosion. Mine ends with a checklist.

The sacred list of the Proper Puerto Rican Lady, not a suggestion, not advice — **law**.

- Ivy League Education (Cornell? ¡*Ay bendito*!)
- Pearls and linen, never sequins ("giving Miami," and we did not do Miami).
- A tasteful yacht, dock in Culebra or bust.
- A husband who looked good in a tax bracket.
- Membership at Caparra Country Club (Sizzler was *not* an option).

If you checked every box, you were supposed to be happy. *Spoiler: You weren't.*

Mami: A Case Study in Checklists & Revenge

Mami checked every box; the yacht, the pearls, the Mass in heels and when the will was read?

$500 and a lifetime of resentment.

She never forgave her brothers. Didn't cry at their funerals. If anyone mentioned them, she'd tilt her head and ask, "*¿Quién*?" "Who?"

That was her P.H.D. in revenge.

Graduation: Orchids, Crutches & Maximum Spectacle

Graduation should have been simple: walk, smile, eat cake. But this was my life.

So, of course it came with orchids, *Dynasty* hair, Oui boutique heels, and medals stacked like a *quinceañera* centerpiece.

- Spanish (I conjugated verbs like a dictator)
- French (fluent in flirting)
- Social Studies (decades of chisme)
- Religion (oh, the irony)
- Science (I won the Piña fair remember?)
- Math? The abyss that hated me back.

And there they were — Mami shining with that familiar white-hot fury — and Papi, proud, balancing on his crutches, watching their Sarito cross the stage; the same nine-pound baby delivered by a hurricane seventeen years before.

Just then, diploma in hand, I remembered Papi's Five Commandments:

- **Focus**: Fire happens.
- **Delegate**: When there's a will, there's a way.
- **Listen & Learn**: Take the lesson, not the teacher.
- **Enjoy Life**: Success is sweet.
- **Be Balanced**: Be a banker, a lawyer, and a poet.

And most importantly, he said: "Charito, if you live by these, nothing, and no one can convince you your dreams don't matter."

At seventeen, I rolled my eyes. Now I see it.

Those Commandments weren't rules.

They were the DNA of this book and the blueprint for surviving the storm.

Curtain Call: The Real Survival Guide

This memoir isn't just stories. It's inheritance; sequined, messy, holy.

The lessons didn't come from Harvard or country clubs. They came from Mami's melodramas, Papi's stubborn fire, and every telenovela that taught me how to cry, slap, love, and survive in pearls.

Life was never normal.

It was always fabulous. And as any heroine knows: survival isn't just making it through; it's making it through with eyeliner intact.

Final Beat: Return to Signal

Fifty-five Episodes.

Fifty-six Laws.

Forgot about Law X.

Not neat.

Not symmetrical.

Neither was I.

And somewhere, that girl born in a hurricane still holds the transistor radio to her ear, tuning through static for a voice that sounds like her own.

She hears it now; crackling but clear.

You survived the storm. Now go make noise.

THE DECODER

Survival Law #55: *Success isn't a checklist. It's a novela. Survive it. Rewrite it. Blind them with sequins.*

A VIEWER'S COMPANION TO LA VIDA DRAMÁTICA

THE LATINA SURVIVAL GUIDE DECODER

(A-Z)

A

Ajo, Limón y Cebolla *n. masc. coll. (AH-hoh lee-MOHN ee see-BOH-yah)* — vegetables

Before Goop, before green juice, before TikTok wellness influencers charged $18 for chlorophyll water, Puerto Rico had Don Bonifacio Olivano.

His self-published masterpiece, *Ajo, Limón y Cebolla,* promised to cure anything — heartache, gout, even government corruption — with those three humble kitchen saints.

- **Ajo (Garlic):** The island's original antibiotic. One clove could lower blood pressure, banish demons, and keep your nosy neighbor from overstaying her visit (garlic breath > holy water).
- **Limón (Lemon):** The detox darling. Allegedly cleansed your liver, whitened your skin, and stripped paint off a Buick. A squeeze of limón cured hangovers and heartbreak alike.
- **Cebolla (Onion):** The drama queen. Cut it and cry out every inherited trauma; eat it raw and your circulation rivals an Olympian's. Place it under the bed and voilà—absorbed *malas energías* (and, inconveniently roaches). In our house, both survived.

Family Lore Cross-Ref:
See Episode 46, where this holy trinity of condiments evolved from folk remedy to family gospel.

Usage Note:
Quoted like scripture. Sore throat? Rub onion on your chest. Boyfriend dumped you? Lemon water at dawn. Haunted by ancestors? Garlic in your purse.

Modern Update:

Don Bonifacio never made the *New England Journal of Medicine*, but on the island, this trinity remains medicine, magic, and melodrama in equal parts.

See also: *Brujería; Home remedies; Abuelo logic.*

Academia San José *n. (ah-kah-DEE-mee-ah sahn-HO- SÉH)*— school

Puerto Rico's finishing school for the elite, where little girls in polyester skirts were trained not just in algebra but in the fine arts of table settings, eye rolls, and Ivy League ambition. If you didn't leave with scoliosis and SAT prep trauma, were you even there?

Usage Notes:
A cross between Catholic discipline and WASP aspiration, Academia San José specialized in producing one of two outcomes:

1. Diplomas fluent in five languages.
2. Women who could balance a gin and tonic while reciting the rosary.

Fun Fact:
The cafeteria pastelillos were more coveted than Harvard acceptance letters — and just as unattainable for the masses.

Modern Update:
Think *Gossip Girl* with better tans, rosaries instead of headbands, and abuelas as the original admissions committee.

See also: *Overachiever central; polyester nun chic; Harvard pipeline in español.*

Amway *n.* (AHM-way) — business

The original Pyramid Scheme Couture, the direct selling empire that turned Puerto Rican marquesinas into cult meetings that stacked with vitamins no one trusted. Proof that island garages invented MLM storage long before Amazon warehouses.

Usage Note:
"I'm going to an Amway meeting = get ready for flat Fresca, folding chairs, and promises of a Lexus.

Fun Fact:
Every Puerto Rican family had one uncle who got roped in. He preached "residual income" until his garage looked like a Walgreens clearance aisle.

Modern Update:
WhatsApp voice notes replaced the Styrofoam cups.
Desperation? Timeless.

Famous Quote:
"This isn't a pyramid scheme. It's a family."
Translation: Run.

See also: *Herbalife; financial ruin with a smile; MLM as cardio.*

Arroz con Dulce *n. (ah-ROHS kohn DOOL-she)* — dessert

Rice pudding, Puerto Rican style, cooked in coconut milk, cinnamon, cloves, and ginger. Served at Christmas to remind you that rice never takes a holiday. Maman's specialty.

¡Ay bendito! *interj. (eye ben-DEE-toh)* — mantra

The Swiss-Army-knife of Puerto Rican expressions, both balm and blade. Literally, "oh, blessed one," but functionally shorthand for poor thing, what a shame, or bless your stupid little heart.

Usage (tone is destiny):

- **Tender**: Grandma, watching you fall off your bike — "¡Ay bendito, nena ven acá!"
- **Pitying (with daggers):** Auntie, hearing you're 30 and still single — "¡Ay bendito!"
- **Cruel glee:** Frenemy, seeing your bad haircut — "¡Ay benditoooo!"

Survival Guide Lesson:
An ¡Ay bendito! can crown you with affection or drag you straight into the jódete category. Context decides.

See also: *jódete; Abuelita logic; Catholic guilt*

B

Bacalaítos *n. pl. (bah-cah-lah-EE-tohs)* — food

Puerto Rican beach gold, giant, fried codfish fritters so thin and wide they double as castanets. The extra-flat ones are called *panderetas* because, yes, they look like tambourines, and after two, you'll be dancing like one.

Eat two and you've basically had Mass, Communion, and the after-party. By the third, you're 80% saltwater, 20% regret, and considering a nap behind a palm tree.

Fun Fact:
They taste best when the grease seeps through the napkin before you've even finished saying, "Dame otra."

See also: *cafetín; mallorcas; tostones.*

Bolo *n. (BOH-loh)* — bingo chip

Not an acronym, not an Amber Alert; just the cultural jewel of every church bingo night. Your special number that when called can break the bingo bank. You scream "¡BOLO!" Like the apocalypse depends on it.

Usage Note:
"¡BOLO! ¡BOLO! Mija, check my card before la vieja claims it!"

Modern Update:
"If you've never screamed BOLO while holding a half-eaten pastelillo — are you even Puerto Rican?

See also: *domino slamming; rosarios y raffles; tía competitive mode.*

Bossu *n., (boh-SOO)* — suitor

Nickname for my first would be Romeo, a young man whose hunchback earned him a lifetime membership in Puerto Rico's nickname economy.

On the island, you weren't Carlos or José, you were Cojo, Gordo, Bizco, or in this case, Bossu (from the French for "hunchback"). Once christened, forever cursed.

Modern Update:
Today *Bossu* would be rebranded as "quirky hot" or "alt-vibe boyfriend" on TikTok. Back then, he was just *el Bossu*, the first boy bold enough to know on my parents' door.

Famous Quote (Family Edition):
¿Ese es el que te gusta? ¡Ay bendito!

Fun Fact:
Jane Austen heroines had Darcys, I had Bossu; hunched, sweaty, earnest, and somehow still romantic.

See also: *chaperones; forbidden suitors; negative x 3.*

Bustelo Coffee *n. prop. (boo-STEH-loh KAW-fee)* —beverage

Born in East Harlem; 1928. More than coffee, an identity in a can. Bright yellow, screaming red, bold enough to stain your soul and your linoleum.

Family Rivalry:

If Café Yaucono was the respectable matriarch, Bustelo was her scandalous cousin in sequins at 10 a.m., the one who flirts with the mailman and starts political arguments before noon.

See also: *Café Yaucono; chisme; revolutions fueled by espresso.*

C

Cabrón *n. masc. (cah-BROHN)* — man

A layered Puerto Rican term that morphs with tone, eyebrow arch, and the level of betrayal involved. At its core, it is the man who got played, or worse, knew he was being played, and still showed up with flowers.

Usage Note:
"Ese tipo es un cabrón." "¡Diablo, qué cabrón eres!" "¡Ay bendito, me dejaste como una cabrona."

Fun Fact:
Originally, "male goat." The horns weren't metaphorical.

Modern Update:
Gen-Z uses *cabrón* the way Brits say "mate" and Americans say "bro".

Famous Quote:
"*Puerto Rico está cabrón.*" — Bad Bunny

Sidebar:
Levels of *Cabronería* (Unofficial Scale)

1. Forgot your birthday.
2. Lives with his mom… and didn't tell you.
3. You're the side chick and his wife follows you on IG.
4. Full-blown Telemundo villain.
5. You forgave him. Again.
6. Welcome to the Cabrona Support Group.

See also: *Toxic Machismo; Bad Bunny lyrics.*

Cafetín *n. masc. (cah-feh-TEEN)* — bar

Roadside sanctum of Medallas, boleros, and frying bacalaítos. Domino tiles slam like gunshots. Men rebuild LUMA from plastic chairs, no tools, just opinions. Women judge from the doorway with doctoral precision. Half bar, half confessional, wholly essential.

See also: *capicú; machismo; abuela denial.*

Caldo de gallina *n., masc. (KAHL-doh deh gah-YEE-nah), —* food

Broth from an older, tougher hen whose flavor is deeper than a beauty-salon rumor. Not caldo de pollo's delicate cousin, this one resurrects the rude.

Fun Fact:
I watched Maman whirl a live black hen into "ingredients." Ten minutes later: garlic, onion, cilantro, and feet bobbing like trophies.

Cultural Note:
Those feet? A delicacy. Also, the reason I once screamed at a Girl Scout petting booth when I saw baby chicks. Permanent trauma served hot.

Famous Quote:
"Cállate y tómate el caldo, esto revive hasta un muerto."

Modern Usage:
"That nap was caldo de gallina for my soul."

See also: *sancocho; brujería ligera.*

Caribe Hilton *n. prop.* (cah-REE-beh HIL-ton) — hotel

Iconic San Juan temple of cocktails, sequins, and questionable decisions. Private beach, public drama.

Usage Note:
Appears in every abuela story that starts "en mis tiempos," and ends with a lipstick smeared alibi.

Fun Fact:
Birthplace of the piña colada. Ramón "Monchito" Marrero says he created it in the Caribe Hilton in 1954, and Don Ramón Portas Mingot said he created it in 1963 in the restaurant Barrachina in old San Juan.

They're still arguing in heaven.

Modern Update:
Wedding backdrop for influencers pretending sequins never left.

See also: *first kiss; piña colada; disco balls; Juliana's.*

Carlos "La Sombra" *n. masc. prop. (CAR-lohs lah SOHM-brah)* — man

Founder of Los Ñetas at Oso Blanco and abuelas bedtime warning. To inmates he was a franchise. To folklore he was proof that shadows don't retire.

Carro público *n. masc. (CAR-roh POO-bli-coh)* — car

Not a taxi, not an Uber; chaotic neutral on wheels. Rosaries on the mirror, merengue at 7 a.m. suspension hanging on by a prayer.

Fun Fact:

Drivers knew your cousin's business before your aunt did.

Famous Quote:
"Te llevo pa' San Juan, pero siéntate al frente que la puerta no cierra."

See also: *last rites for Toyotas.*

Catalina Creel *n. fem. (cat-ah-LEE-nah CRAY-ehl)* —the O.G. of high glam evil.

Matriarch of Cuna de Lobos (1986). Rotating designer eye-patches, zero volume on her voice, maximum volume on vengeance.

Usage:
Calling someone "Catalina Creel" implies flawless, feared, and three moves ahead.

Fun Fact:
Did she lose the eye or just weaponize fashion? Unclear. Effective.

Modern Update:
TED Talk. "Eye Contact is Overrated."

Famous Quote:
"Nunca levanto la voz… Yo solo ordeno."

See also: *gaslight; gatekeep glamour; tia with secrets*

Cerromar Beach Hotel *n. masc.* (*seh-rro-MAR*) — hotel

Hyatt's Caribbean crown jewel of the 70s-80s: golf fairways, waterfall pools, hamburgers that tasted like money, and the Coquí disco; Puerto Rico's Studio 54 with better hips.

Cultural Impact:
Where politicians, celebrities, and locals paraded like novela extras between cabanas.

Modern Update:
Abandoned icon; Olympic pools empty, memories full. A heroine left for dead who still gets quoted.

See also: *Dorado Beach; El Coquí disco; novela-ruins aesthetic*

Chancleta *n. fem.* (*chan-KLEH-tah)* — footwear/fate

Aerodynamic disciplinary device of Latina mothers, accuracy: sniper. Also, a patriarchal metaphor for daughters deemed "not heirs."

Cultural Usage:
"No tiene hijos; solo chancletas." Translation: misogyny disguised as proverb.

Modern Reframe:
She is not a slipper; she is a stiletto in waiting.

See also: *heir myths, walking shame (retired), 500 dollars.*

Chaperones *n. pl. (SHA-peh-rohns*) — guardians

The forever third wheel, usually unpaid, always unamused. Imported from the 19th-century Europe, perfected in Caribbean living rooms.

Usage Note:
"Voy al cine con chaperona" = "I will watch *Ghostbusters* while an older woman stares like I'm about to conceive immaculately."

Fun Fact:
Deterrents? No. Accelerants. Nothing fuels teen lust like the threat of being caught.

Modern Update:
Outsourced to Life360, Find My Phone, and 87 WhatsApp messages from Mami.

See also: *Catholic guilt, forbidden love.*

Chilla *n. (CHEE-yah)* — mistress

The one not invited to Christmas dinner but blowing up someone's phone on Nochebuena.

Alt Etymology:
From chillo (red snapper), a fish that hides in rocks. So does she, behind no-pic WhatsApp accounts named "⍰⍰."

Modern Update:
Playlist by Karol G x Bad Bunny, accountability on mute.

Fun Fact:
In Puerto Rico, having a chilla and ordering chillo are both… customs.

See also: *the other woman, secrets marinated in guilt.*

Closet of Death *n. masc. (CLOH-seht)* — closet/time capsule

The pasillo (hallway) closet in every Puerto Rican household that doubles as booby trap, national archive, and portal to other dimensions.

Contents (documented & rumored):

- Wrapping paper rolls from Christmases past, present, and future
- Extension cords so tangled they could power a small nation; if anyone dared unravel them.
- Cookbooks never opened (The Joy of Jell-O, 1964 edition)
- Tools: one hammer, three bent screwdrivers, rusted nails stored in an empty Café Bustelo tin "just in case"
- Light covers for lamps thrown out decades ago
- World Book Encyclopedia, Volumes A-M only
- Margarine tubs filled with pennies, dimes, and indigenous coin "collections"
- Half-empty bottles of Agua Florida (reserved for blessings and exorcisms)
- A radio that hasn't worked since Hurricane Hugo, kept por si acaso
- Six broken umbrellas, each awaiting miraculous repair
- Artificial flowers in plastic sleeves (Easter, Christmas, funerals)
- Photo albums of First Communions, quinceañeras, and cousins no one can identify
- Rolodex of disconnected numbers (dentists, notaries, "the lady who sewed curtains")
- One shoebox of Woolworth's receipts, because hope springs eternal
- Souvenir fans from every Puerto Rican wedding since 1979
- A bowling trophy no family member admits to winning

- Cracked holy water font shaped like the Virgin of Lourdes (still sacred)
- Three birthday candles melted into the number 8
- A domino set missing the 6/5 tile
- Ziplock bag labeled "important" containing nothing

Usage Note:
Opening the Closet of Death is a full-contact sport. Always cross yourself first. Families treat its contents as sacred relics, even though no one ever finds what they
need.

Modern Update:
Rebranded by influencers as "vintage storage" or "eclectic maximalism." In Puerto Rican homes, still called "el clóset del pasillo" and still lethal.

Fun Fact:
Anthropologists believe the Closet of Death contains at least one artifact from every decade since 1950 and possibly the lost city of Atlantis.

See also: Hoarder chic; pasillo peligroso; Caribbean maximalism

Colonial Imports We Pretend Are Ours *n. pl.* —foods

Edam cheese (queso de bola) in red-wax couture; the turrón that menaces dental work. Props for aristocratic cosplay with Iberian aftertaste.

See also: *turrón; queso de bola; Madrid delusion*

Comemierdas/Jaitonas *n. pl. (koh-meh-MYER-dahs / high-TOH-nahs)* slang

Snobs with no cardio. Literally, the "shit eaters." Functionality: the elite who think Plaza Las Américas is Versailles.

Usage:
"No me saludó… tan comemierda."

Fun Fact:
Implies vanity and cluelessness. The guy who speaks broken English to Puerto Rican waiters? Comemierda.

Modern Update:
Also covers Miami transplants and tag-shy influencers.

See also: *prep-school syndrome; la Sociedad*

Coquí *n.* masc. *(coh- KEE)* — animal/club

Zoological:
Puerto Rico's tiny frog whose chirp lulls the island to sleep.

Sociological (80s):
Legendary disco at Cerromar/Dorado. Velvet ropes, mirrored walls, and men who should've known better.

Personal:
At fourteen, I got in with a fake ID and a gallon of lip gloss. The frog sings you to sleep; the disco wakes you up.

See also: *polyester cardio; bolero at 120 BPM*

Coquito *n. masc. (koh-KEE-toh)* — drink

Puerto Rican eggnog: coconut milk, rum, and secrets. Served chilled, best consumed irresponsibly.

See also: *pitorro; holiday survival; cousins gone wild*

Cowboys and Indians *ph. (KOW-boyz un Eeen-diuns)*—game

Childhood role-play where one kid gets a shiny badge, and the other gets a paper feather and generational trauma.

Fun Fact:
We played it in Puerto Rico too. Then a wise tia whispered, "Mija… tu sabes que nosotros somos los indios, ¿verdad?" Identity crisis unlocked.

Modern Update:
Now called "Settlers of Catan with side-eye."

See also: *cultural appropriation; Taíno Comeback Tour*

Cristina Bazán *n. fem. (KRIS-tee-han Buh-zunh)* —telenovela heroine

Puerto Rican Cinderella, patron saint of elegant suffering. Soft spoken, pearl armored, always one forged will from collapse.

Usage:
"She is very Cristina Bazán" = coiffed martyrdom incoming.

Modern Update:
Hulu limited series *Saint in Pearls: Gaslight, Gatekeep Novela.*

See also: *saint of gaslighting; estúpida-buenaza energy.*

Cuna de Lobos *n. phr. (COO-hah deh LOH_bohs),* telenovela

1986 Televisa classic, glamorous evil in power suits, eye-patch couture set to strings.

Modern Update:
Reimagined every decade because evil ages well.

See also: *Dynasty; executives who think they invented melodrama*

D

Dessert Weapons of Mass Seduction *n. pl. (deh-SERT WEH-pons ohf MAHS dees-TRUH-kshun)* — sweets

Puerto Rican confections that are capable of altering marital status and family dynamics.

- **Guava pastelillitos** — So sweet they've caused engagements, divorces, and one custody battle over the recipe.
- **Flan de coco** — Melts family feuds faster than therapy and cheaper than Prozac.
- **Tembleque** — Coconut pudding that jiggles like Iris Chacón's hips Sunday nights en *El Show de Iris Chacón.*

See also*: flans; tembleques; guava diplomacy; Iris Chacón.*

Día de Reyes *n. (DEE-ah deh RAY-ehs)* — holiday

The Epiphany, January 6, the morning after the all-night Fiesta de Reyes. In scripture, the Wise Men brought gold, frankincense, and myrrh; in Puerto Rico they brought Tonka trucks, Barbies, Atari consoles and proof that Santa Claus was merely a North American understudy.

Tradition:
Children left shoeboxes of grass for camels. By morning the grass had mysteriously vanished; either camel hunger or parental cleanup panic. Families dressed for Mass, feasted on pasteles, pernil, and turrón that glued your morals together like divine penance.

Act II (of course there was one): After surviving our own house party, staff cleared the terrazzo floors of confetti, bones, and empty Veuve Clicquot bottles while we piled into cars for

Villalba or Juana Díaz, where Condado's glitter gave way to parrandas with cuatros, güiros and aguinaldos. The whiplash was glorious: aristocratic hangover meets rural redemption.

Fun Fact: Juana Díaz hosts the island's most famous Reyes parade; live camels, magi in sequins, and pageantry that makes the Rose Bowl look like a PTA picnic.

Survival Rule:
If you can survive Condado at 3 a.m. and Villalba by noon, you're spiritually FEMA-certified.

Personal Note:
My father treated it like it was a holy victory —
Santa 0, Reyes 1.

Famous Quote:
"Aquí los Reyes son los que mandan." — Every Puerto Rican dad, dunking on Santa Claus.

See also: *Fiesta de Reyes (Jan.5); Santa Claus (the understudy); camel logistics.*

Dios Nos Libre *interj. (dee-OHS nohs LEE-bray)* — hex

May the Lord spare us… from whatever fresh chaos you just mentioned. Used by abuelas, tías, and women in rolos as the verbal equivalent of pepper spray.

Usage:
"¿Te imaginas si tu prima se casa con ese tipo? — ¡Dios nos libre! crosses herself and stares into middle distance.

Also applies to tattoos, politicians, and exes with new podcasts.

Fun Fact:

Saying “Dios nos libre” creates a protective bubble of holy shade. Bonus points if followed by a sigh and a dramatic window gaze.

Modern Update:
Now available as a WhatsApp sticker, Etsy pillow, and Facebook caption for cousins who are “going through it.”

Famous Quote:
“Dios nos libre de los hombres casados, los préstamos estudiantiles, y los ex que quieren volver.”— Abuela, sipping Yaucono, with full lashes at 6 a.m.

See also: Virgen Santísima; Ay Bendito; La Señal de la Cruz; Divine Block Button

Doctor Milián *n. masc. (dok-TOR mee-LYAN)* —doctor/guru

Dad’s EST— era self-help messiah whose only prescription was "Focus". Half cult, half fortune cookie, fully licensed by nobody.

Usage:
Invoked whenever Dad wanted to sound mystical and avoid apologizing.

Fun Fact:
His signature quote: “If the sun focuses through a magnifying glass, it burns a hole in the paper.” It was mostly burned-out patience.

Modern Update:
Prototype for today’s influencers who sell clarity candles and cryptocurrency courses. Would have a podcast called “Focus.” Three listeners. All cult members.

See also: *self-help sorcery; TED Talk trauma; The Church of Hustle*

Don Cholito (José Miguel Agrelot) *n. prop. (dohn cho-LEE-toh)* — comedian

Puerto Rican radio and TV legend; part clown, part preacher, full-time caffeine substitute. His morning show began before dawn, revving the island awake with jokes, jingles, and moral lessons disguised as slapstick.

Personal Note:
When I was nineteen, my father arranged for me to appear on *El Show de Don Cholito en la Radio.* Call time **5 a.m.** I arrived in full lip-liner optimism, wondering if this was my big break or an elaborate prank.

Don Cholito squinted through the studio's haze, looked me up and down, and said I reminded him of **Anjelica Houston**. At that hour, I took it as prophecy. In retrospect, he meant I looked like someone who'd already seen too much.

Legacy Venue:
Puerto Rico's *Coliseo José Miguel Agrelot,* lovingly nicknamed *El Choliseo*, the only arena on earth named after a comedian. Bad Bunny now holds court there like the heir to our laugh lineage.

Modern Coda:
What's more Puerto Rican than Don Cholito? Bad Bunny yelling, "Esta es mi casa," on the same stage.
Comedy → reggaetón → cosmic continuity.

Famous Quote:
"No es Don Cholito, es el pulso de mi mañana".

See also: *Radio Reloj; El Choliseo; José Miguel Agrelot; Bad Bunny; fathers moonlighting as talent agents*

E

El Conquistador *n. masc. (el con-KEES-tah-dor)* — hotel

Puerto Rico's Versailles by the Sea. Perched on a cliff in Fajardo, El Conquistador was the five-star playground where excess wasn't optional; it was the dress code. Opened in 1962, it reincarnated under Sheraton, Hyatt, and Waldorf Astoria banners, each promising more chandeliers, more marble and more ways to max out your AmEx.

Why it mattered:
Not just a hotel, a destination. Locals spoke of it like a scandalous cousin, equal parts awe, envy and shade. Families saved for months to splurge a weekend and returned sunburned, broke and spiritually upgraded.

Aesthetic:
Bond-villain lair meets Caribbean flair — cliffside pools cascading into the sea, a golf course unrolling like a green, red carpet, and the pièce de resistance: Palomino Island… on the islet reachable only by ferry. Your tan wasn't complete until you'd been shipped off to an island-within-an-island.

Personal lore:
Estrella and I once arrived on her father's yacht, believing we had transcended class and melanin. We slathered ourselves in Hawaiian Tropic oil, not sunscreen, and spent hours turning like rotisserie chickens under the Caribbean sun.

The trip felt like luxury. The aftermath looked like National Geographic. Weeks later, we were peeling like lizards. Decades later, dermatologists call it what it truly was: permanent sun damage with a view.

Family lore:

- Abuela declared it "too much" yet stole the stationery.

- Tíos closed "business deals" in the lobby where rum flowed like holy water.
- Quinceañeras posed on the grand staircase auditioning for Miss Universe.

Fun Fact:
In the '80s —'90s, "We stayed at El Conquistador" translated to "we'll be bragging about this until Lent."
Modern update: After Hurricane María, it reopened in 2021 with rebirth marketing. Island gossip insists the glamour peaked when the ice buckets looked expensive.

Famous Quote (tourist edition):
"El Conquistador has everything; except reasonable prices." — Every Puerto Rican dad, post-checkout.

See also: *Condado Vanderbilt (old-money cousin; La Concha (party sibling); Oso Blanco (the only fortress with that much gossip)*

Final wink:
If it had a TED talk, it'd be titled *How to Spend Like a Colony.*

Electrolysis *n. (ee-lehk-TROL-uh-sis)* — beauty treatment

Marketed as "permanent hair removal," experienced as the Spanish Inquisition with better lighting.

Process:
Insert a micro needle into each follicle. Zap it. Whisper a prayer to the patron saint of cosmetic suffering. Alleged results: smooth skin. Side effects: scabs, swelling, trauma, and a sudden desire to join Witness Protection.

Clinics:

Run by women with Slavic accents, bulletproof lashes, and the bedside manner of efficient executioners. Motivational poster featured bearded ladies captioned: *This Could Be You.*

Cultural Role:
For many Latinas, not self-care, survival. Skip it and invite whispered comparisons to circus performers. Endure it and walk around with an upper lip that looks like it lost a bar fight.

See also: *Waxing (pain in strip form); bleaching (smells like death; looks like neglect); Sin dolor no hay belleza (the Latina adolescent anthem)*

Final wink:
If Goop sold it, they'd call it *Follicle Shadow Work™* and charge $600 a session.

El General *n. masc. (ehl-hen-ERAHL)* — family patriarch

Not a general, self-anointed commander of cattle, children, and anyone within shouting distance. Born in the 1890s, tempered by San Felipe and San Cipriano hurricanes, El General treated life like a battlefield and his family like raw recruits.

Origin story:
A self-made man who clawed up from scandal. Whispers say his mother was Black, a truth his descendants handled like a contagious disease. Light-skinned enough to pass, he willed himself into real estate, built Puerto Rico's answer to *Home Depot*, and furnished island homes while emptying his own of joy.

Marriage:
New Year's Eve wedding. Maman hated the anniversary on principle. Why toast love if it arrives pre-packaged with a hangover?

Parenting style:
Cattle rancher meets Catholic sadist. Daughters knelt on gravel "for discipline." After all night partying with La Gata, his sons were yanked out of bed at 3:00 a.m. to round up cattle. My mother never mentioned him without a migraine.

Personality notes:
Frugal, domineering, allergic to his daughters' freedom. He controlled what he feared: pregnancy, chaos, and mirrors.

Legacy:
He was a tycoon and tyrant. Proof that Puerto Rican men could build empires from nothing and lose the plot at home.

Fun Fact:
Today he'd be canceled on Twitter and trending on Netflix's *True Crime.*

See also: *patriarchal trauma; gravel rosaries; cattle call at dawn; generational migraines*

Final wink:
His love language was inventory.

El Hamburger *n. masc. (el ahm-bur-GEHR)* — diner

Grease-slick temple in Puerta de Tierra facing the ocean. After the discos closed, sweaty dancers and drunk aristocrats collided here over the greasiest burgers in San Juan. Open until 5:00 a.m., it saved livers and a few marriages from regrettable detours.

Usage:
"Nos vemos en El Hamburger"= surrender to cholesterol and salvation in sesame-seed form.

Fun Fact:
Its neon was a lighthouse for the polyester weary. Politicians, beauty queens, and disco kings, ended here eventually, equalized by grease and exhaustion.

Survival tip:
Order fast. Your hangover depends on it.

Modern Update:
Still standing, it is equal parts tourist stop and nostalgia machine. In its heyday? El Hamburger was the Vatican of 3:00 a.m. burgers.

See also: *Isadora; Juliana's; Flying Saucer; liver triage; polyester afterlife*

Final wink:
If confession came with fires, it was here.

El Vocero *n. masc. (el-bo-SEH-ro)* — newspaper

'70s —'80s tabloid newspaper which served as a public service announcement for collective trauma. Headlines screamed in blood-red above the full body crime photos — no blur, no shame, just breakfast.

Personal Note:

Maman read *El Vocero* daily while clutching a rosary like a fact-checking device. Anytime I dared mention a dream, a plan, or even a theoretical boyfriend, she'd lower the paper just enough to deliver her signature prophecy:

"*Cuando eso pase estaré en la fábrica de botones.*"

(When that happens, I will be in the button factory.)

Meaning, *I'll be dead.*

Back in the day, buttons were made from bones, and apparently so were our metaphors.

Fun Fact:

If it bled, it led. Vendors sold it rolled like a *taquito*, so you wouldn't frighten children on the walk home. Abuelas claimed to hate it yet quoted every headline.

Famous Quote:

"*¡Mira eso, nena! ¡Ay, Dios mío, ¡qué barbaridad! Salió en El Vocero." — Mamán*

See also: El Nuevo Día; The San Juan Star; TV-Guía

El Zipperle *n. obs.* (el-ZEE-pehr-leh) — restaurant

Hato Rey's cathedral of consumption, where steaks were rare, deals medium-well, and marital vows came with a side of rice and beans. Founded in 1953 and demolished in January 2018, El Zipperle wasn't just a restaurant; it was Puerto Rico's answer to the United Nations of Secrets.

Cuisine:
Officially, "Spanish with German flair." Unofficially: whatever the rich ordered after pretending to read the menu. Signature flex? Complimentary tostones with avocado; because nothing says status like free carbs served by a man in white gloves.

Décor:
Think Bavarian telenovela. Tuxedoed waiters in black tails sprinted between "family rooms" (translation: tax deductible trysts) as violins crooned over whispered bribes. The dessert cart's Thousand-Layer Cake was so decadent it qualified for dual citizenship in the Cayman Islands.

Personal Note:
When I came home from Swarthmore, Papi and Don Sixto de la Siesta, Caribbean CEO of ErgoLuxe Beds held our ritual summits

here. Ceasar salads spun tableside. J&B on the rocks. Stories so unbelievable they could've been audited.

After Mami passed, he still booked the private rooms, only now they filled with young Dominican women who wanted his money more than his melancholy. The maître d' knew his drink, his heartbreak, and his credit limit. It was both tragic and fabulous.

Scandal:
Eventually seized by Hacienda for $150 million in unpaid IVU; enough to fund three seasons of a telenovela called *The Auditors of Love.*

Legacy:
Demolished in 2018, ending a 65-year reign of steak, secrets, and sauce-stained dignity. The IRS should've given it a Michelin star for Evasion.

Quote from a chilla (corner booth, 2008):
"He loved his wife but ordered the cake for me. That's when I knew I was the investment."

See also: *Power-lunch purgatory; Michelin Guide to Marital Denial; Hacienda's favorite dining spot.*

Final Wink:
Come for the filet, stay for the audit, and tip well, because ghosts still haunt the check.

Empanadillas *n. fem. pl. (em-pah-nah-DEE-yahs)*— food

Puerto Rico's answer to Hot Pockets if Hot Pockets were seasoned, deep-fried, and blessed by sofrito. You can order the beef, chicken, or pizza (yes, pizza) ones. They scorch the roof of your mouth and still make you order two more.

Usage:
Beach rule: the grease will beat the napkin every time.

See also: *pastelillos, bacalaítos, alcapurrias, sofrito.*

Final Wink:
If you can hold it without dropping oil on your shirt, you're not doing it right.

Escondido *n. adj. masc. (es-con-DEE-do)* — ghost

Literally "hidden." In family life, the person, object, or scandal tucked away when company comes. Could be a cousin, questionable tattoos, a child with questionable volume control, or cash under Abuela's mattress.

Usage:
Tener un escondido is both a verb and a survival tactic. "Deja al nene escondido antes que llegue la suegra. Ese dinero está escondido, no lo toques. Esconde las prendas que viene la sirvienta."

Fun Fact:
Every family has at least one. Some escondidos are human (uncle who drinks too much), edible (secret flan Tupperware), or financial (folded bills inside the Bible).

Modern Update:
On Instagram, escondidos are curated; they appear in one filtered Christmas photo, then vanish like seasonal décor. Bonus category: burner accounts and secret Uber receipts.

Famous Quote:
"Ese es mi primo… pero mejor que se quede escondido." — Every tía at a quinceañera.

See also: *chilla; dinero debajo del colchón; fachada familiar*

Final Wink:
If your family says "nadie lo menciona," expect a slideshow.

Escrava Isaura (The Slave Isaura) *n. (ehs-KRAH-vah ee-SAH-oo-rah)*—telenovela

Brazilian classic (1976, rebroadcast into eternity). Lucélia Santos plays Isaura, the saintliest enslaved woman ever to cry in empire-waist gowns.

Plot vibe:
Born enslaved, raised like a lady. Leônicio, a villain with a graduate degree in obsession, schemes across 100 episodes. *Pride and Prejudice* meets *The Handmaid's Tale* with violins, plantations, and sighing.

Cultural Footprint:
It was a global gateway drug. From Latin American to Eastern Europe to China, poor Isaura went viral long before Netflix discovered subtitles.

Personal Note:
Vero, Cata, and I watched *Escrava Isaura* in Don Vi's van; sunburned, snack-loaded, and spiritually undone. That's where my first survival lessons began: before therapy, before feminism, before subtitles.

Survival metaphor:
Stuck with a tyrant boss, toxic ex, or eternal WhatsApp family chat? Congratulations, you're living in your Isaura era: saintly hair, bureaucratic chains, heroic endurance.

See also: *telenovela logic; martyrdom chic; melodrama export*

Final wink:
If tears earned royalties, Isaura would own *Televisa.*

Ese gato no tiene vergüenza *phr. (EH-she GAH-toh no TYEH-neh vehr-GWEHN-sah) — philosophy*

Said of cats who steal food and people who steal lives; shameless, bold, and usually purring about it.

Usage Note:
Applies equally to a tabby licking his kiwis and a tío borrowing your car for "five minutes" and returning it three days later, out of gas.

See also: *gatera; sinvergüenza; Tracy cat (house CEO)*

Espiritistas *n. pl. (ehs-pee-ree TEAS-tahs) — psychics*

Puerto Rican spiritual mediums equal parts healer, therapist, and ghost whisperer. Think your abuela's therapist meets Miss Cleo, but with more candles and fewer commercials
A person who communicates with spirits, seeking guidance or healing, usually through prayer, trance, or divination.

In Puerto Rico, *espiritistas* come in two main flavors:

- *Intelectuales*: Think book club with ghosts
- *Populares:* Your cousin's neighbor who heals with a rosary, rum and a coconut

Usage Note:
Not to be confused with brujas (though the lines get blurry). If someone tells you, "*Mi tía fue a donde la espiritista,*" it might

mean anything from seeking advice about a breakup to figuring out why the neighbors plants keep dying mysteriously.

Fun Fact:
Espiritismo arrived in Puerto Rico via smuggled books from France, became popular among the elite, and eventually rooted itself in the rural *campos*. Despite the Spanish crown banning it, espiritistas still popped up kitchens, churches and the occasional beauty salon.

Personal Note:
My mother's family comes from a long line of *espiritistas*, women who prayed, poured rum, and negotiated with the dead like seasoned diplomats. By the time *Escrava Isaura* aired, channeling spirits felt less like witchcraft and more like another form of customer service.

Modern Update:
Today, espiritistas are on WhatsApp, charging Venmo donations for limpias and channeling messages from beyond during Facebook lives. Some espiritistas even run full-blown churches.

Famous Quote:
"*La Muerte no es final; es el voicemail espiritual.*" Translation: "Death isn't the end; it's just the spirit world's voicemail."

See also: *brujería; limpias; rezos; la Iglesia según su espíritu; tu prima que siente cosas*

F

(For fear, fractions, and the F that started it all)

Sra. Calcetín *n. fem.* (she-noh-rah kahl-she-TEEN) — sadist

Math teacher, ruler enthusiast, knuckle disciplinarian, sadist. She was the terror of Academia San José's math wing. A woman who believed geometry could be taught through trauma and velocity (of her ruler).

Origin Story:
No one remembers her first name. She appeared one September morning smelling of chalk and
Violetas perfume; the cheap violet scent that still triggers my hives and my fight-or-flight. By Christmas, she'd converted half the class to left-handed writing.

Lesson Style:

- Problem wrong? Ruler.
- Problem right but tone sarcastic? Ruler.
- Ask why x refuses to be found? Extra ruler.

Long Term Side Effects:

- Knuckles permanently concave.
- Fear of fractions, forgiveness, and authority figures named after clothing.
- Flashbacks whenever I smell violet anything.

Personal Note:
In 5th grade I earned a bright red F, my first and only, triggering a *Warning Card* and a family summit that rivaled Vatican II.

Usage Note:
"Sra. Calcetín gave me an F in math class."
Translation: "I'm bad at calculus and emotionally unavailable."

Famous Quote:
"You think life gives partial credit?"
— Sra. Calcetín, circa 1983

See also: *Episode 51; Ruler Trauma; Catholic Math Miracles; Fear-Based Education; F for formative damage.*

Fiesta de Reyes *n., fem. (FEES-tah-da-RAY-ehs) — holiday*

January 5th, the night before the Epiphany, when *Los Tres Santos Reyes*, the Three Holy Magi, brought baby Jesus gold, frankincense, and myrrh (the original luxury gift set). For Latin Americans, this was the holiday, a holy mash-up of incense, Catholic guilt, and camel logistics.

Also happens to land on Armenian Christmas Eve, proving even calendars get confused.

Usage Note:
" *Voy a celebrar la Fiesta de Reyes.*" Translation: "I will be up all-night cutting grass for imaginary camels and pretending my parents didn't buy the gifts I'm about to 'discover'."

Tradition:
Children filled shoeboxes with freshly cut grass for the Magi's camels, then slid them under their parents' bed; as if the camels would politely kneel on terrazzo floors. By morning, the trail of grass always led to the toys. Magic? More like parental vacuuming nightmares.

Fun Fact:
Famously celebrated in Juana Díaz, Puerto Rico, where the Magi parade through the town with all the pomp of a royal wedding, only with more sequins and horses.

Personal Note:

My father's favorite holiday. It outranked Christmas, Santa, and even the Epiphany itself. For him, this was the day religion and razzle-dazzle finally got it right. Every year, our nanny **Lolo** would take **Vero, Cata and me** to **El Morro** to see the live camels; a spectacle equal parts holiness and humidity (*see Episode 16*). The smell of hay, churros, and overexcited camels still sounds like my unofficial religious awakening.

Modern Update:
In some families, the camels have been outsourced to Amazon Prime. Shoeboxes are now Venmo requests.

Famous Quote:
"*No es Santa Claus… son los Reyes.*"
— Every Puerto Rican dad, triumphantly, on January 6.

See also: *Día de Reyes (Jan. 6); Santa Claus (the understudy); Juana Díaz Parade*

Filiberto Ojeda Ríos *n. prop. (fee-lee-BEHR-toh oh-HEH-dah REE-ohs)* — man

A name whispered like family scandal at the dinner table: half patriot, half outlaw, full Puerto Rican legend. Trumpet player by training, revolutionary by trade, and FBI nightmare by destiny.

Backstory:
In the 1970s and 80s, Filiberto co-founded and led *Los Macheteros,* a pro-independence clandestine group. Their most infamous hit? The 1983 Wells Fargo depot heist in West Hartford, Connecticut: $7 million in cash. The kind of number that makes abuelas clutch their rosaries and tías suddenly "remember" they were part of the crew.

Family Lore Cross-Ref:

At one point, the FBI even suspected my father had been kidnapped by Filiberto (Episode 50)

Spoiler: It was less thriller and more telenovela misunderstanding.

Fugitive Years:
Filiberto slipped through FBI manhunts with more flair than a novela villain until September 23, 2005; the anniversary of El Grito de Lares. Surrounded in Hormigueros, he died in a shootout. For some, a martyr; for others, a terrorist; for everyone complicated.

Usage Note:
Say "Filiberto" in Puerto Rico and watch the room split: half whisper *héroe* with reverence, half mutter *terrorista* with disdain, and everyone agrees he looked better in his trumpet-playing days.

Fun Fact:
Once a professional musician, proving that only in Puerto Rico can a trumpet player moonlight as a most-wanted revolutionary.

Modern Update:
His face lives on in murals, protest signs, and niche Twitter threads debating whether to remember him as Puerto Rico's Robin Hood or its Al Capone.

Famous Quote:
"*Puerto Rico será libre.*"
— Filiberto Ojeda Ríos, countless times with more conviction than most people say "*sí*" to dessert.

See also: *Lolita Lebrón; Albizu Campos; El Grito de Lares*

Flamboyanes *n. pl. (flahm-buoy-AH-nehs)* — botany

Puerto Rico's drama queen tree. Bursts into fiery red every summer, just to prove it's hotter than you. Nothing says "I love you" like passing out under a flamboyán in July heatstroke.

Usage Notes:
Ideal backdrop for quince photos, tearful telenovela farewells, or your abuela's rocking chair wisdom.

Fun Fact:
Also called the "flame tree," but let's be honest, it's just showing off.

Modern Update:
Today, it's basically Puerto Rico's Instagram filter.

Famous Quote:
"Meet me under the *flamboyán."*
Translation: Bring a fan and maybe a towel.

See also: *piragua; heatstroke; island nostalgia*

Fried Cholesterol Death Appetizers *n. pl. (frahyd koh-lehs-THE-rohl DETH ap-peh-TEE-sers)* — snacks

The golden quartet of Puerto Rican survival food, designed to clog arteries and silence gossip in equal measure.

- *Alcapurrias*: meat torpedoes of joy.
- *Surullitos*: cornmeal fingers of fried therapy.
- *Bolitas de queso*: fried cheese cannonballs.
- *Pastelillitos de queso y carne:* turnovers fried in oil and Catholic guilt.

Usage Note:

Best eaten scalding hot, standing by the fryer, pretending supplies are scarce while your cousin burns his fingers stealing the last one.

Fun Fact:
At any Puerto Rican party, these appetizers function as edible speed bumps. They slow down the rum long enough to keep the band going until dawn.

Survival Tip:
Never be the last to reach the tray. In the time it takes to blink, abuela will have "saved" the best ones for herself.

See also: *Grease is a Love Language; Cardiologist Avoidance Tactics; Fryer Vigilance Protocol*

Focus™ *v. masc. (FUK-uhs)* — mantra

The all-purpose gospel of the 1970s self-help culture. Imported into Puerto Rican households by fathers who read *Think and Grow Rich* once and never recovered. The belief that all of life's problems, from global recession to bad grades to marital infidelity can be solved if you just "focus harder."

Applications in my house:

- Homework undone? Focus.
- Mother, mid-tantrum? Focus.
- Puerto Rican electricity blackout? Focus (with candles).

Side Effects:
Joylessness, perfectionism, the inability to eat arroz con dulce without someone asking if you're "focused."

See also: *productivity cult; magnifying glass theology; Dr. Milián's retirement plan*

G

Gatera *adj. fem. (gah-THE-rah)* —identity

A household hopelessly devoted to cats. Not just owns cats, but **breathes cats**, decorates with cats, and prefers cats to roughly 80 percent of humanity.

The way some people are oenophiles (wine), audiophiles (sound), or bibliophiles (books), **gateras** are felinophiles — except less academic, more hairballs.

Usage Note:
To call a family gatera is both affectionate and diagnostic. It means they will:

- Interrupt a conversation to discuss a cat's bowel movements.
- Keep lint rollers in every room like fire extinguishers.
- Refer to the cat as *mi hijo* while ignoring actual children in the room.

Fun Fact:
Our clan is unapologetically gatera. Where other families kept guard dogs, we had tabbies sprawled on Mercedes' hoods. Where others hung portraits of ancestors, we displayed glamour shots of our Himalayan Persians.

Modern Update:
Instagram has weaponized the *gatera* identity. What used to be a private mania is now a public brand: cats with their own Reels. TikToks and Amazon wish lists. Being *gatera* is no longer eccentric; it's aspirational.

Famous Quote:
"*Si no le gustan los gatos, no puede ser Buena persona.*"
— Every *tía* vetoing suitors since 1950.

See also: *Crazy Cat Lady (the colonial translation); Escondido; Tracy (house CEO)*

González Padín *n. prop. obsolete (gon-SAH-les pah-DEEN)* — store

The island's department store of record in Old San Juan. Puerto Rico's answer to Macy's, Bloomingdale's— and Christmas all rolled into one. For most of the 20th century, González Padín defined "elegant shopping," from perfumes in crystal bottles to ribboned packages, and counters polished like altars. Shopping there wasn't a transaction—It was ceremony.

Why it mattered:
Their heirs went to Academia San José, cementing the brand's place in the island's upper-middle-class mythology. But for kids, it wasn't the social cachet that mattered.

It was the magic.

Vitrinas navideñas:
Every December, the Old San Juan flagship transformed into a wonderland. The **vitrinas** — lavish Christmas window displays—were pilgrimage sites. Families lined up just to see them sparkle before heading inside to buy ribbons, gloves, or one perfect gift.

For us, it was ritual: Cata, Vero and I pressed our faces to the glass, then ran inside with Lolo, who made every visit feel like a holiday. Afterward, we crossed the street to *Plaza de Armas* for hot chocolate thick enough to patch potholes, and a *quesito* — Puerto Rico's answer to therapy, Botox, and Prozac spilled into one buttery triangle.

Aesthetic:

Shiny counters. Polished floors. Salespeople who wrapped gifts like they were preparing them for the Vatican. González Padín didn't sell things; **it conferred adulthood.**

Family Lore:

- Christmas wasn't Christmas without a trip to the *vitrinas.*
- Abuelas kept the ribbons long after the gifts were gone.
- For many, it was the first place you felt grown-up enough to buy something with your own allowance.

Modern Update:
By the late 1990s, the glamour faded. Today, the Old San Juan flagship is a **Marshalls** — fluorescent lights, bargain bins, and none of the magic.

But in memory, *González Padín* remains the gold standard of Puerto Rican retail elegance.

Famous Quote (family edition):
"*Vamos a González Padín.*"
Translation: Christmas has officially begun.

See also: *Oui Boutique (the chic cousin); La Equina Famosa (menswear altar); Sears (mainland invasion)*

H

Holsum *n. pl. (Haul-soom*) — company/diplomacy

Puerto Rico's most delicious act of class betrayal. Not so much dessert as an edible passport, granting you entry into bingo tables, novenas, and even the fiercest neighborhood grudges. The frosting could survive a hurricane, a blackout, and your cousin's third divorce.

Why It Mattered:
Holsum wasn't just cake; it was class commentary. A store-bought peace offering that said *I was raised right* without having to bake a thing. To arrive without it was social bankruptcy; to bring Entenmann's was cultural treason.

Aesthetic:
A plastic clamshell of moral ambiguity. The logo screamed "*wholesome*", but everyone knew it was mostly preservatives and guilt.

Family Lore:
In our house, bringing a pre-packaged dessert was considered déclassé, an insult to my mother's Cordon-Bleu-by-osmosis baking skills.

"Only working women bring Holsum," she'd whisper, as if the plastic wrap itself carried moral decline.

Naturally those same "working women" arrived at parties in heels, unbothered, with perfect hair and unburned forearms. They were the future.

Fun Fact (a.k.a. Corporate Telenovela):
Holsum arrived in Puerto Rico in the 1950s, imported from Miami. By 1958, the brand was so beloved it set up its own island bakery, feeding our collective sweet tooth *and* class anxiety.

In 1983, U.S. giant Seaboard Corporation bought it — but in 1998, local management staged a novela-worthy coup, buying it back and reclaiming Holsum as a national treasure glazed in independence.

Modern Update:
Today, Holsum employs over 850 people across Puerto Rico—proof that a donut brand can outlast colonialism, heartbreak, and your mom's judgement.

Personal Note:
Despite my mother's disdain, I'd sneak boxes of Holsum donuts to Carmina's house. We'd devour them in secret, high on sugar and rebellion, then hide the empty boxes under her bed — our pastry crimes buried like evidence of teenage joy.

See also: *Bingo-night economics; edible bribes; survival pastries*

I

IBM Selectric *n. fem. obs. (eye-bee-EM she-LEK-trik) —* typewriter

Epigraph:
The typewriter that launched a thousand term papers — and one minor electrical fire.

The diva of typewriters. Introduced in 1961 and instantly crowned queen of the office. Forget clacking keys — this beauty spun a little metal "golf-ball" head that whirled like Studio 54 in miniature, stamping each letter with ruthless precision. Secretaries worshipped it. Executives flexed with it. Novelists swore it made them smarter (or at least more legible).

Why It Mattered:
The Selectric wasn't just technology; it was an attitude. The Tiffany lamp of office equipment. It hummed with authority, purred with precision, and carried the faint musk of existential purpose, and cigarette smoke.

Aesthetic:
Beige body, chrome trim, confidence of a cocktail hostess. Each keystroke came with a satisfying *thwack* and the assurance you were producing something important— even if it was just a passive-aggressive memo.

Family Lore:
My father, proud IBM man, once brought one home: a gleaming Selectric that looked like the future and weighed as much as a small horse. Vero and I, sensing new entertainment, immediately cast it in our game El Cuco — a ghost story meets interpretive dance involving a white bedsheet, dramatic shrieks, and an open glass of water.

The climax: one shriek, one splash, and a typewriter that sparkled like a séance gone wrong.

Papi, unamused, took it to be repaired and muttered, "Next time just pour the water directly on top."

The machine survived — barely — and became my first creative partner: companion of term papers, teenage manifestos, and the earliest verses I ever dared to type. Every sentence smelled faintly of ozone and guilt.

Fun Fact:
The Selectric's claim to fame was its interchangeable "golf-ball" typehead, the original font flex. Swap Courier for Prestige Elite and suddenly you were Hemingway — with a secretary.

Modern Update:
Laptops won, leaving the Selectric in the museum of analog authority. It now haunts vintage shops, writer Instagrams, and the dreams of boomers who still miss carbon copies. Also doubles as an excellent doorstop — or, in my case, a relic of childhood mischief and literary awakening.

See also: Carbon paper (the messy copy machine); *Wite-Out* (liquid regret); *Olivetti* (the pretty cousin); *WordPerfect* (when computers tried to act like typewriters)

Infamia *n. (een-FAH-mee-ah)* —cultural reference/betrayal on steroids, telenovela

Mexican telenovela (Televisa 1981), produced by Ernesto Alonso and starring Susana Dosamantes (glamour weaponized) and Fernando Allende (hair so glossy it had its own lighting budget). The title means, *infamy*, and the plot delivers: betrayals, forbidden love, chandeliers and villains with PHDs in eyebrow arch.

Plot vibe:
Not as global as *Los Ricos También Lloran*, but pure Televisa alchemy — melodrama wrapped in Catholic guild and shoulder pads that doubled as defensive armor.

Cultural footprint:
A textbook Televisa export; less internationally famous, but spiritually militant. Every betrayal came with organ music, heavy eyeliner, and at least one dramatic staircase.

Survival Guide Metaphor:
If your name gets dragged in the group chat or Tia Lucha is "just asking questions" at bingo, *felicidades* — you're living your own *Infamia.* You'll survive but expect at least 50 episodes of side-eye and soft-focus lighting first.

See also*: Telenovela logic; melodramatic eyebrows; Ernesto Alonso Industrial Complex*

Iris Chacón *n. fem. (EE-rees chak- UHN)* — entertainer /cultural earthquake

Puerto Rico's original vedette and Sunday-night-sacrament — the woman who put the island's rear end on the map long before J-Lo was stretching for P.E. Sequins, mink coats and hair that defied humidity and the Pope.

Cultural Impact:
In the '70s and '80s, families gathered like it were mass. Abuelas, uncles, toddlers, and priests sat transfixed as Iris sang "*Tu eres caramelo chocolate*" in a feathered bikini. It was wholesome family programming and free sex education in one.

Showstopper Moment:

The legendary "ass solo" to *Burbujas de Amor*. Puerto Rican living rooms fell silent — only the sound of rosaries dropping onto terrazzo.

International Stint:
May 30, 1984, *Late Night with David Letterman.* She shook maracas and Western sensibilities simultaneously. Scandal ensued; the island beamed.

Rumor Mill:
Breasts allegedly imported. Butt: confirmed local production.

Signature Look:
White mink in August, Rolls idling outside, and a perfect mole above the eyebrow — the punctuation of sin.

Famous Quote (family edition):
"That ass was a national treasure."

See also: *vedette; Juan Luis Guerra; La Bomba Puertorriqueña; J-Lo (the sequel).*

Isadora *n. fem. (eeh-zaa-DOOR-ah)* — nightclub

The velvet temple of *Friday Night Fever*. Isadora was where Condado Plaza marble met polyester, and gossip spread faster than piña-colada brain freeze. Politicians with side lovers, beauty queens still sticky with Aqua Net, and disco kings in platforms all spun beneath mirror balls the size of midlife crises.

Etymology Note:
Named for Isadora Duncan — tragic, glamorous, and fond of scarves — making her the perfect patron saint for San Juan nightlife and poor decisions.

Usage Note:
"Nos vemos en Isadora" translated to sequins, scandal, and somebody's divorce paperwork inching forward.

Fun Fact:
In 1978, tightrope walker Karl Wallenda attempted to cross between the hotel towers. The winds disagreed. He plunged into history — and Isadora's mythology — as the only man to literally fall for San Juan nightlife.

Nightlife Curriculum:
Survive Friday at Isadora, Saturday at Juliana's and Sunday at the Flying Saucer and you earned a PhD in polyester sociology.

Modern Update:
If Isadora existed today, it would be a rooftop lounge with $18 mojitos and LED angel wings for influencers. But the original? Untouchable — frozen forever in glitter, gossip, and 1983 humidity.

See also: *Weekend Disco Circuit; Polyester Saints; Aqua Net Archives; Tragic Glamour*

J

Jacks *n. pl. (JAKS)*— game

The lost sport of sitting on the floor. One rubber ball, a fistful of jagged torture stars, and hours of kneecap endurance masquerading as *fun.*

Origins:
Dates to ancient Greece, Egypt, and even prehistory, when kids tossed animal knucklebones — prehistoric *Squid Game* energy. By the 20th century, shiny metal or plastic versions flooded dime storers and Puerto Rican pantries, imported by well-meaning parents who believed in **character building boredom.**

Cultural Impact:
For Puerto Ricans growing up in the '60s-80s, jacks were a *marquesina* staple; played while mothers fried tostones and chaperones supervised from plastic lawn chairs. Losing a jack under the sofa was tragedy; stepping on one barefoot was a death sentence.

Usage Note:
"Jugamos jacks."
Translation:
"We destroyed our cuticles for glory."

Modern Update:
Occasionally resurrected as a "mindfulness toy" for *millenials* — proof no one under forty knows what boredom is anymore.

Famous Quote:
"Siéntate y juega jacks, deja de molestar."

See also: *retro trauma; Stranger Things nostalgia; marquesina survival kits*

Jíbaro *n. masc. (HEE-bah-roh)* — archetype.

Originally the mountain farmers of Puerto Rico: men in straw hats (*pavas*), with machetes, coffee breath, and an unshakable ability to make a guitar sound like heartbreak.

Once mocked as rural and backward, the jíbaro was eventually rebranded into a cultural icon — **the soulful backbone of the island.**

Usage Note:
To call someone jíbaro can be an insult ("provincial bumpkin") or the highest badge of authenticity, depending on whether you're in San Juan or up in the hills

Fun Fact:
Every Christmas, música jíbara takes over the airwaves — cuatros, güiros and aguinaldos designed to make city kids feel rustic for three months.
(Yes, Christmas in Puerto Rico is the longest in the world: from Thanksgiving to Las Fiestas de San Sebastián in February.)

Modern Update:
Today, jíbaro chic runs the gamut from folkloric carols to Bad Bunny strutting a designer *pava* onstage.

Translation:
What once meant milking cows at dawn is now a Fashion Week accessory.

See also: *pava; cuatro; aguinaldo; Bad Bunny*

Juliana's *n. fem.(jou-LIAH-nahs)* — nightclub

The high-end sequel.

Juliana's at the Caribe Hilton was where old money shook its hips — stiffly, but with conviction.

If Isadora was about sparkle, Juliana's was about **status**. Saturday night here wasn't just a party; it was a masterclass in surviving the aristocracy without tripping over hotel carpet in heels.

Usage Note:
To say "Nos vemos en Juliana's — meant you were either old money, dating old money, or praying no one asked what your last name was.

Fun Fact:
My father was a member, which gave me a front-row seat to the spectacle: mink stoles parked next to martinis, Bee Gees blaring louder than whispered mergers, and ladies balancing tiaras of Aqua Net with deadly precision.

Personal Note:
The Calderonas would chaperone us, solemn as security guards, planted in their reserved booth — eyes scanning, jaws set — until the second round of drinks, when even they surrendered to "*Staying Alive.*"

Felino and the UFOS (crew of San Ignacio gay men) escorted us like sequined bodyguards: all wit, cologne and survival instincts. I wore heels that made me tower — a skyscraper among polyester. I fell a little in love with the club manager; who was in his thirties and thank God, old enough to know better.

Modern Update:
If Juliana's existed today, it would be a velvet-rope lounge with bottle service, $300 champagne "trees," and influencers posing like they owned stock in the Hilton. But in the '70s? It was polyester royalty court, where Bee Gees dictated foreign policy.

See also: *Isadora; Caribe Hilton; polyester diplomacy; the aristocracy in platforms; Weekend Disco Circuit*

Justino Díaz *n. prop. (hoo-STEEN-oh DEE-ahs)* — singer
Puerto Rico's velvet cannon of a voice: the bass baritone who went from San Juan to the world's grandest opera houses and made it look as easy as humming in the shower.

Backstory:
Born in San Juan, Díaz trained at the New England Conservatory and by the 1960s was conquering the Metropolitan Opera with his deep, resonant thunder. He sang everything — Verdi villains, Mozart nobles, swaggering Don Giovannis — often opposite divas who could throw shade sharper than their high Cs.

Why He Mattered:
He wasn't just a singer; he was a *first.* The first Puerto Rican to become a genuine international opera star, proving the island's exports weren't limited to rum, baseball players, and Miss Universe winners. His career stretched decades — a rare feat in an art form where voices burn out faster than political promises.

Modern Update:
In 2022, Díaz received the Lifetime Achievement Grammy Award. Officially entering the pantheon of artists whose résumes require Roman numerals. Island gossip loved pointing out: "*Mira*, he made it all the way from San Juan to the Grammys — and not with reggaetón."

Family Usage:
Whenever a cousin hit a karaoke high note, an aunt would inevitably quip, "*¿Qué te crees, Justino Díaz*?" (*Translation: bring it down, Pavarotti.*)

Famous Quote:
"The human voice is the most beautiful instrument of all." — Justino Díaz, proving you don't need Auto-Tune if you've got God-given brass baritone pipes.

See also: *Ricky Martin; Metropolitan Opera; Coquí*

La Esquina Famosa *n. fem. (lah es-KEE-nah fah-MOH-sah) —* store

Puerto Rico's men's-style altar: where abuelos, papás, and quince chaperone emerged pressed, perfume, and convinced they were God's gift to the double-breasted blazer.

Backstory (sí, real):

Founded in 1924, *La Esquina Famosa* grew from a fabric-and-ready-to-wear shop into a homegrown menswear institution. Shirts that fit. Suits that made even shy accountants strut like they owned the plaza. For decades it also supplied school uniforms to top academies — because style starts with a crisp collar and ends with a name tag, you'll lose.

Golden Era:

By the 1970s-80s, it was a mall canon, listed alongside hair salons that shellacked bangs into aerodynamic miracles. It's where you brought the tie for your first interview and the guayabera your mother swore made you look *serio.*

Fun Fact:

Sí, *La Esquina Famosa* sponsored the 1970s TV game show *Sube Nene Sube*, created and hosted by comedian Luis Vigoreaux. Because even on national television someone had to dress the prizes.

Vibes & Labels:

Caballero con presupuesto pero buen gusto. Polished shirts, dignified tailoring, and ties that whispered — not screamed.

Family Lore Usage:

"Go to La Esquina Famosa and let them measure you. If you guess your size again, I'll disown you."

— Every Puerto Rican mother to every delusional son who thinks "medium" is a personality trait.

Why It Matters:

Three generations learned that dressing *bien puesto* isn't vanity; it's respect — for yourself, the occasion, and the auntie who will check your hem at the church door.

See also: *González Padín; sastre del barrio; guayabera*

La supervivencia es un arte *phr. (la-su-pehr-veeh-VEN-see-ah es oon AR-tay)* —Survival is an art.

If you're still standing, in heels — with matching earrings —it's because you've mastered the discipline passed down by women who smiled while pressure-cooking rage.

Cultural Usage:
Uttered when life derails, but your eyeliner doesn't.
"Your husband left, your cousin stole your identity, and your landlord raised the rent?

"*Mija, la sobreviviencia es un arte.*"

Also heard while:

- Lifting a crying child off a chandelier mid-rosary.
- Lighting a San Antonio candle while drafting a venomous yet polite email.
- Reapplying lip liner before testifying in court.

Implied Meaning:
We didn't survive — we curated survival, with flair, with sarcasm, and occasionally a forged signature.

Modern Update:

Survival now includes therapy, boundaries, and blocking your toxic cousin on WhatsApp. If you did it wearing matching lipstick, congratulations — you've earned your master's.

See also: *High-functioning generational trauma; telenovela-worthy resilience; spiritual warfare in statement earnings.*

La Heredera *n. fem. (lah eh-reh-DEH-rah)* — telenovela Venezuelan melodrama (RCTV, 1982) penned by Delia Fiallo, the queen who could turn a grocery list into tragedy.

Plot vibe:
Innocent heroine inherits not just money but enemies, secrets, and a lifetime subscription to weeping in silk. Cue scheming relatives, misunderstood suitors, and hair with its own plotline.

Cultural Footprint:
A cornerstone of Venezuela's golden export era. Without *La Heredera*, there'd be no *Cristal* or *Topacio*. Proof that in telenovelas, wealth is merely the down payment on suffering.

Survival Guide Metaphor:
Whenever someone insists privilege makes life easier, show them *La Heredera*. Mansions come with mortgages— and conniving cousins.

See also: *Delia Fiallo; martyrdom chic; Venezuelan glam core*

Liquid Courage & Poor Decisions *n. pl. (LEEH-kweed-KAH uns PUAHR deh-SEE-shuns)* — concept

Coquito and **pitorro**.
One sip = karaoke.
Two sips = cousin drama.
Three sips = pistol shots into the sky.

See also: *coquito; pitorro; pistol shots; family therapy; regret.*

Lo sabía *interj.* (loh sah-BEE-ah) — fact

Puerto Rican women's ultimate counterstrike. Three syllables that end debates, silence denials, and vaporize alibis. Translation: *I already knew, cabrón.*

Usage Note:
Husband: "Negativo, negativo, negativo…"
Wife: "Lo sabía."
Translation: Checkmate.

Fun Fact:
Lo sabía requires no evidence — just conviction. Even when wrong, it feels right, and in Puerto Rican households is still admissible in court.

Modern Update:
Now available in text form, complete with ellipses and screenshots: "Lo sabía…"

Famous Quote:
"Lo sabia." — Every Puerto Rican woman who smelled perfume on your shirt before you did.

See also: *Negativo x 3; telenovela logic; abuela's sixth sense*

Los Picapiedras *n. pl. (lohs pee-kah-PYAY-drahss)* —cartoon

Puerto Rico's first cartoon family and a prehistoric guide to middle-class aspirations. *The Flintstones* en español: stone cars, saber-tooth house pets, and more marital tension than your parent's mortgage.

Cultural Impact:
Staple of *Hora de Muñequitos* ritual, where we learned bowling, slapstick, and fossil-powered capitalism.

Dubbing Lore: Fred Flintstone became Pedra Picapiedra, voiced by Jorge "El Tata" Arvizu, later Arturo Mercado, proof that Latin American dubbing could outperform the original.

Personal Note: English Fred's "Yabba-Dabba-Doo!" always sounded flat. But Pedro? That grunt carried the weight of every Puerto Rican dad who's ever yelled, "¡La cena está lista!" at sunrise.

See also: *Hora de Muñequitos; Don Gato; El Chavo del Ocho; Pacheco; Tío Nobel; dinosaur labor rights.*

Los Ricos También Lloran *prop. n. (luhs REE-kuhs tum-beeUHn YOH-ran)* — Mexican telenovela

1979 soap-opera opus: rich people's tears, class war disguised as love.

Translation: *The Rich Also Cry.* And oh, did they —on yachts, in mansions, into monogrammed Dior pillows.

Usage: Describing any life of luxury that's also a train wreck. "Very *Los Ricos También Lloran*" = crying in couture.

Fun Fact: Veronica Castro became a household deity, proving mascara streaks photograph beautifully when they cost $80.

Modern Update: Picture Eiza González as misunderstood heiress, Bad Bunny as gardener with secrets, soundtrack by heartbreak and reggaetón.

Famous Quote: Even pearls stain with tears.

See also: *elite pain; crying in couture; emotional capitalism.*

Los Tres Reyes Magos *n. pl. (lohs trehs RAY-ehs MAH-gohs)* — biblical figures

Puerto Rico's original influencers: three travelers who managed a cross-continental collab with no GPS, no Expedia, and one and one star as their Wi-Fi signal. They brought gold, frankincense, myrrh — but in Puerto Rico, they brought Tonka trucks, Barbie Dreamhouses, Atari consoles, and the annual reminder that Santa Claus was the gringo understudy.

Cast of Characters:

- *Mélchor*: Dark-skinned king, crowd favorite in Juana Díaz parades. Abuelas whispered about him like a telenovela lead.
- *Gaspar:* Middle child energy; brought frankincense and identity issues.
- *Baltazar*: Silver-fox energy; patron saint of dramatic entrances.

Tradition: On January 5th, kids cut grass for invisible camels, placed it in shoeboxes and woke up to magic. It wasn't just a holiday; it was a moral exam: generosity, faith, and manual dexterity with scissors.

Personal Note: My father loved *Los Reyes*. He said Santa came with receipts, but the Reyes come with faith. On January 6th, he'd light up like a kid himself, insisting we honor the real holiday. To him, Santa was American marketing; Los Reyes were sovereignty. He clung to them the way he clung to his ideals: stubbornly, proudly like a true *independentista* in a linen guayabera.

Cultural Significance & Resistance

After the 1898 U.S. invasion, Puerto Rico's Dia de Reyes evolved from a Catholic celebration into quiet rebellion; our glittery act of defiance wrapped in hay and devotion. When Santa Claus started creeping into local malls, *Los Reyes* became a cultural counterpunch: "Keep your jolly colonizer. We already have kings."

Scholars call it "cultural preservation." We call it "not letting the gringos steal January." The Reyes Magos symbolized not just faith but identity: Spanish Catholic roots braided with African and Taíno spirit. Mélchor, the Black Magi, became especially iconic; the image a stand-in for the rural Puerto Rican everyman, the jíbaro carried pride instead of gold.

Even in diaspora, families cling to the ritual; grass, shoeboxes, and the faint smell of evaporated milk, because it's the one tradition that still feels entirely ours. No mall Santas, no Hallmark cards, just homegrown magic on a humid morning.

Modern Update: These days they show up in pickup trucks, speedboats, or Facebook Live, sequins brighter than ever. They don't just bring gifts; they bring memory, resistance, and receipts from 1898.

Survival Note: To be Puerto Rican is to know your real gifts came from Los Reyes, not Santa. Identity wasn't sealed at baptism; it happened the morning you tore open your toy and your father said, "*Aquí los Reyes son los que mandan.*"

Santa vs. Los Reyes: A Comparative Study in Colonial Trauma and Glitter

(Excerpt from the unaccredited Universidad de la Calle Madrid Department of Cultural Pettiness)

Category	Santa Claus	Los Tres Reyes Magos
Nationality	North Pole (via Coca-Cola headquarters)	Bethlehem → Caribbean GPS
Arrival Method	Breaks into your house. Leaves crumbs.	Follows a star. Leaves blessings and hay residue.
Transportation	Reindeer union	Camels with union issues
Branding	Red suit, white beard, corporate sponsorship	Sequins, crowns, and Catholic guilt
Cultural Symbolism	U.S. consumerism wrapped in jingles	Puerto Rican defiance in gold lamé
Music Cue	"*Ho,Ho,Ho*"	"*Alegría, alegría, alegría…*" (and bongos)
Gift-Giving Logic	Naughty or nice list	Divine grace and your abuela's intercession
Religious Affiliation	Pagan-turned-mall-mascot	Biblical with a hint of rebellion
Socio-Political Function	Colonial distraction	Cultural resistance, also sparkly
After-Party Snack	Cookies and milk	Arroz con dulce, café and moral superiority

Thesis: Every time a Puerto Rican kid leaves grass for camels instead of cookies for reindeer, a tiny piece of cultural sovereignty is restored. Santa sells; *Los Reyes* save.

Conclusion: History proved what our abuelas always knew; faith travels better on a camel than a sleigh.

M

Machota *n. fem. (mah-CHOH-tah)* — tomboy

From macho but with a feminine ending. A coded — and usually shady—word for lesbian. In family gossip, it comes with the classic tía disclaimer:
"*Si se vistiera más feminina, she would change.*"

(*Translation: "If she dressed more feminine, she would change." Spoiler: she wouldn't.)*

Now a whole TikTok aesthetic, side-eye included.

Usage Note:
Often whispered at *bautizos* or weddings, right before the tías ask why you're still single.

Fun Fact:
Like all good slurs, it's been reclaimed. Today, *machota* is less insult, more aesthetic: short nails, button-downs, confidence.

Modern Update:
From whispered judgment to trending hashtag. The word that once got you side-eyed at a *boda* now gets you 50K followers and a girlfriend who owns a toolbox.

Famous Quote:
"Allá va la machota con su jevita."
Usually delivered with side-eye and extra lipstick on the glass.

See also: *tortillera; marimacha; patriarchy; abuela denial.*

Mallorcas *n. pl. (mah-YOR-kas)* — pastry

Puerto Rican heaven in powdered sugar. Sweet, coiled bread rolls descended from the Spanish *ensaïmada* and adopted by Puerto Ricans as if we'd invented them. Dusted generously with confectioners' sugar (think edible snowfall), *mallorcas* can be eaten plain — or, if you're spiritually ambitious, sliced, toasted, buttered, and elevated to divine-chair levels.

Origins:
Imported from Mallorca, Spain, then reinvented in Puerto Rican panaderías where flour, butter, and Catholic guilt collided in the early 20th century.

Cultural Impact:
Getting a proper *mallorca* was a pilgrimage. In Torrimar, it was Panadería Pepín. In Ocean Park, Kasalta (where President Obama once risked powdered sugar on his tie). In Old San Juan, Cafetería Mallorca — the OG temple. Each guarded its recipe like nuclear codes.

Usage Note:
"Voy pa' Kasalta a comerme una Mallorca.
Translation: *I am about to achieve nirvana, one buttery crumb at a time.*

Fun Fact:
Powdered sugar on your shirt wasn't an accident; it was a badge of honor. You wore it into meetings, onto dates, into history. (Some of us still have the shirts. Vintage now.)

Recipe (survival version):
Not the secret one — that's guarded by *abuelitas* with rolling pins — but close enough to singe your eyebrows Not the secret one, that's guarded by *abuelitas* with rolling pins, but close enough to singe your eyebrows with joy:

- 3 ¼ cups flour
- ¼ cup sugar

- 1 packet yeast
- ¾ cup warm milk
- 2 eggs
- ¼ cup butter (softened)
- Pinch of salt

Mix, knead, let rise. Roll into spirals, bake at 350F until golden. Dust with enough confectioners' sugan to trigger a snow advisory. Best served warm, with butter or ham & cheese.

Modern Update:
Now photographed more than eaten. Instagram has turned them into powdered props. But one bite still makes you believe in God — or at least in gluten.

Famous Quote (family edition):
"Nada más rico que una mallorca con mantequilla y café." — Every Puerto Rican abuela every morning of your childhood.

See also: *café con leche; Panadería Pepín; Kasalta*

Manjares *n. masc. (man-HA-ris)* — food; emotional leverage

Puerto Rican desserts so rich they qualify as both inheritance and weapon. Custards, flans, *tembleques, brazos gitanos* — culinary bribes designed to shut you up, cure your fever, and keep you loyal to the family all at once.

Metaphysical side effects:
Instant forgiveness. Prolonged sugar coma. Increased likelihood of saying "*coño, qué rico*" through tears.

In our house, *manjares* weren't recipes; they were contracts.
You ate — you obeyed.
You disobeyed — you didn't get seconds.

Moral:
Never argue with someone holding a flan.

Mantecaditos *n. pl. (man-the-cah-DEE-thos)* — cookie
Puerto Rico's must dangerous cookie. Also called, *polvorones*, but only amateurs call it that. These thumbprint shortbreads — made with butter, Crisco (or lard), sugar, flour and almond extract — are topped with sprinkles, guava, or that sacred maraschino cherry slice. One bite and they'll relocate immediately to your hips. Zero regrets.

Usage Note:
"Did you call la *señora* that makes the *mantecaditos*? I need three dozen for gifts." (A.K.A.: for me)

Fun Fact:
Often traced back to *Cocina Criolla* by Carmen Aboy Valldejuli — the gold standard of classic recipes that even fairy-kingdom elves follow religiously.

Modern Update:
Yes, gluten-free and vegan variations exist. They taste like nostalgia-free-cardboard. Vegan mantecaditos are regret in cookie form.

Famous Quote:
"If *mantecaditos* are wrong, I don't want to be right."
— *Every abuela ever.*

Recipe:
Beloved adaptation based on Valldejuli's original straight from Puerto Rican Cookery courtesy of Kitchen Gidget.
https://www.kitchengidget.com/2018/12/08/mantecaditos-puerto-rican-cookies/

See also: *polvorones; lard-ettes; manjar de dioses; comas navideñas.*

María la del Barrio *n. fem. (ma-REE-ah-lah-del- BAH-ree-OH)* — novela heroine.

The barrio's chosen one: half street fighter, half saint, all drama. Proof you can lose your man, your baby, and your memory — but never your dignity. Played by the one and only Thalía, 90's telenovela royalty: all heart, zero apology.

Usage Notes:
To call someone a *María del Barrio* is an honor: the unbothered glow-up from nothing to ¿qué miras estúpido? greatness. She's the girl who shows up to your brunch in a thrifted crop top, slaps your cheating cousin, and still gets proposed to by the millionaire.

Fun Fact:
María literally threw Soraya Montenegro into a pile of trash. Yes, she deserved it. María lost her memory, her baby, her man (twice) — never her dignity.

Modern Update:
She'd be a viral TikTok queen today, exposing cheaters with live receipts. Sponsored by a sustainable fashion. Always trending.

Famous Quote:
"¡Maldita lisiada!" — Wrong queen but María made that line possible.

See also: *saint with hoops; Latina Cinderella; empathy with edge; TikTok saint; chaos with a conscience.*

Marista *n. (mah-REES-tahs)* — school

The Catholic boys' school in Torrimar, Puerto Rico. Eternal rivals to Colegio San Ignacio. If San Ignacio was Romeo, Colegio Marista was Mercutio: louder, cooler, and a little dangerous.

This wasn't just basketball or volleyball — it was a culture, fought in polo shirts and rosaries. San Ignacio boys looked like future senators. Marista boys came in like future DJs, entrepreneurs, and hustlers.

On any given weekend, you'd find the two tribes colliding at house parties, beach bonfires, or quinceañeras; their school colors invisible but unmistakable in the way they circled each other on the dance floor.

Insider Gossip:
Mothers swore they'd never let their daughters date a Marista boy.
Translation: every family reunión had at least one secret Marista boyfriend.

Fun Fact (Institutional Version):
Founded in 1964 by the Marist Brothers. All-boys, until 1983. Back then, no girls — only rumors, tournaments, and imported swagger.

See also: *San Ignacio rivalry; quinceañera politics; polo-shirt wars.*

Marquesina *n. fem. (mahr-kay-SEEN-ah)* — driveway
The marquesina wasn't a driveway —it was a stage for social hierarchy in Puerto Rico. The material of your floor spoke louder than your last name:

- *Raw cement*: surviving, not thriving. Laundry lines and emergency baptisms happened here.

- *Smooth cement*: upward mobility. Kids could roller-derby without bleeding.
- *Tile*: Holy Grail. Dentists, lawyers, cousins in politics. Bonus points if the tile matched your bathroom.

Usage Note:
"Voy pa' un party de *marquesina*."
Translation: *I will return sticky with sweat, reeking of Sprite, and possibly pregnant.*

Fun Fact:
Mothers scrubbed marquesinas until Vatican clean — just for a '89 Crown Vic to park on it. The goal wasn't cleanliness. It was optics. A spotless marquesina could elevate you from nobody to Rotary-Club material.

Modern Update:
Now a CrossFit gym (cousin bench pressing with cinder blocks), nail salon (tía's side hustle), Costco storage unit, confessional booth, and therapy office — sometimes at the same time.

Famous Quote:
"Que no bailen encima del carro, por favor." —
Every uncle, at every marquesina party, before someone inevitably twerked on the hood.
See also: *quinceañera; discoteca casera; carro público; class warfare in the tile form.*

Mayaguez & Aguadilla *n. plur. (my-ah-GWENS & ah-gwah-DEE-yah)* — towns

On Puerto Rico's western edge, Mayagüez insists on gravitas — university energy, crab festival, and gossip delivered like peer-reviewed footnotes.

Aguadilla flirts — surfboards, sunsets, piraguas, scandal by the sea.

If Mayagüez writes the thesis, Aguadilla spills the tea.

N

Negativo, Negativo, Negativo *interj. (neh-gah-TEE-voh, neh-gah-TEE-voh, neh-gah-TEE-voh)* — no

Puerto Rican male defense strategy. The de facto national motto of men when confronted with accusations of infidelity, wandering eyes, or the mere suggestion that another woman exists. Less phrase, more **choreography**: wide eyes, hand to chest, tragic sincerity.

Usage Note:
Wife: "Estabas Mirando a esa mujer, ¿verdad?"
Husband: "¡Negativo, negativo, negativo!"
Translation:
"I was meditating on your divine perfection, mi reina."

Fun Fact: Functions like duct tape — sloppy, transparent, and briefly effective if applied before witnesses arrive. Entire marriages, baptisms, and political campaigns have survived on "deny, deny, deny."

Famous Quote:
"Negativo, negativo, negativo."
— Every Puerto Rican dad, tío or boyfriend caught looking at a waitress, 1960-present.

Modern Update: Now available via WhatsApp voice note, complete with dramatic pauses. Some men have even upgraded to emoji shorthand: 🙅🙅🙅.

Personal Note:
When my father sat in his wheelchair, an anonymous caller whispered that he was having an affair with his secretary. My mother didn't wait for fact-checking — she went full primetime.

While she raged, Papi kept repeating, "*negativo, negativo, negativo,*" like a malfunctioning prayer machine. The more she shouted, the louder he denied, until the living room sounded like a war between Telemundo and the Vatican.
Later, we learned the caller was just someone's bored cousin. Still, the scene stayed burned in me: love, pride, and rumor locked in a telenovela death match.

Proof that in Puerto Rico, denial isn't just defense — it's choreography.

See also*: machismo; excuses; perreo; lo sabía*

Novela Stock Exchange *n. (noh-VAIL-ah STUHK ex-CHAIN-ge)* — market

The Invisible Wall Street of Latino family drama.

Opening bell: Sunday misa
Closing bell: Bingo night.

Analysts: your tías.
Regulation: nonexistent

Current Market Trends:
$CHISME (Gossip Futures): always bullish.
$INFIDELIDAD (Infidelity Options): volatile, high yield.
$ABUELA (Matron Holdings): stable dividends of rosaries & guilt.
$SLAP: (Face-to-Face Commodities): aggressive buy during sweeps week.

Insider Trading: mandatory

Market Motto:
If you didn't hear it on Univision, it's still in pre-production.

Personal Note:
I cried easily, which made me a natural actress — and my mother's favorite critic. If I teared up mid-argument, she'd sigh, "*Aquí viene la novela*," as if I were walking onto a set instead of surviving her fury.

When she was enraged, she'd add, "*Don't cry or I'll hit you harder.*"
So, I learned to perform silently: tears on delay, cue them later when the house went still. That's where I discovered the first rule of melodrama.

Emotion without permission becomes art.

O

Oratoria *n. fem. (oh-rah-TOH-ree-ah)* — cultural blood sport

Puerto Rican competitive public speaking — part speech-and-debate, part melodrama, wholly fueled by Catholic guilt, colonial baggage, and Aqua Net.

Cultural Impact:
At elite schools like **Academia San José,** *oratoria* wasn't extracurricular; it was gladiator combat in blazers.

Categories included:

- **Poetry**: Weep until they hand you a trophy.
- **Comedy**: Always loud, rarely funny.
- **Essay**: Mock-trial theatrics, closing arguments at fourteen.
- **Original Writing:** Melodrama with footnotes

Because empire never dies, performances were in Spanish, English, and the occasional pretentious French. Winning wasn't just about medals — it was social currency. Half of San Juan's lawyers, politicians, and anchors cut their teeth here. The other half married someone who did.

Personal Note:
After performing, we'd huddle backstage like caffeinated debutantes — hands clasped, mascara trembling, hearts pounding like conga drums. The emcee's countdown felt like the Miss Universe finale:

"*En tercer lugar…*"

We started screaming before he finished. I usually snagged first or second, but the real win was when our all-girls school obliterated **San Ignacio, Perpetuo and Marista.** Nothing hits like girls power in patent-leather shoes and rosaries.

Usage Note:
"Ella ganó en oratoria."

Translation:
Brace yourself — she's about to run for office.

Survival Guide Lesson:
Oratoria was never about diction; it was domination. If you could cry on cue, smirk in three languages, and quote **Martí and Shakespeare** in the same breath, you ruled the cafeteria.

See also: *Catholic guilt; prep-school syndrome; political starter kits.*

Oso Blanco *n. masc. (OH-soh-BLAHN-koh)* — prison
Puerto Rico's answer to Alcatraz — same despair, worse humidity. Officially *Presidio Estatal de Río Piedras*, but everyone called it **Oso Blanco**, the White Bear.

Built in the 1930s to be modern and humane, it quickly became the most violent penitentiary: a place where justice went to die and shivs were passed around like communion wafers.

Why It Mattered:
Every Puerto Rican kid grew up hearing,
"*No termines en Oso Blanco.*"

Parents dropped it into lectures, the way others threatened military school. By the 1970s-80s, Oso Blanco was infamous for riots, overcrowding, and escapes, so cinematic they made telenovelas look underwritten.

One inmate fled dressed as a woman, others tunneled out with the confidence of method actors.

Aesthetic:

- **Outside**: whitewashed fortress, like a colonial wedding cake.
- **Inside**: hell with mosquitoes.

Family Lore:

- Abuela swore even mentioning it at dinner brought *mala suerte*.
- Every cousin's cautionary tale ended with:" *...y si no estudias, te vas pa' Oso Blanco.*"
- Taxi drivers used it as shorthand for danger: "Ah no, eso está cerca de Oso Blanco."

Fun Fact:

Dubbed *the Alcatraz of the Caribbean*. Unlike Alcatraz, no one's selling T-shirts. But in 2008 Rapper **Voltio** did the next best thing — turned it into a concert venue.

En Vivo Desde Oso Blanco was half-documentary, half-redemption arc; reggaetón meets repentance. Prisoners nodding to beats instead of sermons. Puerto Rico collectively whispered, "*At least someone got out with a record deal.*"

Modern Update:

Closed and demolished in 2000s, developers dreamed of condos or a convention center (because of course). Still the White Bear still growls in the collective psyche.

Puerto Ricans never forget their folklore — especially when it involves shanks, bad plumbing, and one unforgettable rap show.

Famous Quotes:

"*Más vale estudiar que terminar en Oso Blanco.*"

— Every Puerto Rican parent, forever.

See also: *La Princesa Prison; Escondido; Carlos "La Sombra"*

Oui Boutique *n. fem. obsolete (wee boo-TEEK)* — store
Before Gucci had a flagship in Condado and before Instagram invented "influencers," Puerto Rico had ***Oui Boutique*** — the crown jewel of Hato Rey retail.

Run by **María Zipperle** (yes, of the famous El Zipperle restaurant family.) *Oui* wasn't just a store; it was a **social filter**. If you could shop there, you belonged.

Aesthetic:
Small, chic, and intimidatingly quiet. European labels hung like holy relics. Saleswomen with perfect blowouts and arched brows, could size up your credit limit faster than a loan officer.

Why it mattered:
For the fashionable elite of the '70s–'90s, *Oui* was the only place to shop. If you wore *Oui,* people would know. If you couldn't afford it, you pretended you "didn't like that style."

Oui wasn't just clothes — it was armor for cocktail parties, charity galas, and the endless carousel of San Juan gossip.

Family lore:

- Tías swore by its authority: "Si no lo compraste en Oui, mejor no lo uses."
- Abuelas kept the shopping bags to reuse —maximum flex, minimum waste.
- Daughters begged for *Oui* dresses for quinceañeras; mothers replied, *"Cuando te cases."*

Fun Fact:
The French name was intentional; sophisticated, slightly smug, and confusing enough that one cousin spent years believing it sold children's clothes called *Wee Boutique*.

Modern update:

Long closed, but its ghost still haunts San Juan closets. To this day, some women look at Zara the way their mothers looked at Kmart — tragic resignation.

Famous Quote (unofficial):
"Oui darling, or nothing at all."

See also: *González Padín; La Esquina Famosa; Condado boutiques*

O Summary – Performance, Punishment & Pretension
Every Puerto Rican family was a **stage**, a **courtroom**, and a **boutique**.

Oratoria taught us to perform emotion. **Oso Blanco** reminded us of what happened when the performance failed. **Oui Boutique** taught us how to dress for both outcomes.

Between the microphone, the cell block, and the fitting room, we learned that presentation wasn't vanity — it was survival.

Cry beautifully.
Obey selectively.
Accessorize strategically.

Because on the island, sincerity without style is just noise —and no one gets a standing ovation for that.

P

Pac-Man *n. masc. (PAK-man)* — a game.

Japanese arcade game (1980) starring a yellow circle who eats pellets, fruit and ghosts.

In Puerto Rican childhood: the default Halloween/UNICEF costume when your parents were broke, crafty, or both. Made of poster board, tempera pain, and Scotch tape —equal parts iconic and humiliating.

Our parents called it creativity; we called it *public humiliation with a glue stick.*

Usage Note:

Worn by Estrella to UNICEF World Day, where she shuffled across the courtyard chomping the air while a classmate in a blue bedsheet ghost chased her. Instant legend, cardboard splinters included.

Modern Update:

Today, Pac-Man is retro chic: $49.95 on a T-Shirt at Urban Outfitters. Back then, our DIY versions peeled school **paint** and left bruises on our thighs.

Fun Fact:

Pac-Man was originally "Puck-Man" in Japan, renamed for the U.S. release because teens kept vandalizing the machines to read "F***Man." Puerto Rican mothers never knew this; they just saw a yellow circle and thought: "¡Perfecto para la parada de UNICEF!"

See also: *Leia Buns; Flamenco Trauma; Arcade Addiction; Childhood Cosplay Gone Wrong*

Pacheco *n. male (Pah-CHEH-co)* — entertainer

Alias: The Saint of Wholesome Chaos / *El Santo de Caos Infantil*

Era: When afternoons came with morals, jingles, and a side of diabetes. Pastel-suited televangelist of good manners.

The man, the myth, the after-school exorcist of bad behavior: Pacheco who could silence and entire island of hyper children with three divine words: ¡*Cámara, por favor*!

Armed with cartoon, courtesy, and Holsum sponsorship, he ruled Puerto Rican living rooms like a benevolent dictator of decency. Every episode began with a smile so pure it could bleach uniforms and ended with thousands of kids mailing in crayon drawings like moral receipts.

Cultural Note:

He wasn't alone. No prophet ever is. Behind him scurried his cherubic sidekick, *El Enanito de Holsum*, a polyester blur forever sprinting with a tray of powdered donuts — the sugar dusted archangel of chaos.

Together they embodied the island's unofficial religion: **Carbohydrates & Catholic guilt.**

Across the dial, Tio Nobel counter-programmed with nautical madness and confetti. Their rivalry was our first televised custody battle:

- **Pacheco**: cookies, morals, hugs.
- **Nobel:** boots, prizes, mild trauma.

Personal Field Report:

In our house, 4:00 p.m. meant war:

I was Team Pacheco. Vero was Team Nobel. The TV dial was the battlefield. When Pacheco whispered, ¡*Cámara, por favor*! I straightened my posture like the Virgin Mary was watching. When Tio Nobel screamed, "¡*Arriba la alegría*!" Vero threw cheese curls at the screen.

El Enanito Holsum ran laps with his tray, sprinkling us all in ghostly donut dust. By 4:30 the carpet looked like a **crime scene at Dunkin' Donuts.**

Modern Usage:

"Tan dulce que parece Pacheco." Used for someone so wholesomely nice you suspect they're hiding bodies or baking cookies.

Fun Fact:

Pacheco once convinced thirty thousand people to bike through San Juan in matching T-shirts, proving that even chaos can be cardio when led by a saint in a powder blue blazer. The island never needed therapy; it had Pacheco and donuts.

See Also: *Tío Nobel; El Enanito Holsum; Maratón de la Esperanza; Public Television Feelings*

Palangana *n. fem. (pah-lawn-GAH-nah)* — object

A washbasin also (bizarrely) called pato ("duck") which made no sense unless you count its tragic double-duty as a chamber pot for lazy Victorian-era midnight pee breaks.

Usage Note:

Families once kept them under the bed for "emergencies," Let's just say: porcelain was a privilege.

Fun Fact:

Adding insult to indignity, *pato* also became a cruel nickname for homosexual men back in the day. Proof that language, like plumbing, eventually evolves-but not always fast enough.

Famous Quote:

'Busca el pato, nena."Equally horrifying whether they meant the chamber pot or the gossip about your tío.

See also: *chamber pot; pato (slur); bad branding*

Pan de Agua *n. masc. (pahn deh AH-gwah)* — food

Puerto Rico's sacred carb: crisp crust, soft steamy center, and a fragrance that could resurrect the dead.

Fun Fact:

Impossible to get home intact. Traditionally slathered with butter while still hot, preferably in the car, parked crooked outside the *panadería.* By the time you got home, the loaf looked like it had been mugged.

Famous Quote:

"No toques la puntita, esa es de Mami."

(*"Don't touch the end piece; that's Mom's."*)

Modern Usage:

Used to describe anything irresistibly warm, or nostalgic. "That hug felt like fresh *pan de agua* straight from the oven."

See also: *pernil; mantequilla; café con leche; pan sobao; panadería milagrosa*

Pasteles *n. pl. (pahs-THE-lehs)* — holiday dish

Not cake. Not pastelillo. Puerto Rican haute cuisine disguised as a boiled plantain tamal. Filled with pork, chicken, raisins and olives; wrapped in a plantain leaf; boiled until you're sweating patience you don't have.

Warning: Eat hot. Cold pasteles may cause intestinal unrest and family feuds.

Pava *n. fem. (PAH-vah)* — hat

The Puerto Rican jíbaro crown: wide-brimmed straw, built for sun, rain, and unsolicited gossip.

Once humble campesino gear, now a high-fashion statement.

Usage Note:

Me puse la pava.

Translation: "I am both preventing heatstroke and declaring my jíbaro heritage in one fabulous gesture."

Fun Fact:

Before Coachella, the pava was political. In the mid 1900s, it became the unofficial merch of **the Partido Popular Demócratico (PPD)**. Imagine voting with accessories.

Modern Update: Bad Bunny resurrected the pava, turning a campesino's workwear into a runway-ready crown. What once said "plátano harvest" now says, "front row at Fashion Week, con orgullo."

See also: *jíbaro; guayabera; sombrero; Bad Bunny's closet.*

Pernil *n. masc.* (pehr-NEEL) — roast

The roasted pork shoulder of the gods. Marinated in garlic, adobo, and every ounce of your mother's passive aggression. Skin roasted to chicharrón-level crispiness, meat falling off the bone like your Tía after three coquitos.

The secret ingredient? Every unspoken family resentment, roasted to perfection.

Pique *n. masc. (PEE-keh)* — condiment

Puerto Rican potion of the fire and pride, made by fermenting chili peppers, garlic, and pineapple rinds in recycled rum bottles. Not "hot sauce" — ancestral medicine.

My **dad** and Cundo Flechazo poured it on everything "*pa' que coja vida*" (so it comes alive). Burns the tongue, heals the soul, and doubles as truth serum after midnight.

Famous Quote:

"Esto no pica; esto revive" (This doesn't just burn; it resurrects.)

See also*: ají caballero*

Pisicorre *n. (PEE-SEE-coh-reh)* — minivan

From *pisa y corre* ("step and run"). Puerto Rico's iconic white vans: part shuttle, part sauna, part survival test.

Cultural Impact:

If Americans had yellow buses and sitcom nostalgia, we had pisicorres: gladiator chariots careening through Santurce and Río Piedras. Mothers handed us over daily; fully aware the drivers only knew two speeds: *demasiado rápido* and *más rápido.*

Usage Note:

"Voy en pisicorre."

Translation: "If I make it alive, I'll see you in homeroom."

Fun Fact:

Seatbelts were decorative, if they existed at all; survival depended on grip strength and prayer. If OSHA had visited, they'd have needed therapy.

Modern Update:

Today Uber exists, but no app can replicate the chaos, danger and efficiency of the pisicorre. White vans still haunt San Juan traffic; aging relics of a less regulated, more exhilarating era.

Famous Quote:

"Apúrate que se va el pisicorre."

See also*:* carro público; marquesina parties; parking lot *Hunger Games*

Pitorro *n. masc. (pee-TOH-rro)* — drink

Puerto Rican moonshine. Also known as *cañita*, and as the reason your Tía danced on a table last Christmas.

Distilled illegally from sugarcane: fiery, unregulated, and guaranteed to singe your throat on the way down.

Usage Note:

Pitorro isn't bought; it's bestowed. A cousin shows up with a recycled bottle of clear mystery liquid and whispers: "Es casero." Translation: this is either the best drink of your life or instant blindness.

Flavor profile:

Tastes like rocket fuel, improved only by parcha, tamarind, or gummy bears soaking at the bottom.

Fun Fact:

During Prohibition, *pitorro* was the drink of resistance. Today, it's the drink of every holiday party, wedding, or wake where people swear, they'll "just have una copita" and wake up three days later in Bayamón.

Family Love Cross-Ref:

See Episode 46, Don Bonifacio Oliviano not only preached Ajo, Limón y Cebolla as cure all, but also distilled his own *pitorro* — medicine, magic, and hangover in one bottle.

Modern Update:

Now sold in artisanal shops with tasting notes, proving gentrification even found our hangovers.

Famous Quote:

"Eso no es ron... eso es *pitorro.*"

See also: *Medalla Light; coquito; resaca; cañita*

Plaza Las Américas *n. (PLAH-sah lahs ah-MEH-ree-kahs)* — mall

The Mecca of shopping, not of dating. The Caribbean's largest mall: Puerto Rico's temple of air-conditioning, handbags, and inter-class anthropology.

Cultural Impact:

Where families strolled, women compared purses like battle armor, and teens discovered that not all malls were created equal.

- Boys from La Merced? Forbidden.
- Boys from San Ignacio? Future sons-in-law.

If you wanted suitors with orthodontics, you migrated to *San Patricio Plaza* — the catwalk of future hedge-fund managers.

Favorite Stores:

La Femme (for dresses that decided your social class.), Novus (because shoes made the snob). Clubman (gentlemen's luxury), and Orange Julius (universal sticky diplomacy).

The Real Sacrifice:

Parking. A *Hunger Games* of circling, cursing, and territorial rage. Many left Plaza not with new shoes but with fresh enemies.

Usage Note:

"Voy pa' Plaza." Translation: "I will be seen, judged and possibly ignored — and certainly cursed at — in the parking lot."

See also: *comemierdas; San Patricio Plaza; Orange Julius; hangovers; parking wars*

Puerto Rican Elite Institutions *ph. (pweh-toh-REE-kahn eh-LEET in-sti-TOO-shuns)* — places

The holy trinity of privilege: **Academia San José** (education), **Caribe Hilton** (social life), and **El Zipperle** (business). Together, they formed the Bermuda Triangle where old money met new scandal, and everyone pretended to be European.

To belong was to exist above the island's messy reality; to not belong was to wait outside the gates, dreaming of piña coladas and alumni connections.

Fun Fact: Entire family reputations rose or fell based on whether their daughter's quinceañera made it into *El Nuevo Día.*

Now they survive mostly in photo albums, where children in lace socks look like miniature senators.

Today their alumni run half the island — and the other half's therapy sessions.

See also: *country clubs; rosaries; generational denial*

Raymond Chandler *n. (RAY-mahn-CHAHN-dler)*—author

American novelist, father of the hard-boiled detective; accidental patron saint of Puerto Rican boys recovering from experimental surgeries in Fajardo.

While other kids obsessed over baseball cards or Beatles records, **Leopoldo Oliviano** read *The Big Sleep*, *Farewell My Lovely*, and *The Long Goodbye* as if they were survival manuals, Chandler gave him a toolkit: trench-coat confidence, sarcasm as armor, desire as puzzle and swagger as mobility aid.

In family lore, this was the pivot. Books of philosophy gave Papi gravitas, but Chandler gave him style. He stopped being "the boy on crutches" and became our own Philip Marlowe — except instead of a gun, he carried orchids, Lorca poems, and a dangerous smile.

See also: *noir; survival manuals; Papi; orchids; Lorca poems*

Reina de Saba/ Queen of Sheba Cake *n., (RAY-nah-day-SAHbah) — cake*

Chocolate Almond Decadence with a side of *chisme*.

A French chocolate-almond cake made famous by **Julia Child**; delicate enough to collapse in you breathe too hard near it, rich enough to convince your in-laws you've been to Paris.

Usage Note:
Served at dinner parties where hosts want to imply, they own a passport. In Puerto Rican gatherings, however, it was shorthand for: "Who does she think she is? La reina de Saba?

Fun Fact:

Julia Child called it one of her favorite cakes. For her, it was elegance. For Tia Gladys, it was arrogance.

Modern Usage:
Found in food blogs. Whole Foods bakeries and occasionally in a marquesina at a cousin's birthday party — right next to the flan de queso everyone actually finishes.

Famous Quote:
"¿Quién se cree que es? ¿La reina de Saba?"
— uttered any time someone overdoes it, whether it's cake, jewelry, or opinions.

Julia Child's Recipe
(a.k.a Puerto Rican dinner party one-upmanship, adapted from *Mastering the Art of French Cooking* via Food.com)

Ingredients:

- 4 oz semisweet chocolate, melted with 2 tbsp rum or coffee
- ½ cup unsalted butter (softened)
- ⅔ cup sugar (divided)
- 3 eggs, separated
- ⅓ cup finely ground almonds
- ½ cup cake flour, sifted

Buttercream Glaze:

- 2 oz semisweet chocolate, melted with 2 tbsp rum or coffee
- 5-6 tbsp unsalted butter

Directions (*abridged for gossip breaks*):

Preheat oven to 350°F. Butter and flour an 8-inch pan.

Melt chocolate with rum/coffee; let it cool — like your temper.

Cream butter and sugar until pale; add yolks, chocolate, almonds.

Beat egg whites to soft peaks; fold in gently (and judgmentally).

Bake 25 minutes; center should tremble like family secrets.

Cool, glaze, and serve at room temperature — with drama.

Tía's Gossip Note:
"¿Viste? Ni quedó bien cocinado en el medio."
"¿Eso es un bizcocho? Ay, por favor. Dame flan."

Survival Note:
If the center's raw, drown it in Café Bustelo and gossip. It'll go down smoother than your cousin's engagement news.

S

Safari Park (Dorado*) n. masc. (sah-FAH-ree-PAHRK- doh-RAH-doh)* — zoo

Puerto Rico's short-lived attempt at a Serengeti-by-the-Sea. The pitch: glamorous African safari, Caribbean-style. The reality: animals blinking like they'd wandered onto the wrong novela set.

Imagine giraffes in disbelief, a hippo with a calcium deficiency, and an Arctic fox wondering if he'd missed his connecting flight to Alaska. The **Sociedad Protectora de Animales** and the **Department of Natural Resources** eventually stepped in because — surprise — running a zoo requires money.

The Donkey Incident:

Forced to climb a towering platform only to bellyflop into a tiny pool below, as if starring in a budget *Cirque du Soleil: Dorado Edition.* Somewhere, Evel Knievel was jealous.

Fun Fact:

Local lore still whispers about zebras spotted wandering Dorado after the park closed. Were they real? Were they cows with good lighting? In Puerto Rico, both are possible.

Modern Update:

Today, Safari Park survives as mythic punchline: the place where you saw "lions" while eating piraguas, and where every uncle swears, "*Se escapó una cebra, te lo juro.*"

Famous Quote:

"Safari Park fue tremendo… hasta que el burro se tiró de la plataforma." — every tía laughing so she won't cry.

See also: Isla de Cabras (actual goats, no budget issues); Parque de las Ciencias (more rockets, fewer zebras)

Saddle Shoes *n. pl. (SA-dl-shooz)* —footwear

Footwear of discipline, class, and blisters. Two-tone prep-school leather shoes designed to suffocate both feet and individuality.

Origins:

Created in the early 1900s as men's athletic shoes, they galloped into women's wardrobes by the 1930s, when teen girls paired them with bobby socks and poodle skirts. By the 1950s, the were stamped into the DNA of American prep culture: wholesome, repressive, and fashionably stiff.

Puerto Rican twist:

Imported as ASJ Catholic school uniforms, they screamed "good family" and whispered, "orthopedic trauma."

Cultural Impact:

Wearing them meant two things:

1. You had status (these weren't Payless flats; they had to be polished within an inch of their lives).

2. You had no independence (you were literally laced to conformity).

Usage Note:

"*Póntelos.*"

Translation: "Suffer but look respectable."

Fun Fact:

Cheerleaders wore them in the U.S.; in Puerto Rico, they signaled you were one family fight away from being called *comemierdas.*

Modern Update:

Resurfaced today as ironic retro fashion or $600 runway couture that still gives you bunions.

Famous Quote:

"If they're dirty, you're grounded. If they're clean, you're miserable."

See also: *Prep School Syndrome; Uniform trauma; comemierdas*

San Ignacio *n. (sahn eeg-NAH-syoh)* — school

Colegio San Ignacio de Loyola, the Jesuit-run Catholic prep school in San Juan, Puerto Rico. The island's equivalent to Andover, Exeter, or Eton — where ties, privilege, and ambition were baked in along with the Mass schedule.

If Marista boys swaggered like Mercutio, San Ignacio boys postured like Hamlet: dramatic, ambitious and convinced they were destined for tragedy or Congress. It incubated Puerto Rico's future governors, senators, bankers and Ivy League legacies; its alumni list read like draft picks for Harvard, Yale, Princeton, and Georgetown.

Everything that comes with all-boys prep culture came standard: Jesuit priests as spiritual drill sergeants, intense basketball-court rivalries, whispered locker-room scandals, and overly brotherly weekend "bonding" that made mothers whisper and daughters' swoon.

Insider Gossip:

Mothers pushed their daughters toward San Ignacio boys, describing them as "future husband material."
Translation: Expect snobbery with your bouquet of roses, plus a mother-in-law who'll ask where your grandfather studied law.

Fun Fact (Institutional Version):

Founded in 1952, modeled after elite Jesuit schools worldwide, with a mission to form "men for others." What it formed was Puerto Rico's political and business class — with enough Latin homework and tennis to make sure no one forgot where they were headed.

Social Commentary (see Episode 52):

Felino, our gay fairy godmother and lifelong consiglieri, also graduated from San Ignacio, along with his merry crew of UFO's (Unidentified Flying (H)ombres). They became our unofficial bodyguards and nightclub escorts, shepherding us through Juliana's, Isadora, and The Flying Saucer with the reverence of saints and the discretion of sinners.

Mami and Cata's mother adored them; Mami felt relieved we were *escorted but not defiled.* We felt like debutantes with better lighting and sharper contour.

See also: *Marista; Ivy League pipelines; polo-shirt wars; mother-in-law approval ratings*

Sandwichitos de mezcla *n. pl. (sahn-gwhee-CHEE-tos deh MEHS-klah)* — sandwiches

Puerto Rican crack in triangular form: tiny, crustless white-bread sandwiches stuffed with a neon-orange cheese-meat-pimiento-mash that could survive a hurricane, a blackout, and three generations of gossip.

Usage Note:

Mandatory at every quinceañera, wedding, *bautizo*, Christmas party, baby shower, bridal shower, or vaguely social event. Show up without *mezcla* and you'll be disowned.

Fun Fact:

Born out of Puerto Rican ingenuity with U.S. Army surplus (Spam + Cheez Whiz = cultural alchemy). We turned rations into haute cuisine.

Modern Update:

Still headlining the buffet table, now often wrapped in Saran-Wrap pyramids like little artifacts from a civilization powered by gossip and mayonnaise.

Famous Quote:

"No puedes comer solo uno."

Translation: "You can't eat just one." Which is why you'll end up eating seventeen.

See also: tripleta; medianoche; pastelillos; family cholesterol

Sato *n. masc. (SAH-toh)* — dog

Puerto Rican shorthand for a scrappy stray mutt: street smart, hurricane-proof, and usually better at surviving than you. Can also refer to a feral man with similar survival skills and grooming habits.

Fun Fact:

Every airport rescue campaign starts with a *sato* and ends with someone crying on Instagram.

See also: *perros realengos; island resilience; bad-boy energy*

Sin Ti *n. (seen-tee)* — song
Literal translation: *Without You.*

Bolero written by **Pepe Guízar**, made eternal by **Los Panchos**, and responsible for generations of Latin American women weeping into their *cafecito.* With just three guitars and harmonies smoother than rum, Los Panchos managed to bottle loneliness and longing into a three-minute anthem.

For my father, it wasn't background music; it was artillery. After books and poetry had softened my mother's resistance, he deployed *Sin Ti.* (*See Episode 9)*

Crutches or no crutches, when a man sings, "*sin ti no podre vivir jamás*" (without you, I could never live) while looking directly into your eyes, you start to believe him. In our family mythology, this was the final *coup de grâce* — the moment bolero and bravado fused into seduction strategy.

See also: *bolero; Los Panchos; cafecito; tears; seduction strategy*

Sor Juana Inés de la Cruz *n. (SOHR, HWA-nah ee-NES deh lah KROOz)* — nun

A 17th century nun, poet, and intellectual from New Spain (Mexico) who became the OG feminist of the Américas. Imagine Beyoncé with a quill, writing sonnets instead of singles, while dragging men in perfect rhyme.

Usage Note:
Invoked anytime you need receipts that women in Latin America were out-thinking men centuries before hashtags.

Fun Fact:
She entered a convent just so she could read books all day. Same, girl.

Modern Update:
Would 100% have a Substack, a viral TED Talk, and two million TikTok followers dissecting *machismo* in iambic pentameter.

Famous Quote:
"*Hombres necios que acusáis a la mujer sin razón…*"
Translation: "You foolish men who accuse women without cause." A.k.a. the 1600s version of *boy bye.*

Modern Moral: Before feminism had merch, it had Sor Juana.

See also: *feminism; La Malinche; Frida Kahlo; receipts*

Telenovela Logic *phr. (the-leh-no-veh-lah loh-heek)* —cultural framework/ survival philosophy

The unwritten rules governing Latin-American soap operas —and by extension, our actual family lives. Equal parts incense, intrigue, contour; catechism with better lighting.

Telenovela logic explains why:

- No secret stays buried
- Villains always own chandeliers
- Women cry rivers of mascara without smudging.

Core Principles:

- **Amnesia Clause:** Every head injury = plot twist
- **Evil Twin Mandate:** If someone looks familiar, relax, it's the twin.
- **Class Warfare Doctrine:** Poor-but-noble heroine vs. rich-but-miserable heir. God's favorite matchup.
- **Rosary Rule:** No sin goes unpunished, unless you're fabulous.
- **Episode Inflation Law:** Every problem demands 80 episodes and 300 tears.

Cultural Impact:
From Mexico to Brazil, Venezuela to Puerto Rico, novelas were master classes in exaggerated living and free acting lessons, sex ed (sort of), and therapy (absolutely not).

Survival Metaphor:
Life is a novela.
Your boss? The villain.
Your cousin's quince? Filler episode.
Your divorce? Season-finale cliffhanger.

Famous Quote:

"Esto no se acaba hasta que la villana se caiga por las escaleras." ("It's not over until the villain falls down the steps.")

See also: *Infamia; La Heredera; Escrava Isaura; Los Ricos También Lloran; melodramatic eyebrows*

The Flying Saucer *n. (flahy-ing SAW-ser)* — nightclub

A disco that looked like a UFO crash-landed on Isla Verde Beach and never left. By Sunday, the sequined survivors of Condado staggered into its dome for one last spin under the strobe lights. Equal parts disco, crash site, and confessional.

Usage Note:
"See you at the Saucer," meant you had no plans to respect Monday, Mass, or your liver.

Fun Fact:
Sunburnt playboys and broken-heeled debutantes circled the floor like glamorous zombies. Legend says more confessions were whispered there than at San Juan Cathedral.

Survival Rule:
If you crawled out alive on Sunday, you could face anything; Monday, hurricanes, or your tías rosary.

Modern Update:
Today it'd be an Airbnb dome titled, "Retro *UFO Vibes* by the Beach."
Back then, it was the final boss level of the Weekend Disco Circuit.

See also: *Isadora, Juliana's Weekend Disco Circuit, glamorous zombies.*

The Haircut Trope *ph. (deh-HARE-kut trohp)* — trope

In novelas, scissors equal storyline. From Cristal's Victoria Ascanio slicing her past to *Yo Soy Betty la Fea's* braces -to-boss glow-up, haircutting isn't cosmetic — it's cathartic.

Personal Note:
My bathroom meltdown was less "rebirth," more "crime scene." Still, every short-haired heroine deserves her pilot episode.

See also: *Infamia; La Heredera; Telenovela Logic; Bad Hair Decisions*

The Latina Survival Beauty Kit
(1978- 1988 edition)

ELECTROLYSIS
"Permanent hair removal!" a.k.a. medieval torture by Russian aestheticians moonlighting as interrogators. Result: swelling, trauma, and a lifelong milk-mustache of healing cream.

CHAMOMILE / MANZANILLA HAIR LIGHTENER
Brew tea, soak arm hair, achieve "sun-kissed fuss." Classmate Gigi Goldstein took it full head. Outcome: *rubia broom chic.*

NOXZEMA COLD CREAM
Smelled like Vicks' sluttier cousin. Promised clear skin; delivered menthol rash and mime confidence.

BABY OIL + HAWAIIAN TROPIC OIL
Glaze yourself like lechón and roast under Caribbean sun. SPF was science fiction.

SUN-IN
Promised California blonde. Delivered nuclear-orange streaks.

NAIR
"Who wears short shorts?" after smelling this chemical tragedy.

VASELINE ON EYELASHES
"Natural mascara." Result: sticky lids + mosquito buffet.

AQUA NET

Held bangs through hurricanes; doubled as mace; blamed for ozone holes.

PREPARATION H (Under-Eye Miracle)

Trade secret of Barbarella-era models. Dab hemorrhoid cream under your eyes to shrink puffiness before a date, shoots, or a moral collapse. Aside from Max Factor, Mazola-oil injections and models shooting heroin, this was my mother's "This-is-it, modeling-career" moment for me. I emerged radiant, chemically preserved, and smelled faintly of regret and eucalyptus. (*See Episode 31*)

Editorial Note:

Every heroine needs a makeover; ours came with burns, rashes, and PTSD in a jar.

Survival Tip:

Sin dolor, no hay belleza.

Beauty mostly gave us trauma with tweezers.

The Rocky Horror Picture Show *ph. (ROCK-ee HOR-or PIK-chur SHO)* — film

A cult classic... except in Puerto Rico.

Why Americans Loved It:

Rebellion in fishnets.

Why We Didn't Need It:

We already had Iris Chacón, Drag, feathers, scandal included. Puerto Rican families didn't whisper about sex; they ignored it— then panicked if you held hands.

Personal Note:

When I finally saw it, it felt like an inside joke. Why cosplay camp when your aunt already shows up in bingo in a boa?

PR edition Quote:

"Time warp? Cariño, we've been living in one since 1898."

See also: *Iris Chacón; marquesina parties; cultural lost-in-translation (See Episode 30)*

The Rules *obs. (deh ROOLS)* — book

That pastel 90s "manual" that claimed the way to land a man was to act endangered; rare, elusive, and preferably silent.

- Never accept a Saturday date after Wednesday.
- Always end the call first.
- Be mysterious = never eat carbs in public.

We treated it like scripture, then wondered why we were hungry and alone by the landline.

Survival Note:

If a book tells you to vanish to be loved, donate it and buy yourself a sandwich.

The San Juan Star *n.* **(sahn-HWAN stahr)** — newspaper

The defunct English-language daily for people who believed reading in English made them slightly taller.

Household Edition:

My father treated like scripture; Mami treated like scripture; Maman treated it like a guest list; reading obituaries with her *cafecito*: "*Mira este, se murió también.*"

Usage:

"Maman read the obituaries in The San Juan Star like she was checking attendance."

See also: *El Nuevo Día; bilingual delusion; press freedom; colonial hangover*

The Weekend Disco Circuit *phr. (deh WEEK-end DEES-ko SIR-kweet)* — party circuit

In '70s-80s San Juan, survival was judged by heel height and hangover.

Friday: *Isadora* at Condado Plaza — polyester, gossip, and tragedy (Karl Wallenda literally fell into legend there).

Saturday: *Juliana's* at the Caribe Hilton — old money swaying to the Bee Gees and insider trades.

Sunday: *The Flying Saucer* — the UFO of Isla Verde where sequined zombies twirled till dawn.

Final Boss:

El Hamburger, Puerta de Tierra, burgers, gossip, and grease as sacrament. If you made it there by 5 a.m., you were immortal.

Circuit Rule:

Dance all weekend → survive anything: hangovers, hurricanes or tía side-eye at Mass.

Tío Nobel *n. masc. (TEE-oh NOH-bell)* — TV host

Cuban-born Nobel Vega, the trusted captain of Puerto Rican after-school TV (El Show de Tío Nobel). Always in naval regalia, commanding a green-screen sea that looked like lime Jell-O having a meltdown.

Cultural Note:

Rival to Pacheco, half the island yelled, "¡*Más muñequitos*!" while the other half, "¡*Cámara, por favor*!" Antenna direction = political ideology.

Personal Note:

4:00 p.m. meant Bay of Piglets at home. Vero was Team Nobel. I was Team Pacheco. Dad would yell, "Turn off that capitalist clown and bring me the tambourine boy!" Translation: holiday exorcism with cowbells.

Modern Usage:

"Don't go full Tío Nobel." = Stop turning life into a televised toy giveaway.

Fun Fact:

Retired to Miami and allegedly commands Publix shopping carts like naval vessels.

See also: *Pacheco; Remote Control (Extinct Species); Bozo Migration Patterns*

Tostones *n. masc. pl. (tohs-TOH-nehs)* — food

Twice-fried plantains: crispy outside, tender inside. Proof that some things deserve a second chance, and a dash of salt.

Usage:
Side dish, snack, or family weapon.

Fun Fact:

Some of us used them as crackers for Beluga caviar; others baptize them in *ajilimoli* (garlic, olive oil dressing) and whisper novenas of cholesterol.

The true heretics? They put ketchup on them. Those people are still in witness protection. In family lore, a cousin once showed up with Heinz and was promptly exiled to Bayamón.

See also: *mofongo, arroz con gandules, bacalaítos*

Traqueteo *n. (trah-keh-THE-oh)* — slang

Hands, hustles, and everything you shouldn't be doing.

- **PG-13 edition:** Marquesina make-outs
- **R-rated edition:** smuggling kilos instead of kisses.

Cultural Impact:

Teenagers whispered it like a dare; adults used it to lecture.

Usage:

Romantic: "Se fueron detrás de la marquesina a traquetear."

Criminal: "*Está metido en traqueteo con los del caserío.*"

Fun Fact:

One word, two sins: lust and commerce.

Famous Quote:

"*Aquí no quiero ni traqueteo ni traqueteos.*"

— Every abuela ever.

See also: *apestillarse; chaperones; narco-novelas*

Whopper de Burger King *n. (HWAH-per deh BUR-ger KEENG)* — burger

The holy grail of Puerto Rican fast food in the 1980s-90s; more popular than Mc Donald's and practically a sacrament after First Friday mass. Flame-broiled, oversized, and wrapped in the aura of American cool.

Usage Note:
A reward Mami dangled after dragging us through Catholic guilt and polyester uniforms. Heaven was spelled W-H-O-P-P-E-R.

Fun Fact:
One Burger King even had a giant metal slide beside it. I once flew down in a burlap sack, scraped my forearms raw trying to brake and still thought it was worth it for that burger.

Modern Update:
The slide may be gone, but so is our cholesterol score.

Famous Quote:
"Después de misa, Burger King."

See also: *McDonald's; First Friday Mass; trauma disguised as treats (Episode 11)*

APPENDIX

SURVIVAL LAWS

(For those who made it to the credits)

SURVIVAL LAWS

Act I – Hurricanes, Handguns & Holy Ghosts

Born in a hurricane, raised by matriarchs with chancletas, and haunted by ghosts who won't take a hint.

Survival Law #1: The American Dream has no warranty — especially if you're Puerto Rican.

Survival Law #2: Born in a storm? Congratulations, chaos is your sibling. Learn to braid the wind

Survival Law #X: Never stomp on a queen's hat unless you're ready for the trash.

Survival Law #3: When life feels impossible, pretend you're in a telenovela. If you can't survive it, at least give it ratings.

Survival Law #4: Survival isn't muscle; it's stamina. Outlast everyone at the table.

Survival Law #5: Family feud? Duck first, ask questions later.

Survival Law #6 Never underestimate the counted-out. Disability doesn't cancel strategy.

Survival Law #7 Beware of the mother who stomps. Her ankles hold ancestral fury, culinary sorcery, and the discipline of a general.

Survival Law #8: If love knocks, don't just open the door. Expect the full orchestra.

Survival Law #9 In Puerto Rican families, every victory comes with collateral damage.

Survival Law #10 Laugh at death once, and marriage feels less like destiny than endurance.

Survival Law #11: Ghosts don't scare me. Relatives with business plans do. But a *sopa de plátano* and a San Judas candle can make even death feel negotiable.

Act II – Madrid Street: Dynasty with Beans

Bingo rivalries, communion meltdowns, and double-trouble aunts. The real dynasty isn't in *Dallas* — it's in Torrimar.

Survival Law #12: Respect the neighborhood ghost. He always knows more secrets than the living.

Survival Law #13: If your street runs like a telenovela, lean in. Even your nostalgia deserves a theme song.

Survival Law #14: Paranoia counts as survival. *Uno nunca sabe.*

Survival Law #15: Spot the frauds, savor the recipes and never mistake a costume for a crown.

Survival Law # 16: Not every savior wears wings. Some wear aprons, smear aloe on your wounds, and teach you that love can survive shame, laughter, and even bad pyramid schemes.

Survival Law #17: Never underestimate a diva —especially when she's heartbroken. Glamour fades, but survival always looks fabulous under pressure.

Survival Law #18: If you can survive chaos, heartbreak, and ghosts, you can survive anything. Just bring heels— the devil respects stilettos.

Survival Law #19: If your family party doesn't require a helmet, elastic pants and a referee with poetry skills, was it even a fiesta?

Survival Law #20: If you bleed long enough, you stop apologizing for the stain.

Survival Law #21: Fold your insecurities into a cootie catcher and remember: you're the fortune, not the paper.

Survival Law #22: On Madrid Street, survival wasn't about picking tragedy or comedy—it was dancing both in sequins.

Act III – From Disco Balls to Chicken Inn

Privilege collapses under the weight of polyester disco, stolen luggage, and Crystal Fontaine's tragicomic fall.

Survival Law #23: When life casts you as Saint Joseph at eight, wear the beard and own the role. Dynasties fade; destiny does not.

Survival Law #24: In my novela, villains plot, fortunes collapse—but the heroine? She survives.

Survival Law #25: Snow looks magical until it soaks your socks. Choose survival over suede.

Survival Law #26: At fourteen, sequins and borrowed choreography count as confidence. The mustache comes off; the shame never does.

Survival Law #27: Beauty fades, but electrolysis pain is eternal. Choose your battles; some scars are invisible but still burn.

Survival Law #28: Hair bleach is temporary. Polaroids are forever.

Survival Law #29: Grace won't save you from gravity—or bad taste in boys. Dolls may be fragile, but they endure.

Survival Law #30: A bad first kiss is a blessing. It lowers expectations for everything after.

Survival Law #31: You can survive polyester, pizza caves, and Catholic guilt. What breaks you is always the thing no one sees.

Catholic repression, cursed slambooks, fake Russian royals, and neurosurgeons who should've kept their tongues to themselves.

Survival Law #32: Life's a pair of saddle shoes —squeaky, stiff, humiliating. Learn the code, play along, and graduate with your dignity intact. The rules don't change; only the uniforms.

Survival Law #33: Trapped with hormone-crazed teens? Forget logic. Play a telenovela; puberty bows to a dramatic slap.

Survival Law #34: Science may impress the judges, but *chemistry* always steals the novela.

Survival Law #35: In Puerto Rico, survival isn't defensive driving — it's strategic bribery.

Survival Law # 36: A medical degree can't save you from gossip. Family scandal spreads faster than malpractice suits.

Survival Law #37: When life demands a talent show, crown yourself and perform. Delusion is just confidence with better lighting.

Survival Law #38: Repression always leaks —sometimes in graffiti. Bring rosaries, Wite-Out and a plausible alibi.

Survival Law #39: Every masked ball crowns a Cinderella. But survival belongs to the rebels and the weirdos.

Act V – Cats, Curses & Other Inheritances

Ghost landlords, garlic-scented pueblos, fierce titis, and aristocratic cats who lived harder than Hemingway.

Survival Law #40: Parents can block cleavage and dodge truth, but repression always reruns. The sequel's called real life.

Survival Law #41: Survival is the only medal that never tarnishes.

Survival Law #42: First love and the sea share a talent for wreckage. If you're lucky, all you lose is a lamp.

Survival Law #43: A bad haircut is temporary. Learning to live with yourself takes longer to grow back.

Survival Law #44: One dance isn't a marriage. A "yes" isn't forever. And silence will betray you faster than a fake ID ever could.

Survival Law #45: *Echoes of Silence*: Secrets don't stay buried. They wait for the worst moment to resurface— usually mid-salsa. Silence, like cement, keeps the whole cracked structure standing, until the day it doesn't.

Survival Law #46: If your family recipe involves urine, call it artisanal. Every generation ferments its own cure — some with prayer, some with *pitorro,* and some with laughter disguised as memory.

Survival Law #47: If they call you *fiera*, wear it. Claws out, heart steady. Survival isn't handed down — it's hand built.

Survival Law #48: Be suspicious of anyone who calls green eyeshadow "natural." They're hiding bigger lies and probably own a friendship tiger.

Survival Law #49: Survive like a cat — claws out, eyes open, landing on your feet every time. Protect the secret. Guard the heart. And when silence comes, purr louder than fear.

Act VI – Sequins, Scandals & Survival Laws
Mob math, confessional breakdowns, strip-club bookkeeping, and the eternal scam of success. Sequins never fail.

Survival Law #50: Never fear a SWAT team. Fear an interrupted *merienda.*

Survival Law #51: If life's equations never add up, trust your instinct, not the numbers. The answer is never in math; it's in survival.

Survival Law #52: If your bed shakes, pray it's the motor—not the money laundering.

Survival Law #53: Barbershops are confessionals. Tip well; your secrets depend on it.

Survival Law #54: Fold your insecurities into a cootie catcher, slip them in your pocket, and remember: you're the fortune, not the paper.

Survival Law #55: Success isn't a checklist. It's a novela. Survive it. Rewrite it. Blind them with sequins.

Collected from Episodes 1-55 of The Latina Survival Guide.

SEASON TWO PREVIEWS

SWARTHMORE

(Episode 201)

COMING SOON ON RMP STUDIO™
THE LATINA SURVIVAL GUIDE
SEASON TWO: THE EXILE

Premiere Date: TBD (a.k.a. whenever therapy clears me)

Rating: Telenovela for Mature Audiences with Parent Issues

Genre: Coming-of-Age Meets Culture-Shock Meets Catholic Hangover

---

TRAILER SCRIPT

(Voice over + Quick Cuts)

NARRATOR V.O.

Every telenovela heroine must eventually leave the island.

She packs her pearls, her sequins, and several generations of unprocessed childhood trauma…

… and boards a plane to **Swarthmore College.**

CUT TO:

Stone halls.

Snow.

Silence.

Somewhere, an organ plays **Pachelbel's Canon in D minor** as my tan evaporates on impact.

QUICK MONTAGE:

- Louis Vuitton trunks sinking in snow like **Titanic II: The Colonial Edition**
- Roommate from hell: blonde, nude, emotionally unavailable, majors in sarcasm.
- Mandatory swim test—I dogpaddle like a Cuban refugee in Dior
- First frat party: beer pong, Bauhaus, and existential regret.
- My first penis: Smaller than promised, sadder than expected, carrying the emotional weight of several unfinished conversations.

NARRATOR (V.O.)

I came for enlightenment.

I got mono, culture shock,

and a minor in *Feminism for the Bewildered.*

VOICES OVERLAP (rapid cuts)

"Don't drink the punch."

"Patriarchy is a construct."

"Who brought *pastelillos* to the Women's Center again?"

NARRATOR (V.O.)

By mid-semester I was

half-whore,

half-nun,

and 100 percent over it.

THE DECODER

Survival Law #201: Exile isn't glamorous. It's homesickness with tuition and acne.

COMING SOON

Where sequins meet socialism.

Where the telenovela heroine learns to swim through patriarchy in heels.

Where "finding yourself" costs

$100,000 a year plus therapy.

NARRATOR (V.O.)

Stay tuned.

Because apparently…
redemption has a meal plan.

END OF BROADCAST

EPILOGUE

CHANCLETA NOTES

CHANCLETA NOTES FOR THOUGHTS YOU SHOULD PROBABLY KEEP TO YOURSELF

Some stories land softly.
Others come at you flying.

Use the pages that follow for the thoughts, memories, side-eyes, realizations, and reactions this book stirred up.

No witnesses. No footnotes. No apologies.

www.ingramcontent.com/pod-product-compliance
Lightning Source LLC
LaVergne TN
LVHW041313150826
845673LV00004B/1313

* 9 7 8 1 9 6 9 7 4 5 0 8 9 *